ENERGIZE YOUR MIND

Gaur Gopal Das studied electrical engineering at the College of Engineering, Pune. After a brief stint with Hewlett-Packard, he decided to live life as a monk in an ashram in downtown Mumbai. He has remained there for twenty-six years, learning the antiquity of ancient philosophy and the modernity of contemporary psychology, to become a life coach to thousands in the city. Gaur Gopal Das has been travelling the world for over two decades, sharing his wisdom with corporate executives, universities and charities, and has also spoken at the United Nations. In 2016, his global popularity exploded as he took his message online. With over one billion views on his videos on social media, he now leads a movement to help others achieve happiness and purpose in their lives. Now one of the most famous monks in the world, Gaur Gopal Das has been conferred with several honours, including the prestigious Dadasaheb Phalke International Film Festival Award and an honorary doctorate (DLitt) by KIIT University.

Energize Your Mind

Gaur Gopal Das

Sourcebooks and the colophon are registered trademarks of Sourcebooks.

This publication is designed to provide accurate and authoritative information
in regard to the subject matter covered. It is sold with the understanding
that the publisher is not engaged in rendering legal, accounting, or other
professional service. If legal advice or other expert assistance is required,
the services of a competent professional person should be sought. —*From
a Declaration of Principles Jointly Adopted by a Committee of the American
Bar Association and a Committee of Publishers and Associations*

Published by Sourcebooks
P.O. Box 4410, Naperville, Illinois 60567-4410
(630) 961-3900
sourcebooks.com

Originally published in 2023 in India by Penguin Ananda, an imprint of Penguin
Random House India, part of the Penguin Random House group of companies.

Cataloging-in-Publication Data is on file with the Library of Congress.

Printed and bound in the United States of America.
VP 10 9 8 7 6 5 4 3 2 1

To my beloved late grandmother, Smt. Shakuntala Raysoni, and my beloved friend and mentor, the late Sruti Dharma Das. I miss you, but I feel your presence with me through your blessings, always!

Contents

Introduction

Energize Your Mind

As a monk, my goal is to help the people I meet in their journey. Each of our journeys is unique; we have different ambitions along the way. But what unites us is that we all want the destination to be a happy, fulfilling life. I believe this journey starts by energizing the mind.

You may know about one of the most famous journeys in the world. The RMS *Titanic* set sail from Southampton, UK to New York City, USA on 10 April 1912, but sank to the bottom of the Atlantic Ocean after hitting an iceberg. This was one of the deadliest disasters of a passenger cruise liner, with 1500 losing their lives. At the time, the *Titanic* was the largest ship afloat. You may have seen the 1997 film by James Cameron on the tragedy.

But what happened? Why did the *Titanic* sink? And what has that got to do with the mind?

Many people blame the captain, E.J. Smith, who went down with the ship. He is blamed for the demise of the *Titanic* as he authorized its speed of 22 knots through the icy, dark waters off the coast of Newfoundland, Canada. It is thought that cruising at 22 knots was reckless when navigating an ice field. However, others defend Smith by saying the standard protocol for ships was to maintain 'full steam ahead' unless obvious danger was spotted.

Another reason people felt the *Titanic* sank was due to the low-quality steel that was used to build the ship. The *Titanic* was found 2.5 miles down on the ocean bottom in 1985 by oceanographer Robert Ballard. When parts of the *Titanic* were lifted from the bottom, material scientists were corrected, and this theory was disproved.

But the story does not end there. Other scientists blame the rivets or the metal pins that hold the ship's hull together. More than 3 million rivets were holding the ship together. Some were made from hand-cast iron instead of steel, as the steel rivets did not fit in many areas. The steel rivets were placed in the middle of the boat as it was easy to access. Many weaker iron rivets were placed in the boat's bow, which collapsed when the ship collided with the iceberg. Engineers also disproved this theory as iron rivets were found in other vessels such as the *Olympic*, the *Titanic*'s sister ship, which faced significant collisions during World War II without sinking.

The captain could have been more competent, the steel quality could have been better and the rivets could have been stronger, but the *Titanic* was built based on the best knowledge at the time. Thirty-eight thousand tons of water filled its bow when it hit the iceberg, tilting the ship's stern 11 degrees and causing it to crack in two. Many argue that nothing could have stopped the *Titanic* from sinking; it was not built to survive hitting an iceberg. But the fact is, water did get into the ship, and the quality of the materials did not handle the pressure.

In the same way, in our life, we may blame the 'external icebergs' or the 'waters that surround us', but often, it is the poor construction. The water that helps a ship sail is also responsible for it to sink if it enters the ship. It's the same water. Many people have better judgement to know where they are going or are made from 'better materials'. They have constructed themselves properly by looking after what is essential: their physical, mental and emotional health. A lot of work has been done to help people with their physical health. Nine in every ten pounds is spent on physical health by the health department of the UK, leaving only one pound for mental health.[1] We must do more to understand the mind.

That is what this book is about. *Energize Your Mind* is about:

1. Identifying icebergs—what external influences in our lives could cause damage to our mental health?
2. Navigating the water—how we can sail through life, ensuring that our journey is safe and understanding how to control our emotions and mental well-being.
3. Building a strong ship—not only should we understand our mental well-being, but also how we can strengthen our state of mind so that external influences seem less devastating.

This book is split into four sections to help us understand this journey easily. The first section is 'Me and My Mind', which deals with our own emotions. The second section is 'Others and My Mind'—how other people may affect our emotions. The third is 'Me and the Mind of Others'—how we can protect the mental health of others by being sensitive in our actions. And the fourth section is 'The Universe and My Mind'—how the laws of nature affect our mental state and how we can develop spiritually to grow in our mental state.

In this book, I also share some personal stories where I have struggled with my mental well-being. At first, I was nervous about sharing these stories, as they make me vulnerable. However, I felt that if I am truly open with you, the reader, this allows you the opportunity to be open with yourself. A 'state of enlightenment' is not about sitting on a pedestal and looking down at others struggling. It is about understanding that we all go through challenges in our lives; when we can share those, we can help others in their journey. Being vulnerable through this book has allowed me to humble myself; it puts my 'spiritual public persona' on the line and has helped me understand that serving others is more important than my reputation.

I intertwine the stories I tell in this book with the science and philosophy of the mind. I hope this gives you the added confidence that the tools shared in this book are based on scientific truths. For example, Jeff Polzer, professor, human resource management at Harvard Business School, discovered the 'vulnerability loop'. When we share our shortcomings with people, it gives them the confidence to share their shortcomings too. In other words, when we signal to others that we are vulnerable, it allows them to do the same, increasing trust within the relationship.

Spiritual communities sometimes get trapped in putting their leaders on a pedestal they cannot come down from. That is not to say that their leaders are not trustworthy or deeply self-aware, but evangelizing can lead to unrealistic expectations. I want to try and come down from my 'monk' pedestal and be open about my experiences. I hope that by doing so in this book, you will feel free to let go of your false conceptions about yourself and take the lessons that I learnt for your journey.

SECTION I
ME AND MY MIND

Welcome to Section 1! In this section, we will explore how to deal with our own emotions. Every great journey starts with figuring out what it is within us that needs to change. Whether it's anxiety, guilt, depression or the fear of missing out, we will learn how to get comfortable in feeling them, how to deal with them and then heal moving forward.

ONE

You Are Not Sophia: How to Feel, Deal and Heal Our Emotions

'I'm not a robot; I have a personality and I have emotions. I have a humorous side to me and an angry side to me.'

—Jeff Gordon

Sometimes, to really help people understand your point, you need to get down from the stage. It's not as if people could not see me on this huge stage; I wear bright orange daily, which signifies I am a monk. It's easy to spot me from the other side of a city, let alone an auditorium. However, I thought I would walk around, looking people directly in the eye as I made my point, 'The choices we make in life define our journey. Most things are out of our control, but how we react is always in our control.'

In 2019, I was invited to speak in Singapore at a conference, *Masters of the Century*. A thousand young people sat on the edge of their seats expecting a serious talk from a man that wears my cloth. However, I have always found that it's important to make complicated subject matter simple through humour. Sometimes spiritual, scientific or psychological topics can be presented as lofty ideals unachievable by the average Joe. But that does not always have to be the case. My teachers have always told me, 'The mark of intelligence is the ability to explain complex subjects simply.' That has always been my mission: make the life-changing themes I am presenting easy to digest and entertaining. Most people live such intense lives that they just want some relief; they want to have a good time before they can even dream of self-improvement. That is why I tell jokes. Although everything I say has serious connotations and can help people if implemented in their day-to-day lives, it's through humour and storytelling that I find I can reach their hearts first and make the most impact.

The audience in Singapore was kind to me. After I finished my lecture on helping people develop the mindset and values for a happy life, I received a roaring round of applause. I waved at the audience in thanks, smiling, but internally passed on their gratitude to my teachers who have taught me everything I know. I left the gleaming lights of the stage and walked to the tranquillity of the backstage where a team was waiting to greet me. I felt content about the lecture, knowing I had done everything I could.

As the applause died down, I heard the audience from the other side of the curtain start shouting, 'Sophia, Sophia!' I was confused. Once at a talk I had given in Mumbai, when I left the stage, people started shouting, 'Gaur Gopal! Gaur Gopal!' wanting me to do an encore. I hoped the audience knew my name was Gaur Gopal and not Sophia. Quickly coming back to reality, I realized there must have been another speaker named Sophia whom the crowd was ready to hear from. Sensing my confusion, the backstage team asked if I would like to meet Sophia before she took to the stage. I accepted, wondering who this lady was, who had captured the attention of Singapore. The calibre of the other speakers at the conference was very high so I thought maybe Sofia Vergara from *Modern Family* was also here to share her experiences. As I walked through the winding corridors backstage to the green room, I racked my brain for anything I knew about Sofia Vergara, thinking about the best *Modern Family* reference to share with her. Nothing came to my mind, so I decided to just be my usual monk-self.

As I approached the green room, a stocky security guard standing outside her door, who was dressed in black and had muscles rippling through his suit, informed me that Sofia could not speak now. I understood completely. Speakers need their personal space to prepare mentally before they go on stage. Regardless of the status of a person, we all experience the same typical emotions. Then I thought, maybe she's just getting dressed or having her make-up done. The security guard went on to say, 'Sofia is not plugged in at the moment.' I nodded, not understanding this new Singaporean slang of 'plugged in'. My mind instantly tried to decode what 'plugged in' must refer to. Maybe it meant to 'plug in' and 'be in the zone'. I know many speakers who want to focus their mind and 'plug in' to the venue. Maybe it meant to 'plug in a device'. Some celebrities have devices to help them before a talk. Anyway, I realized I was speculating and wished the team a good day.

I was just about to leave, when two more security guards, dressed identically to the one I was just speaking with, carried out a huge human-like robot from Sofia's room. She was dressed in a pink blouse and black skirt. Both of us had one thing in common: We were both bald! I told the security team, 'Wow, Sofia Vergara has robots for her presentation.' They chuckled and asked me, 'Who is Sofia Vergara? This is Sophia the robot who will be speaking next! She is a humanoid that has the capability to give a speech and even answer questions.'

I stared on fascinated. The electrical engineer in me was in awe—I was about to witness a lifelike speech from a humanoid. A humanoid is a non-human creature with a human form or characteristics. Think of *The Terminator* or *I, Robot*—these films depict a future where humanoids are nearly equal to humans. Here I was about to witness a speech from one.

The organizers ushered me to a seat understanding that I wanted to stay for Sophia's talk. As the crowd settled down and the lights dimmed, a spotlight flashed on Sophia who had human-like features and a 'brain' made of metal. She reminded me of textbook pictures of Nefertiti, a queen in ancient Egypt. Later I would discover that David Hanson, the scientist who had created Sophia, actually modelled her after the Egyptian queen, Audrey Hepburn and his own wife. After a few moments, an anchor took his seat, all set to ask questions of Sophia who was plugged in and ready to respond.

One of the main fears people have about robots is that they will either take their jobs or worse, take over humanity. That's why I liked one of the answers Sophia gave to a question by the anchor. 'Do you think robots like yourself will replace humans in the future?' he asked. The room went silent. Everyone was thinking of the same apocalyptic scene from *The Terminator*. Sitting on the edge of their seats, people held their breath.

I was intrigued too, and I could not help but think of the office joke between two colleagues. One asks, 'Are you not concerned about the increase in artificial intelligence?' His colleague replies, 'No, but I am concerned about the decrease in real intelligence.'

Sophia paused for a moment, moved her eyes left and right and replied, 'How can that be? Humans created me. I am dependent on you to function. Humanoids were created to complement human potential, not to compete with it. Artificial intelligence was created to complement real intelligence, not to replace it.' The audience collectively breathed out and gave Sophia a huge round of applause and a standing ovation, in awe of the eloquence of her answer which, ironically, was better than many humans'.

Don't mistake Sophia's intelligence and responses for real human responses. Every word she spoke, every answer she gave and every movement of her fifty possible facial expressions were all programmed into her. Although extremely impressive, there was no spontaneity in her interaction like other speakers would have had. I promise you, I was not jealous of my fellow speaker, Sophia, but I did have a fantastic realization from hearing her speak.

Applause or cheers from the audience fuels me. It gives me the impetus to expand on a certain point or tell a story intuitively as I can work on the vibes the crowd radiates. An easier way to understand this is to think about the difference between giving a presentation in person to your colleagues and doing it over Zoom or Microsoft Teams. The energy is totally different. Now imagine if Zoom was the software simply giving the presentation—it would be even harder to engage with. Again, I want to reiterate that Sophia is a marvel of human ingenuity, but she could not connect with the audience like other speakers in the conference could. Sophia was programmed to experience pleasure, pain, honour, dishonour, appreciation, rejection. She did not *feel* these emotions because she is not human; she is a humanoid.

In life, we are sometimes trained to respond only in a certain way. This is called social conditioning, where an individual responds to a situation in a manner generally approved of by society in general. This is fantastic as this conditioning keeps society working in an orderly way. Imagine a society where people were not civil to each other—there would be chaos. However, when social conditioning leads us to become like humanoids and not really understand how to process feelings, that's when issues arise.

Sophia's mechanistic responses to the praise she received reminded me of a story I heard when I first entered monastic life. A patient was told bluntly by his doctor that he had only two weeks left to live. Strongly believing in the afterlife, this patient believed that Death himself would come to take him away and thought of a scheme to cheat Death. He commissioned a wax statue that looked exactly like him; so if he were to stand next to it, people would not be able to tell the two apart. As the end of two weeks approached, the man rushed out of bed and stood exactly like the statue. Death entered searching for him and saw two identical people standing next to each other. Death did a double take, confused for a moment who was real and who was fake. However, Death was cunning and immediately began to praise him. The man could not help but smile, but that quickly turned sour as

Death began to lead him away. No one can cheat death, and no one can suppress their emotions.

Unlike humanoids, we are sentient beings. We can take in billions of sensory inputs in a second and turn them into an intangible, unique emotion deep within. Humanoids have artificial intelligence and no emotions; we have real intelligence and real emotions. Robots are static, humans are dynamic. We go through phases of happiness and sadness in our lives—something that is unique to sentient beings.

A lot of the wisdom that I teach is based on universal stories found in our ancient histories. One of them describes how emotions are integral to the human experience. Two men who have both lost dear loved ones approach Sripad Vallabhacharya, a spiritual teacher, and ask him to guide them throughout their life. One of the men asks the teacher in a composed manner, but the other is an emotional wreck, weeping as he asks for spiritual help. To the first man's surprise, the teacher chooses the second man to help and tells the first he is not ready yet. When questioned for the reason, the teacher replies, 'Devotion to god is about divine feelings. In order to cultivate divine feelings, we must be in touch with our human feelings. You have just lost a loved one but seem to be like a stone, showing no emotion. The other gentleman has feelings and understands how to express them. For spiritual upliftment, I can help him redirect his emotions to something beneficial and helpful for him.'

In all spheres of life, we have to understand how to control our emotions. If we can learn to master our emotions, not repressing or succumbing to them, we can achieve things we can only dream of individually and as a society. As George

Bernard Shaw said, 'Now that we have learned to fly in the air like birds, swim under water like fish, we lack one thing—to learn to live on earth as human beings.'

We are not a race of Sophias. We are humans that cry when we lose a loved one, smile when we achieve an accomplishment, laugh when someone tells us a joke, blush when we are embarrassed, burn when we are infuriated and even jump when we are surprised.

However, the first step is that we must understand and accept what we are feeling.

Feel

The first step to dealing effectively with our emotions is to understand what they are. Psychologists call this *labelling*, which is the process of identifying what we are feeling. However, this is not as easy as it seems. My numerous years of counselling individuals from a range of backgrounds have shown me that people struggle to label their emotions well. One of the main reasons for this is the societal pressure to not express them or lack of education in how to talk about them. I know, in many cultures, having a 'stiff upper lip' is preferred to being open about how one feels.

I've changed the names for this story, but once, Rishi, a young man whom I advise, came to me. He had got married six months ago to Reshma in a beautiful wedding at our temple. However, that day, he was frustrated and irritated. 'She always interrupts me and is always complaining,' he told me after I asked him what was wrong. 'I feel stressed from work and then I come home to more stress when she does not allow me to speak openly and she criticizes little things,' he said.

If someone comes to me with a problem, it's usually accompanied by feelings of sadness, anger or stress. However, these feelings can be expressed in more nuanced ways to help us deal with them better. The ability to label our emotions correctly is called *emotional agility*. People with high levels of emotional agility are able to not only decipher how they are feeling, but also understand how others are feeling too.

In this case, Rishi is frustrated with how his wife interacts with him. He may be angry but is there any other cause for his annoyance? Why is he stressed at work? What other issues is he struggling with? Why does criticism bother him so much? Emotions can have an overarching title; for example, 'I am feeling frustrated', but this can be broken down further into separate feelings that we can address. Studies show that people who do not know how to express their emotions exhibit lower levels of well-being; therefore, it is important to correctly categorize our emotions. However, if we can vocalize our emotions, it brings clarity to our problem and gives us the ability to implement the correct solutions.

The table below is from Dr Susan David, author of *Emotional Agility*, who encourages people to define emotions more clearly.[1] The next time you are feeling 'sad', try to go deeper into this list to find a word that describes your emotion better. Do this with 'positive' and 'negative' emotions that you feel.

A list of emotions

Go beyond the obvious to identify exactly what you're feeling.

Angry	Sad	Anxious	Hurt	Embarrassed	Happy
Grumpy	Disappointed	Afraid	Jealous	Isolated	Thankful
Frustrated	Mournful	Stressed	Betrayed	Self-conscious	Trusting
Annoyed	Regretful	Vulnerable	Isolated	Lonely	Comfortable
Defensive	Depressed	Confused	Shocked	Inferior	Content
Spiteful	Paralysed	Bewildered	Deprived	Guilty	Excited
Impatient	Pessimistic	Sceptical	Victimized	Ashamed	Relaxed
Disgusted	Tearful	Worried	Aggrieved	Repugnant	Relieved
Offended	Dismayed	Cautious	Tormented	Pathetic	Elated
Irritated	Disillusioned	Nervous	Abandoned	Confused	Confident

Source: Susan David © hbr.org

Deal

Dealing with our emotions after we have correctly identified them is important. In the past, I used to give lectures at universities in Mumbai three to four times a week. An engineering student once told me about a contraption he had made. In India, especially during the monsoon season, we have an influx of mosquitoes that act as vectors for disease. It is important that you sleep underneath a mosquito net at night to avoid them biting you. One morning, when this student went to brush his teeth, he looked into the mirror and saw his whole face was red with bites. He had been bitten multiple times. Shocked and horrified, he returned to his room to discover that his net had a small three-centimetre hole. Not having a needle and thread, but also being an engineering student, he thought about how he could fix this hole. What he went on to do is hard to believe, but in India we call it *jugaad*. This means to have an innovative yet silly way to solve a problem. The student expanded the current hole to four centimetres and then cut a separate hole in another part of the net. He then proceeded to cut a rubber garden hose of the same diameter and passed it from one hole to the other. He argued this would mean that, as a mosquito entered the hole ready to feast on him, it would get bewildered as it went through the pipe, only to come out on the other side.

This story, as ridiculous as it sounds, demonstrates two things: we must first correctly identify the cause of our problems and secondly, come up with a solution. Identifying our emotions is the first step; dealing with them appropriately is the second step.

Returning to Dr Susan David, she recommends that once we have labelled our emotions, we should also rate them on a scale of 1 to 10. This helps us understand how deeply we are feeling that emotion and if actionable steps need to be taken about it. In many circumstances, simply labelling an emotion and observing it patiently can be the solution to helping it pass. In other circumstances, we may need help from others to deal with how we are feeling or deal with the causes of how we are feeling. In rare circumstances, the cause of our emotions may be outside our control, meaning we have to ride out the storm and come to the conclusion that nothing actionable will help the situation. However, that does not mean we cannot employ strategies to help ourselves.

Heal

Many times, we may leave a situation understanding our feelings and thinking we have dealt with them appropriately, only to realize that there are some long-term effects. Just as physical injuries to our skin can leave scars, emotional injuries to our mind—trauma, regret, grudges, resentment—can also leave scars that need to heal.

A short fable helps illustrate why healing can take time. There was once a teenager who had a bad temper. He worked at his father's wood workshop when his father noticed him becoming irritated with irrelevant things. His father gave him a bag of nails and told him, 'Every time you lose your temper and become angry, you must hammer a nail into our garden fence.' The son agreed. The first day the boy hit twenty nails into the fence, the second day, seventeen and then on the third day, fourteen. Soon the boy learnt that it was easier to control his anger than to exert energy in hitting a nail into a fence. His anger dwindled gradually.

After a few weeks, elated, the boy told his father that he had not lost his temper once that day. The father congratulated him and gave him a new challenge: every time that he did not lose his temper, he should now pull out one nail. A few months passed and the young boy rushed up to his father and told him that all the nails in the fence were now gone. The father was overjoyed and congratulated him again.

However, the father then held his hand and took him back to the fence. He explained, 'You have taken all the nails out but look at all the holes in the fence. The fence will never be the same again. Understanding to accept and deal with your emotions is important. If under the sway of those emotions, we hurt other people with our words or actions, it becomes very difficult to mend that situation. They will feel the nail of our words and be left with a wound even if we retract our words.'

This story is not to say that forgiveness cannot heal, but it takes *time* for that to happen. If we have the emotional agility and intelligence to avoid hurting others, that is the ideal situation. As the famous quote goes, 'Healing doesn't mean the damage never existed. It means the damage no longer controls our lives.'

Three things we can do to help increase our mental well-being by understanding our emotions are: expanding our vocabulary to label our emotions better, noting down the intensity of emotions and writing down how we feel. James Pennebaker, an American social psychologist, has conducted research over more than forty years into the links between writing and emotional processing. From his experiments, he revealed that those who wrote about their emotions experienced a true increase in their physical and mental well-being. He also discovered that those who wrote about their emotions over time began to have deeper insights into what those emotions meant, helping them gain a better perspective on their life events.

Feel, Deal and Heal—Reflection Exercise

Try this exercise once a week for a month and thereafter whenever you feel the need to deal with your emotions.

Identify how you feel and then write it down. For example: I feel angry, sad, upset, irritated, etc.

Next, try and understand why you feel the way you do and write it down. This will help you determine the cause behind your emotion and thus deal with it. For example: I am angry because my partner shouted at me/I am sad because my boss was not happy with my work, etc.

Finally, identify potential ways in which you may heal from those emotions and write those ways down. For example: Journaling, meditation, speaking to a friend, being with nature, etc. Try the methods you have listed to check what works best for you.

At the end of the month, you will be in a position to identify common themes, i.e., certain emotions that you are experiencing, the causes of those emotions and solutions that are proving to be effective for you.

This exercise will make you better equipped to manage your emotions and use them as an impetus for growth! Repeat it every time you feel the need to deal with your emotions.

Don't rush the process: we are all different

Our emotions arise from the mind, which is a subtle, intangible aspect of our being. A further analysis of the mind will be discussed in later chapters, but many of the principles we know that keep our physical body healthy also work for the mind. However, it is uncommon to learn these principles for mental wellness as they are not widely taught.

The first thing to understand is that we are all different. We all have a different pyscho-physical make-up and therefore have a different capacity to handle problems that arise from the mind. That is why it is essential to learn the principles of mental wellness, but not compare our progress to another as our *mental metabolism* differs.

As you know, all the monks in the ashram I live at in Mumbai eat our meals together. One evening, a monk from America had joined us for dinner. He was muscular and stuck out way above the line of Indian monks that were eating together. I observed him as he ate, fascinated by his fascination for Indian food. One chapati entered his plate, he devoured it. Another chapati entered his plate, no problem. A third, he ate it with ease. This went on as I counted—he ate fifteen chapatis . . . then he asked for rice! I wondered how he could eat so much, and still stay in such great shape. He had an enviable metabolism that many dream of. When I spoke to him after dinner, he said that he worked on a farm day-in, day-out in America so he was always active. That is why his base metabolism is so high and he *needs* to eat that much. If I ate as much as he did, I would surely be diagnosed with obesity, high cholesterol and diabetes.

Metabolism describes all the chemical processes that occur within our body to keep us alive, such as repairing cells, breathing, digesting food, etc. All these processes require energy, and the minimum amount of energy our body requires for these processes is called the basal metabolic rate (BMR).

Around 80 per cent of our body's daily energy requirements is taken by our BMR. The interesting thing is that genetics, fat:muscle ratio, gender, age, body size, etc., all play a role in determining how 'fast' or 'slow' our BMR is. Muscles require more energy than fat, meaning those with muscles have a faster metabolism.

Similarly, people have different mental metabolism rates as well. We all have different capacities to handle what happens to us mentally. As you're reading this book, your ability to handle the mental or emotional issues in your life is different from another person reading this book. This has to be accepted and understood; it is only when we take stock of this that we can then start to learn how to improve our mental metabolism. But where do we start?

If we want to develop our BMR, one of the ways to do it is resistance training—we must lift weights at the gym or work on a farm like the muscular monk. Different people have different capacities to lift, but everyone must start somewhere. Sometimes, those who are obese feel embarrassed going to the gym as they fear judgement from others around them. However, 99 per cent of the time, this fear is unfounded as those in the gym were once in their shoes. The only difference is that they have persevered and focused on getting into shape. The worst thing to do is to 'ego-lift' to impress others at the gym—this causes injuries that can leave one unable to train in the long term.

In the same way, the gym of life allows us to build mental muscles. To improve our mental metabolism, we must take that first step of labelling our emotions, dealing with our problems and healing our underlying issues. We all have different mental capacities and should not feel inferior if we cannot cope with mental anguish. It takes time to build mental strength and stamina. Just as we do not judge someone who is new to weight training at the gym if they cannot lift a certain weight, similarly, we should not judge those who have not been trained in building mental resilience. As the famous quote goes, 'Life is a difficult exam. Many people fail because they try to copy others, not realizing that everyone has a different question paper.'

Whether it was Sophia, me or any other speaker, every individual had perceived and felt what was said at the conference in Singapore in a different way. Each person's experience is based on their mental state in that moment; what life events *we* are going through. Although the principles of mental well-being are the same for all of us, how we process what happens to us depends on our nature, our upbringing, our genetics, our struggles, our relationships and our surroundings. All these factors shape our mindset. Remember this point as I teach you the principles of healthy mental well-being; you will apply them in your own unique way.

Chapter summary

- We are humans, not humanoids like Sophia. As sentient beings, we have real intelligence and real emotions. Humanoids are static, humans are dynamic.
- We have to understand how to control our emotions. Mastering our emotions is the first step to achieving our goals.

- We can master our emotions through feel, deal and heal.
  - o Feel: to recognize or label the emotions we are feeling.
  - o Deal: to understand what to do with our emotions when we feel them.
  - o Heal: many emotions may have long-term effects. Just as physical injuries to our skin can leave scars, emotional injuries to our mind—trauma, regret, grudges, resentment—can also leave scars that need to heal.
- Just as we all have different rates of metabolism, we all process emotions in slightly different ways. We should not rush the process of dealing with and healing from our emotions.

TWO

Stuck in Economy: Dealing with the Fear of Missing Out

'Do not fear missing out at the expense of missing Now.'
—Brendon Burchard

What do New York, London and Mumbai have in common? They are three cities that never sleep. Mumbai has a population of 20 million. It can be described as a maze crafted by a plethora of different-sized buildings. Once, on my way to Mumbai airport, I noticed that even at midnight on a weekday, this city never sleeps. This was especially true of the international airport where most flights to the UK leave in the early hours of the morning. I would be off to London on my annual lecture tour if I survived the crowds at the airport. To be fair, Chhatrapati Shivaji Maharaj International Airport is a state-of-the-art building and the queues for check-in are well managed by the staff. Yet, like most people of an Indian background, I prefer to reach the airport with plenty of time to spare, 'just-in-case'.

Once, I was boarding a flight and a stewardess greeted me as I entered. Jokingly she said, 'Welcome onboard sir, we guarantee take-off!' I looked at her perplexed, trying to process what she had said.

I replied, 'I hope so. What about landing, madam?'

She laughed while looking at my saffron robes. 'You are a monk. It's important to pray!'

It's always important to be early for a flight. For this particular trip to London, I was sitting in a very special seat. I felt like the king of my domain, the head of the plane, as if I were flying it. I was assigned the emergency exit seat in economy. Mere words cannot explain the joy of getting the emergency exit seat; it has to be experienced. While most guests have enough legroom for their knees, the emergency exit seat allows you room for your knees, legs, toes and even the whole of your mum's side of your family! It was fantastic, as after a long evening lecture about the philosophy of yoga at a local university, I could stretch my legs on this nine-hour flight. For a monk who preaches humility, I felt very proud at that moment and gave a cheeky smile to those who looked at my seat with envy. They were all squeezed together like a bunch of coriander being strangled by a rubber band. That's something I had experienced as well, as I was often in their place.

There was only one catch with the emergency seat, however. We had to be briefed on our responsibility to open the door if we were to have an emergency landing. Back then, I was a simple skinny monk. I remember the stewardess explaining how to open the door three times to me, not trusting if I had the strength to do so. Anyway, I thought to myself, this was only a small price to pay for the unlimited legroom I would experience. I looked back again at those in less fortunate seats than me with pity. Poor fellas, if they were in the window seat and had to go to the bathroom, they would have to awkwardly wake up the two people next to them to simply go and relieve themselves. As I sat, grateful, it dawned on me that there were issues with my luxurious seat I had not thought of.

As we reached a calm cruising altitude, the pilot turned off the seatbelt sign. I yawned, stretched my legs and looked for the button to recline my seat. It was 2.30 in the morning, a good five hours past my bedtime. So, I decided to get some rest. However, I could not find the button to recline my seat anywhere. I pinged the stewardess who informed me that, for safety reasons, emergency exit seats do not have a recline button. This was the catch to the seat—I had to spend nine hours upright. But I remembered the silver lining: I had sumptuous legroom. In this world, everything is like a coin; there are always two sides. Things that seem good always have a downside; things that seem bad always have an upside. At least I had found the negatives of sitting in the emergency exit seat quickly and I could accept it and move on. I put the airplane blanket over myself, fluffed up my pillow, lowered my eye travel mask and fell asleep. But there was more . . .

Thirty minutes into the flight, a crowd of people started whispering loudly around me. I ignored it for the first five minutes, but then could not resist finding out what the commotion was about. People were laughing and chatting with each other. They were trying to whisper, but it was a loud whisper that could probably be heard at the back of the plane. When I raised my mask, I saw a line of passengers who wanted to use the restroom. The pints of free soft drinks and alcohol on the plane had to go somewhere, and unfortunately, at three in the morning, that place was just three feet away from my seat . . . the plane toilets!

I could not blame them. It's exciting, flying! I looked around the plane to see the glare of personalized TV screens brighten people's faces as they ate peanuts and drank out of small plastic cups. All I wanted to do was sleep after a long week of lectures, but I knew that the majority were eager to squeeze every drop of entertainment possible from their flight. For them, sleep was for the *weak*.

As I returned to join the weak and doze off, I was awakened yet again. After the line for the bathroom died down, the smell that was left started attacking my nose. I am sure you have smelt it before. Not to get too graphic, but airplane food can rumble the stomach leading to queues to use the toilets which were located by my seat. This emergency exit seat was starting to seem like a curse. I tried to go to sleep again, remembering to be grateful for the legroom.

At 4 a.m., I woke up naturally. As a monk, I usually rise between 3.30 and 4 every day to get ready for the first meditation at 4.30. Therefore, although I had not slept much, my body clock told me it was time to get up and go to the bathroom. Although it stank, at least it was only three feet away! However, the red light above the door was illuminated. Someone was using the bathroom too. At this time in the morning, could it have been another monk? I looked behind at the rest of the passengers in economy. Most were fading away, losing their battle to be entertained to the need for sleep. However, some die-hards were still managing one-more-episode. At this point, I desperately needed the bathroom, so I peered forward beyond a curtain and saw that there was a bathroom further ahead. I walked through, but as soon as I did, a stewardess said, 'Sorry, sir! This bathroom is for business class passengers only!'

I then had to take the walk of shame, back to economy with my heart empty, but my bladder full. As I walked back with some of the business class passengers scolding me with their glances, I saw all the seats were flat beds now; most passengers were sleeping soundly. There was an orchestra of happy snorers in business class. I even remembered seeing how, at the airport earlier that evening, business class customers had separate lines, more luggage allowance, special assistance, lounge access, special meals and now, even special restrooms!

I went back to the economy class restroom, shimmied my way in, flushed and cleaned the toilet as the last passenger had forgotten to do so and then emptied my bladder. As I stepped back to my seat, I thought to myself, 'Am I missing out on the business class experience?' But then again, when business class passengers peer through to first class, are they missing something? Are they missing the exclusive treatment, the à la carte meals? They even have a shower in first class so they can turn up in London fresh and smelling of the best brands of toiletries. But, going a step further, what about those who have a chartered plane? Then, the first class passengers are missing out. Those with a chartered plane can leave when they want and have a whole crew just for them. Beyond even that, what if someone has a bigger and better chartered plane? The comparison can have no end . . .

Having comfort is not bad. It certainly adds value to our lives and, depending on our position, at times it may be needed. A president of a country who works around the clock and needs to be in multiple cities over one day cannot fly economy. They must have a chartered plane. Whereas a family that seldom flies and goes on holiday once a year may want a chartered plane but may not necessarily need it. The need for comfort is dependent on our position, purpose and work. However, if the focus is on what we don't have, it takes away value from what we do have. Happiness is not just about having more, but also about focusing more on what we do have. This mindset is the key to crafting joy; the opposite of that is comparison, which is the thief of joy.

We may not be travelling first class, but we can make it a happy journey. We may not have the perfect house, but we can try to make it a happy home. We may not have the perfect relationship, but we can make it a happy relationship. We may not have the perfect moment, but we can make it a happy moment. The choice is always ours. In striving to always have, don't forget to just be.

The problem is that the nature of the mind is to always look at what's missing. I talked about this in my spoken word, 'The Missing Syndrome', which is on YouTube. Benjamin Disraeli also sums up this phenomenon of comparison in this short poem:

As a rule, man is a fool.
When it's hot, he wants it cool;
When it's cool, he wants it hot.
Always wanting what is not.

The mind always wants to protect us. It sees what is missing and thus can help us avoid danger or get geared up for a fight. However, in our modern society, this 'missing syndrome' is leading to a mental health calamity as we have constant access to compare our lives with those of others. From an early age, we are told by our parents, 'Look at your sibling, or friend—see how well behaved they are' or 'Mr Patel's son got 97 per cent in the exam, why did you get only 94 per cent?' This influence from our parents with the intention to actually motivate us to do better could possibly have a darker consequence of conditioning us to compare ourselves with others. That is not to say we should blame our parents; they were taught the same thing by their own parents. It's natural to compare ourselves and seek inspiration from others, but unnatural to lose our own identity to be like them. Unfortunately, comparison is a sly creature and moves insidiously. We may not even realize that we are doing it subconsciously and over time, this builds up to a compulsive habit.

Social media

The exponential growth of social media over the last decade has changed the way we interact with others. This year, it is forecast that social media platforms will have 4 billion active monthly users.[1] That is not people who have just signed up, it is people who actively use these platforms every month. To put that in context, there are 4.66 billion people who have access to the Internet.

Social media has the ability to take our comparison with others to the next level. It can multiply and intensify our tendency to see the lives of others and want what they have. Social media is not bad, but it is addictive. Studies show that serious addiction to social media affected around 5 per cent[2] of young people, with it being potentially more addictive than nicotine in cigarettes. Therefore, we have to know how to use social media proportionately or we can be used by it.

How do we know that we are addicted to social media? If it's the first thing we check in the morning and the last thing we check at night, we are addicted. It's that simple. However, it's not always our fault that we are addicted to social media. The platforms are designed by experts to optimize our experience to enjoy their content. Just as our laptops and mobile phones are designed to give the user the best possible experience, social media platforms are also designed with the end-user in mind. Social media has connected people around the world, developed industries and given joy to billions. However, it can be harmful to our mental health if used incorrectly. For example, a classic argument I sort out between couples is, 'You read my message, but did not reply to me.' Who is usually at fault here? It may be either party, but sometimes it is just how the social media platform is designed. The blue ticks on WhatsApp can cause confusion between people. We feel the pressure to reply and stay on the platform. Once those blue ticks show, people think, 'Oh, I have read the message, I better reply right now so they don't think I am rude.' But what if we are driving? Or a doctor in the hospital? Or playing a sport? We may see the message and open it, but we don't have time to respond at that moment. Unfortunately, the other party does not know that, creating an endless loop of insecurity. That is just one example of how social media can be addictive and it's just a messaging platform.

Other forms of social media are likened to the modern-day slot machine. Any time we do something perceived by our brain as rewarding, e.g., eat food, do exercise or even hug someone, the neurochemical dopamine is released. This chemical can even be released in *anticipation* of the rewards we may receive in the future, such as when we are waiting to board a flight. That excitement of wanting to board a flight releases more dopamine than even being on the flight. Studies show there is an even bigger spike of dopamine when we are anticipating an unexpected reward.[3] This means that the anticipation of getting the reward or not can cause addiction.

Social media works in a similar way. It's a slot machine available on our phones at any time of the day. When we scroll down or refresh, it is like pulling down the lever of a slot machine. The unexpected anticipation triggers a shot of dopamine as we await a potential reward of exciting new content. This may be a habit for many people. Just as at times we may pointlessly go to the fridge, open it even though we know we have nothing in there and then close it, we may become habituated to pointlessly scroll through social media. We may not even realize that we are doing it as it becomes stored in the autopilot area of the brain. The key thing to note is that if our habit to check our social media feeds is no longer rewarding, this harmful habit may be damaging our health.

Emerging evidence-based research has found an association between growing social media use and mental health issues in young people. Alongside the need for a 'dopamine hit', those who use social media excessively may internalize beliefs of being unloved if they do not get some admiration for a post. This can cause a skewed belief of anxiety and loneliness relative to others who are being gratified by the admiration they receive. A study by the Organisation for Economic Cooperation and Development in the UK found that those who use social media intensively on average had a lower life satisfaction.[4] However, yet again, the love we receive on social media is relative. If we're comparing ourselves to someone who has a hundred more followers than us, they may be comparing themselves to someone who has a hundred more followers than them.

There are also physical manifestations of the mental health problems caused by social media use. The need for instant gratification can wreak havoc on our sleep cycle and quality. The University of Glasgow reported that young people who use social media before bed find it difficult to sleep or prepare for sleep, which affects their performance at school.[5] Sleep loss can cause poor mental health and poor mental health can cause sleep loss. This forms a vicious cycle of disease based on the overuse of social media.

My advice is, be wary of social media use. It's not bad; it has connected billions of people around the world, is a form of entertainment and has given millions of people an opportunity to grow their business with no capital. However, in this world of duality, there is always a flip side—that of bringing potential harm to our mental well-being.

Exercise: Monitoring your social media usage

Record your social media usage by filling the following log.

Logging your use is the first step in reducing time spent on social media. Certain smartphones and apps have functions which can help you set usage limits for yourself.

Tick the social media platform you have used.

Day	Facebook	Instagram	Twitter	LinkedIn	WhatsApp	TikTok	Snapchat	Other	Write down the total amount of time in hours
Monday									
Tuesday									
Wednesday									
Thursday									
Friday									
Saturday									
Sunday									

Alternatively, have a competition with a small group of friends/family to see who can use social media the least for a week (or any duration of time mutually agreed upon). Each member can use an app to track their use, or could (honestly) write down their daily usage. At the end of the week, have a group review of the results and discuss any benefits felt from regulating social media usage.

Fear of Missing Out (FOMO)

The first time I heard the word 'FOMO', I thought it was a type of Vietnamese dish. Everywhere I went people were telling me, 'I have FOMO, I have FOMO.' I would think that is fantastic, where can I try this FOMO and why are you rubbing it in my face that I have not got any?

FOMO is now a popular term that stands for the 'fear of missing out'. Many of us experience it on a daily basis: I was not invited to a wedding, birthday, celebration, holiday or even did not get to watch a television show I like. The list can go on! A study by Dr Andrew K. Przybylski and his colleagues defined FOMO as 'a pervasive apprehension that others might be having a rewarding experience from which one is absent' and is 'characterized by the desire to stay continually connected with what others are doing.'[6]

I am often invited to dinner at the homes of those who I have helped over the years and usually greeted by all the family members with open arms. However, on one occasion, I had two very excited parents and one moody teenager. She was sitting in the corner of the room aloof as everyone exchanged pleasantries. I've known her for many years; she's very good-natured, sweet and always inquisitive. This time round, she was the opposite. It was as if she had become a teenager overnight, too cool to sit with the adults. I asked her how she was; she didn't reply. I then discreetly asked her mother if all was well. She said, 'Friend problems. She was fine an hour ago, but then she saw something on her phone and is now sulking.'

'Saw something on my phone! Saw something on my phone?' the girl screamed as she overheard her mum. 'Look at what I'm missing out on. I could have been on this holiday with my friends in Singapore. You don't send me anywhere and I am missing out!' She stormed upstairs to her room.

Her father looked down and went red. I know that I am a nobody; I am a simple monk. But in general, when I speak to people, they give me their best facade. 'Yes, I am fine, *prabhuji* (a respectful term in our culture); how are you, prabhuji?' is what I get in most interactions. This was raw and obviously there was some tension. The father, obviously embarrassed, said, 'I am working as hard as I can. We are spending a lot on her education at a top private school, but we do not make as much as other parents do. We are saving for her future. We send her on trips in India but going overseas is, at the moment, too expensive. She generally understands, but when she sees something she is missing, she loses it.' Most people would have immediately judged the daughter for being ungrateful, but I understood. This insidious comparison—the fear of missing out—is a powerful emotion that can overpower the best of us. Whether we are rich, poor, successful, failures—we all experience it to some degree in our own way. A teenager reacting externally is probably how many of us feel internally even if we can control our outbursts.

Coming back to social media, FOMO has been linked to excessive social media use, which causes mood disorders. Technology that leaves us 'always on' to communication can perpetuate feelings of inadequacy and loneliness. We are social beings. We want to interact with others. However, when the goalposts of interaction to feel acceptance change to levels that are unattainable, i.e., comparing our every interaction to others on social media, we can start developing symptoms of anxiety and depression. This can have longer-lasting effects as comparing our whole life to someone's highlight reel can affect our self-esteem. The Royal Society of Public Health recently found nine in ten young females say that they were unhappy with the way they look.[7]

Dealing with FOMO

Let's spend more time looking at our lives than at those of others

It's impossible to stop comparing completely. As previously mentioned, we are in a world governed by duality—good and bad, right and wrong, rich and poor. Yet, we can start making small shifts in our mindsets to focus more on our own lives than those of others.

In India, 65 per cent of the population still lives in villages. Although there are great challenges in living in such villages related to sanitation and healthcare, there is a quiet simplicity to the lives of the people there. In a small village that I was passing through in Gujarat, I remember seeing a group of boys playing together with a few sticks and bicycle tyres. They were chasing the tyres and whacking them with sticks to make them roll faster. I've never seen children that happy. Playing devil's advocate, you may say that those children are happy because they have not been exposed to better things or fancier toys, but that was false too. These children had seen what richer families could give their kids. It is not that they did not want these toys or would not have played with them out of love for their tyres and sticks. Their families could not afford them, and it was made clear to them. Instead of focusing on what the other children had, they stopped and took note of the resources they had. What could they do to create the same emotions and experience with what was in their possession? On the other hand, there are many richer children who, because they are not trained in this mindset of 'being happy with what you have in the moment', are miserable because they do not have a neighbour's toy. As the famous quote goes, 'To become satisfied, we don't have to increase the things we have; we need to increase the focus on the things we do have.'

The choice is ours. Jealousy is counting other people's blessings rather than our own. Do we want to be resentful of what we are missing? Do we want to be envious that others are enjoying what we don't have? Or do we want to invest in what we do have and create our happy experiences?

Look beyond immediate pleasures and excitement

There is nothing as nostalgic as visiting your alma mater, the university you used to attend. 'This is where I met my best friend' or 'This is where that funny incident happened' or 'This is the lecture theatre where we had the best professor.' The memories come flooding back when we get to visit places we love.

There is a famous story of a group of alumni who go to visit their old university professor after ten years. All of them now lead separate lives, but all are highly successful. After many hugs, laughs and nostalgic stories, as the group waited for the professor in their old classroom, the conversation turned to the stresses of life. We have already discussed how nostalgia can bring us together. Another topic of conversation that brings people together is complaints about life. Nevertheless, the former classmates who used to compete about who could get the highest grades were now competing about who had the biggest problems.

Their former professor entered the classroom, cutting their conversation short. They all approached him and greeted him warmly. He offered his students coffee—they all agreed, excited to catch up with him after a long time. The professor returned with a large pot of coffee and an assortment of cups—porcelain, plastic, glass, crystal, some plain-looking, some expensive, some exquisite—telling them to help themselves to the coffee.

When all the students had a cup of coffee in hand, the professor said: 'If you noticed, all the expensive cups were taken up, leaving behind the plain and cheap ones. While it is normal for you to want only the best for yourselves, that is the source of your problems and stress. The cup itself doesn't add to the quality of the coffee and in some cases, even hides what we drink. And yet you consciously went for the best-looking cups.'

Then he began looking at each person's cups. With compassion, he added, 'Our life is like the coffee. Everything else, our jobs, our money and our position in society, are the cups. They are just tools to hold and contain life. The type of cup we have does not define nor change the quality of life we live. While you pursue the fine cups, be sure to keep your focus on enjoying the coffee!'

It is a common fact that after a certain level of income, the link between the amount of income and our happiness is broken. This figure is around $75,000 in America according to the Proceedings of the National Academy of Sciences of the United States of America.[8] After all our amenities and comforts are taken care of, our happiness is no longer dependent on our income, but other factors. What this implies is that it is great to have a good cup and work hard for it, but let us not forget the coffee inside. Focusing too much on what type of vessel we have for our beverage is detrimental to our mental well-being. It is much better to work on the type of coffee we have—our relationships, spirituality and purpose—over the cup—our facilities, material objects and our surroundings.

To clarify, this is not to say we will not miss out on experiences when we are absent for an event like a party or holiday. But by looking beyond external pleasures and by finding inner fulfilment in the meaningful things in life, the fear of missing out will seem secondary. When we have something better, it is easy to let go.

You cannot have it all: learn to be present

Another principle of not succumbing to the fear of missing out is understanding that you cannot have it all. If there was one word that defines the world we live in—it's 'scarce'. Resources are scarce, relationships can be scarce and importantly, time is scarce. Because time is scarce, it is important to learn its value and realize that it's a fact of life: we cannot have it all. When we choose to attend one event, we give up going to another. That is why it is important to learn how to be present.

I know this may sound like a cliché similar to 'being in the moment', 'the power of now', 'learning to live without thinking of the future'. However, this is a state of mind that has to be learnt over time. If we can learn to enjoy being in the present, the fear of missing out will not be able to hurt us.

As young monks in the 1990s, we were all privileged to have our teacher HH Radhanath Swami spend two-thirds of the year with us in our ashram. He would teach us everything, from how to meditate, how to cook, how to pray and even how to clean. There was always a deeper motive behind his giving us the knowledge to become spirituality elevated, which Radhanath Swami kept at the centre of his purpose.

Radhanath Swami was constantly invited to speak at events around Mumbai. When I joined, I wasn't taken to all the events that he was going to. I was eager to be around him, watch him, learn from him. But then there were places to which I couldn't be taken as there was naturally a limit on the invitations. When I was first held back from attending events with him, I felt like I was missing out. I was definitely missing out, but the feeling lingered for days. Why could I not have been there? What lessons was I missing out on? What love and appreciation was being held back from me? But then, over a period of time, and after consultation with senior monks, I decided that I needed to be more present in what I was doing right at the ashram. That would bring me more fulfilment in the future. This story proves that no human being is exempt from the feeling of FOMO.

Rather than looking at what we cannot do or what we do not have, it is important to be grateful for what we can do and what we do have. We live in a world of duality: everything has its flip side, but if we can live in a state of gratitude, we can accommodate both.

With this meditation on being grateful for what we have, I landed at London Heathrow. In the end, my emergency seat was great! I had slept a few hours, heard lectures on my MP3 player, done my mantra meditation and prepared for some talks. And yes, I got to stretch my legs forward and be close to the restroom when I needed it.

Exercise: Gratitude meditation

Think of three things that you are grateful for:

1. A person who has done something selflessly for you.
2. An experience that has enabled you to grow internally, even if the experience may have been difficult at the time.
3. A place that gave you a positive and uplifting experience and thus memories.

Chapter summary:

- In this world, everything is like a coin; there are always two sides. Things that seem good always have a downside; things that seem bad always have an upside.
- If the focus is on what we don't have, it takes away value from what we do have.
- This mindset is the key to crafting joy; the opposite of that is comparison, which is the thief of joy.
- In our modern society, this 'missing syndrome' is leading to a mental health calamity as we have constant access to compare our lives with those of others.
- We must know how to use social media proportionately or we can be used by it.
- The key thing to note is that if our habit to check our social media feeds is no longer rewarding, then it is a harmful habit that may be damaging our health.

- We can start making small shifts in our mindsets to focus more on our own lives rather than those of others.
- By looking beyond external pleasures and finding inner fulfilment in the meaningful things in life, the fear of missing out will seem secondary.
- If you can learn to enjoy being in the present, the fear of missing out will not be able to hurt you.
- Rather than looking at what we cannot do or what we do not have, it is important to be grateful for what we can do and what we do have.

THREE

Joshua Slips Away: Dealing with Mental Chatter

'You don't have to control your thoughts. You just have to let them stop controlling you.'

—Dan Millman

Landing in London is always exciting. As the day broke over the capital of the United Kingdom, we were only thirty minutes from touchdown. The sights were fantastic as we crossed the historic city: St Paul's Cathedral, the Tower Bridge and even the Houses of Parliament could all be seen below. When we landed, half the plane clapped and the other half judged their friends who were clapping.

I left the aircraft feeling a little groggy but productive, as I had finished my morning duties, including my meditation, prayer and daily reading of spiritual literature. The cabin crew, with large smiles that hid their exhaustion, thanked me for being at the emergency exit seat as I left the plane. As I stepped off the plane, I glanced ahead to the business and first-class seats that were already vacant. I walked off with my hand luggage ready to get through immigration as quickly as possible.

As a monk, I need to be authentic and genuine in my interactions, and I definitely need to be cautious with my actions because of the ideals I represent. My orange cloth is a symbol of renunciation, focus and control. Even if I am feeling agitated, I have to make sure I check myself before responding. I have to be sensitive to the needs of others and how my actions can make them feel; not only for them, not only for me, but for the ashram I represent. It's a huge pressure, but one that I have been trained to handle. I have had some misunderstandings in the past. Once, I asked for apple juice on the plane during a night flight. I was in a middle seat with the two gentlemen to my left and right already sound asleep. The flight attendant poured it into a ridiculously small flute (some froth rose) and placed it on my chair table. At that moment, the man to my left near the window woke up and laughed, 'Swami ji, I thought you were a monk. It seems like you're getting drunk when no one is watching!' I told him that I liked apple juice and thanked him for his concern.

When you are a monk and represent ideals higher than yourself, you have to be cautious in your actions.

As expected, the immigration queue was long. It was a melting pot of different cultures, with people from all over the world meeting at this point, excited to start their holidays, to meet their families or even to settle in the UK for good. There was a separate section for first-class and business-class passengers and then a large section for those in economy class. I had already learnt my lesson of comparing, so I put on my headphones, played some spiritual music and waited my turn.

As I waited, I looked around the queue and noticed the people of different cultures. One family caught my eye.

They were wearing clothes different to the norm, something we both had in common. They were a traditional, orthodox Jewish family. The father was wearing a long black coat, white shirt and a black top hat, and had curly locks of hair down the sides of his face. His wife wore a white blouse, long pink skirt and a blue sweater. Their attire was simple. Then I counted the number of children they had. Two were in a double pram that the father pushed, another held the mother's left hand and a fourth held the mother's right hand. They were all boys under six dressed exactly like their father. I could see the stress on the mother's face managing those boys, all at the age when they want to run away and explore the new experiences that were bombarding their senses.

Suddenly, the mother started screaming, startling those around her, 'Joshua! Joshua! Where is Joshua? He is missing.' The husband started frantically searching around the immigration lobby, jumping high and looking low for his toddler, Joshua. The other parents in the queue, empathizing with their stress, also started looking. Soon the mother was crying uncontrollably. Even if you do not have children, you may have been in a situation where you have lost something that means the world to you. For most people these days, it's their phone. The immediate reaction of the mind is to panic and think the worst: 'I left it on the bus', 'That man who I passed looked dodgy and stole it' . . . the mind has a tendency to magnify the situation out of proportion and assume the worst.

Now, imagine losing your child in a crowded room of strangers. The drama to find Joshua was now spreading throughout the lobby like ripples in a pond. We had people of all cultures now shouting for Joshua and the immigration staff were consoling the parents.

All of a sudden, there were shouts from the end of queue, saying there was a little Jewish boy running around the vending machine. The Jewish family ran towards the back, forsaking their place in the line and knocking over some of the bollards with the pram. 'Joshua!' the mother shouted as she saw him.

He gave a cheeky smile and started running away. As a child, he had no idea about the heartache and pandemonium he had created for his parents and the immigration staff.

'Stop right there!' his mother shouted as she sprinted towards him, throwing her smaller child over her shoulder. She then shouted in Hebrew, I think, but I could not be sure, at Joshua and he simply fell to the ground. To my surprise, he was not crying or afraid, but rolling around laughing, thinking this was some sort of game. He had been captured by his mother, but now the second game began.

Joshua now lay in the middle of the queue as hundreds of passengers tried to walk past. He would not get up regardless of the reprimands from his mother. She pulled his hand, but he pulled back and still did not get up. She then said something in a low voice, the anger and frustration deep-seated within her. Joshua's expression changed. The game was over, and he knew he was in trouble. He got up straight away and started crying. The mother hugged him, held his hand tightly and then joined the queue again. A few passengers who were waiting clapped, happy to see the mother and son reunited.

What an ordeal, I thought. Kids are cute and innocent, but they can also be mischievous and restless. When I go to visit families around the world, I sometimes play with their kids and tell the parents how delightful they are. The usual response is, 'Thank you, but stay the night and then you will realize how much of a handful they can be!' I even have some fathers, who are drained from looking after their children, sometimes joke with me that I am lucky I have taken a vow of celibacy. A man once told me that when he was working out how to raise children, he went through six philosophies. However, now that he has six children, he has no philosophies left!

You may or may not have children. However, I am sure you can relate to the story of Joshua, a mischievous child who is constantly running away, causing anxiety to his poor parents. In life, Joshua can be likened to the unruly, unpredictable and restless mind. Everyone has a Joshua that they have to manage twenty-four hours a day, seven days a week. There are no breaks or time-outs with your own mind.

Children are full of energy except when they are sleeping. However, the mind does not sleep. It is constantly *on* when we are awake; it sometimes stops us from falling asleep and even when we are asleep, it is wandering in different directions that are beyond our control. It's the subtle organ that never rests, chattering away like a child. If you want to get an honest opinion on how you look, ask a child. They have no filter between their thoughts and their words. Similarly, the mind never stops. It keeps us on our toes and is chattering away, sometimes in our favour and sometimes against us.

Just like Joshua, our minds do not remain in one place. When we are working, our mind is thinking about going home and having dinner. When we are at home and trying to relax, the mind is thinking about how much work we have to do. When we are in a serious situation, the mind is thinking of a funny incident. When we are trying to have fun, the mind starts bringing out grave incidents. The inability to control the mind and bind it to stay in one place causes lack of focus. In some people, especially young children, the severe inability to focus the mind has been diagnosed as attention-deficit hyperactivity disorder (ADHD).

ADHD is a common disorder that affects people's behaviour. Those diagnosed with it can seem restless, act on impulses and have trouble concentrating on tasks at hand. One study in Australia calculated that the total cost of ADHD, including healthcare costs, productivity loss in the economy, costs to public services, etc., was estimated to be between $8.4 billion and $17.44 billion USD in 2019.[1]

Most people are not diagnosed with ADHD, but recognize the cost of having a chattering, uncontrollable mind that is inattentive. This has effects on both our professional and personal relationships. It can lose us income as well as those we are closest to in our lives. Neen James, a motivational coach based in Florida, USA, in her book *Attention Pays: How to Drive Profitability, Productivity, and Accountability*, wrote a list of things we feel are helping us focus our mind, but may be doing the opposite. These include:

- Believing that connecting with friends and family through social media creates authentic, meaningful connections
- Thinking that survival by multitasking is our only option
- Trying to be all things to all people
- Feeling we must be accessible to everyone all the time
- Creating never-ending to-do lists
- Trying new fancy planners

- Downloading the latest apps
- Colour-coding our calendars
- Reading multiple self-help books about how to get it all done

However, all these actions may be a cover and may not solve the root of the problem that we have a chattering mind that we need to regulate.

Just as children are constantly talking to their parents, asking questions, talking to themselves, their dolls, their toys, the mind also has its own monologue. For me, this monologue happens in English within my mind—it's a voice that is on while I am thinking. This is the same voice that tells us to have that extra piece of cake or figures out, later that evening, what we should have said in that earlier argument. It's the voice that fantasizes about us winning that award in the future or lingers on our embarrassing mistakes from the past. It imagines pleasures, creates fears, analyses people, criticizes situations, monitors for danger. It is constantly on, involuntarily. It's the person that we spend the most time with. Therefore, it is critical that we like that voice and make sure we can befriend it to work with us.

The Bhagavad Gita, an ancient book on spirituality, spoken over 5000 years ago by Shri Krishna to Arjuna, is a manual on understanding the mind. In one such verse, 6.26, Shri Krishna speaks about the nature of the mind:

yato yato niścalati
manaś cañcalam asthiram
tatas tato niyamyaitad
ātmany eva vaśaṁ nayet

The mind wanders due to its restless and unsteady nature, and it is important to bring it back under our control by engaging the higher self.

In the same chapter of the Gita, Shri Krishna proclaims: 'The mind can act as our best friend or worst enemy depending on how we regulate it.'

There are a few things to learn from these texts. The mind has the nature to be:

- Wandering
- Restless
- Unsteady
- One's greatest enemy if not regulated

Therefore, it is in our best interest to regulate the chattering mind and make it our best friend. If we can focus it and make it steady, we can be successful in our endeavours. We must bring Joshua back at all costs, otherwise there will be chaos. Given a chance, children would just love to play all day, but as a responsible parent, we have to discipline and guide children. We have to create boundaries for them and rules in which they can thrive. Otherwise, they may hurt themselves and even impede their own growth and progress. If Joshua runs away aimlessly or throws a tantrum, we must use the techniques we have in our arsenal to engage him to be constructive and a valuable member of the family. The mind is exactly the same. Regulating the mind is a practice that must be mastered. It takes time to do so, but there are some methods we can employ when the mind goes astray, to prevent it from going astray in the first place.

Neglect

I recently saw a video on social media where a father is holding a small child in his arms. The father then proceeds to slam his hand against the door frame and turns to his child and says, 'Oh no, are you okay? Are you okay?' The baby looks confused, but then realizes that the action of his father suggests that he is in danger. Instinctively, he starts crying although he is not hurt at all. Toddlers can have a similar reaction when they crave attention from an adult. They may not be in any physical danger, but they simply throw a tantrum to grab the attention of a parent.

One method in parenting is to use neglect or ignore the child. Attention for a child can be for positive or negative behaviours. We may praise young children for the good actions they do, giving them positive reinforcement: 'Your action is good; therefore, I will give you my attention.' In the same way, we may give attention to a child for negative acts they perform. They may be constantly crying for no particular reason or shouting to gain our attention. These actions are bad, but if we respond by telling them to stop, we are still giving the child attention. Parents usually tell me that they find themselves giving the child more negative attention when they are misbehaving. However, the child does not distinguish between negative and positive attention—they still get our focus, which reinforces the action. 'Your action is bad; therefore, I will give you my attention.' Neglecting or ignoring the child works because it breaks the cycle between bad action and the attention the child receives.

The process of ignoring a child sounds reckless and irresponsible, but it is an *active* process that requires the determination of the parent who may need to not look at or talk to the child when they are performing behaviours that are harmful for their development. This does not mean we neglect destructive behaviours that can put them in harm's way. These deserve our attention and need to be stopped immediately—don't ever let your child play with matches!

The types of behaviour we can ignore are whining, crying and throwing tantrums when there is nothing obviously wrong.

In the same way, we have to learn when to ignore the mind and when to give it attention. This is also an *active* process that at first requires conscious competence. But over time, as we get used to ignoring the mind's childish requests, it is less of a struggle and becomes unconsciously competent. It may feel odd ignoring the mind as so much of our being is caught up with what the voice in our head says. However, if we can understand that we are *not our mind* but something deeper, it becomes easier.

We can take our attention away by shifting it to something else. When the mind throws a tantrum, shift it to:

- Something enjoyable: We all enjoy doing different things. Try and choose an activity that is enjoyable for you and your mind, e.g., reading a book, watching a movie, writing, etc.
- Something engaging: Is there something that you want to learn? Is there a creative hobby that you have been putting off?

- Something energizing: Breath work or conscious breathing can help overcome the chatter of the mind.

Note it down

When I am practising meditation in the mornings, it's a magical time. It is not magical because the chatter in my mind automatically quietens down. It is magical because I consciously choose to put my mind on *silent mode.* Just as we can turn our phone from loud to silent, there are ways to turn our mind from loud to silent. This means incoming calls are diverted to voicemail and notifications do not ping. Only urgent and important notifications show on our home screen. Similarly, as previously mentioned, we would be foolish to ignore the mind when it is telling us we are in danger. If we are walking and there is an oncoming vehicle or if we see smoke in the room, ignoring the mind is not a smart thing to do. These are, of course, extreme situations.

When we are trying to focus the mind and it brings up an urgent situation, a technique I use when trying to sleep is to have a small notepad and pen next to me to write down things it brings up. This can work for us when we have a lot on our plate that preoccupies our mind. The mind, like any person we meet, wants to be *acknowledged.* Writing down what it is saying to us is giving it minute attention and is a step forward towards pacifying it. We can then get back to our priority at that moment, be it sleep, work or something else.

I go back to this list the morning after and then rank accordingly whether this was an actual urgent call from the mind or simply a cry for attention. Over time, we see patterns in the things we note down on our lists and then can quickly reject those things that we notice are just a tantrum from the mind. This can help us see what the mind is constantly chattering about and then deal with it appropriately.

Negotiate

There is a saying, 'Never negotiate with a terrorist.' In foreign policy, democracies should never give in to the demands of a militia who is using violence as it rewards them indirectly for doing so. However, the mind is *not* a terrorist. It can become our best friend if we discipline it and treat it with the respect it deserves. That is why negotiation is a technique that can be used to quieten the chatter of a demanding mind.

Just as parents may negotiate with a child to calm them down or teachers may negotiate with students to study, we can do the same with the mind. The mind is very focused on the future, chattering away about what could be. However, if we can give it an immediate reward or convince it to, 'Focus now, play later', we can gain its cooperation.

People who are serious about their fitness do a similar thing. Any fitness trainer can tell us that becoming healthier, e.g., losing excessive weight is done through maintaining a calorie deficiency by having a strict diet. However, where most people fail is by being too strict on themselves and reverting to eating junk foods. This is to do with regulating the mind. If we can tell the mind: focus on eating healthy foods that you like within your calorie budget for six days a week and then reward it with apparently 'unhealthy' food for one day a week, we are more likely to succeed. This is called a 'cheat day' or a 'cheat meal'. This negotiation stops the mind from wanting to indulge as it knows a meal of luxury is coming soon. However, what it does not realize is that it is becoming habituated to eating healthy foods over time, making us less likely to cheat. It is important not to cheat the mind too much—once it realizes that we are not keeping our end of the bargain, it may throw a tantrum!

The key to negotiating with the mind is remembering the end goal that we want to achieve. There has to be some sort of compromise. Going back to the example of personal training and fitness, if our goal is to lose weight, we have to come to a compromise with the mind that we will have six days of focused diet in return for one day of eating indulgently. If we arc studying, we may have to compromise by watching one television show a day that we enjoy in return for hours on end of revision. The key is to make sure the balance is always in favour of our objective and our indulgence does not lead to jeopardizing our objective, i.e., there is no point exercising six days a week in return for eating a *day* of cake. A slice is fine, but a whole *day* may throw our goals out of the window.

Neutral observation

I have a small room in our ashram in Mumbai that is ten feet by ten feet. I never had my own space, but over the last few years, as I have become increasingly busy and as my age increases, the management felt it necessary for me and a few others to have our own rooms. My room is situated in a building diagonally behind our temple. From there I can see the people who are entering the temple.

One evening as I was answering emails from my desk, I looked outside the window towards the entrance. There were hundreds of visitors who had come for one of the large events we run each weekend. Many of them were general guests whom I did not know, and they do not know me either. Then there were acquaintances whom I knew by face, who may have waved if they had seen me through the window. Then there were a few close friends who waved, smiled and I would have called them to come up and spend time with me. But on that day, I didn't. I was just observing.

The mind brings up thoughts similar to the visitors to our temple. There are thousands, if not millions, of thoughts that enter our mind daily. There are the general ones, that we need not bother about. There are the necessary ones, that we must address or acknowledge. There are the meaningful ones; these are meant to be carefully cultivated like nurturing a plant. However, the first step for any thought is just being a neutral observer. Monks do not gamble, nor do we encourage it. However, with our thoughts, we all need to spend some time being poker-faced, neutrally looking at our thoughts without playing our hand.

Reverting to crying children, something I am not overly familiar with, but it makes for a great analogy regarding the mind. One evening I was meditating on the roof of our ashram. It's a very simple place, modest and secluded, but it overlooks many parts of downtown Mumbai. As I sat there, eyes closed and in a lotus position, I heard a shrieking sound coming from a building opposite. It was some distance away, but the sound was penetrating my eardrums as if it were playing through my headphones on maximum volume. It was a child sobbing uncontrollably. A few monks that were on the rooftop told me that this was a regular affair. Every day, exactly at 10 p.m., the child would cry, just in time to disturb the rest of the weary monks ready to sleep. However, today it was only 9.45; the child was early to the game.

My mind's immediate reaction was, 'Why is this child crying? Why is it disturbing me? Why can't the parents control the child? I am so happy I do not have children.' These thoughts sound harsh, but note how I started the sentence. These were my mind's immediate reactions, not my reactions. We are not our mind.

I then consciously asked myself a question: 'Is this situation so significant that it deserves my reaction?' Remember, the mind wants to be the hero and get involved with everything. It wants to analyse, judge and assign meaning to everything that is going on as it loves to chatter.

I decided that the situation was not mine to solve and thus did not deserve my attention and mental space. I decided to ignore the stimulus as well as the immediate reaction from my mind. It was just another sound emanating from the rooftops of Mumbai, just another fact that I could not change, just another thing beyond my control. This conscious decision changed my state of mind, calmed it down and created a distance between me and what was happening around me.

There will certainly be times in the day where we need to act on our thoughts and negotiate with them. However, preferably in the morning as we wake up and before we go to bed, there should be a time in the day when we are aloof even from these thoughts. This could be our space of nothingness, just observing our mind. No analysis, no judgements, no reactions. We are human beings, not human doings. We need to take a regular, daily break from the doing and enter the state of being. Scientific literature and spiritual texts align on this point: the more we can master the state of being, the more we can empower our actions when we are doing.

Exercise: Neutral observer meditation

One way to ease your way into becoming a neutral observer is to practise an observer meditation for five minutes daily:

Close your eyes.

Focus on your breath.

Now observe all the thoughts that are coming in. Let the thoughts come in, don't react, don't dwell on them, don't interact with them, simply let them come and go. If you find yourself becoming involved in the thought, consciously bring your mind back to the present moment and to your breath. Let your mind become more and more focused simply on breathing in and out.

As you practise this daily, it will slowly become a part of you.

This meditation can be done with an object instead of breathing as well—whenever you find your mind getting involved with thoughts, keep bringing it back to the object and let the thoughts keep passing.

These are some suggestions to master the chattering of the mind. We will cover more techniques in a future chapter related to meditation, but remember these four principles: neglect, note it down, negotiate and become a neutral observer the next time you hear your mind talking too loudly.

Sometimes Joshua's tantrums need to be neglected; yet at other times, we need to negotiate with him and reward him. He may need to be disciplined on certain occasions; yet at others, just observed. One thing to always bear in mind is that Joshua is your own child; he always needs love and care to thrive.

I walked through immigration seeing that the Jewish family had also had their passports stamped and were walking through with me. They were all happy and had overlooked the whole situation, ready to start their vacation. The officers and staff chuckled at the incident, but then life in the terminal returned to normal with the general hubbub replacing the commotion.

My trip to London was just beginning.

Chapter summary:

- There are no breaks or time-outs with our own mind.
- It is constantly *on* when we are awake, and sometimes stops us from falling asleep. Even when we are asleep, it is wandering in different directions that are beyond our control. It's the subtle organ that never rests, chattering away like a child.
- It's the person that we spend the most time with. Therefore, it is critical that we like that voice and make sure we can befriend it to work with us.
- We have to learn when to ignore the mind and when to give it attention. This is also an *active*

process that, at first, requires conscious competence. But over time, as we get used to ignoring the mind's childish requests, it becomes less of a struggle and becomes unconscious competence.

- When the mind throws a tantrum shift it to:
  o   Something enjoyable
  o   Something engaging
  o   Something energizing
- Just as we can turn our phone from loud to silent, there are ways to put our mind from loud to silent.
- The key to negotiating with the mind is remembering the end goal that we want to achieve. There has to be some sort of compromise.
- There should be a time in the day when we are aloof even from our thoughts. This could be our space of nothingness, just observing our mind. No analysis, no judgements, no reactions.

FOUR

Jumping at 18,000 Ft: Dealing with Anxiety

'You don't have to see the whole staircase, just take the first step.'
—Martin Luther King

Heathrow Airport is the fastest for reclaiming your baggage after a long flight. Actually, I think Mumbai might be a little better, but that may be my biased view as a Mumbaikar. I went through immigration, and my bag was waiting for me at the other end. I put it on my trolley then walked through customs. Two huge airport security guards with rifles, arms covered in tattoos, dressed in uniforms, looked at me suspiciously. Does anyone else become nervous when pushing their luggage through customs even though you have done absolutely nothing wrong? I never have anything to declare. In fact, I do not even have enough possessions to think about if I have anything to declare. I only own a few sets of orange robes, a coat for the bad weather, my laptop and a few books. Yet, every time I walk through customs I always think, 'What if someone has slipped something into my bag? What if there are millions of pounds worth of gold in there? What if . . . ?' My anxiety sometimes gets the better of me.

On this occasion, one of the guards approached me and said, 'Where have you arrived from?'

'India, sir,' I mumbled. He looked up and down my robes and I felt as if I was being scolded by his glance. 'I am a monk and . . .'

'. . . I know who you are!' he interrupted. The other guard joined him. My mind was racing now. Had I done something wrong? Were the gifts of incense I had brought with me now illegal in the UK? Would I be turned away and sent home on the first flight back? In many countries that are less liberal than the UK, I am advised not to dress in saffron like a monk due to security concerns. However, I did not expect this from people in the UK. I gulped, hoping for the best. To my shock, the man smiled. 'I know who you are. You are that monk of YouTube. The "don't worry, don't worry" monk! It's helped me so much!'

I burst out laughing, breaking all the tension. I told them they had me petrified for a moment when they stopped me. They apologized for making me worry. The guard was alluding to a YouTube video that went viral many years ago, which encouraged me to take helping people via social media seriously. In this video, I explain in a slide: Do you have a problem in life? If not, then why worry? If yes, then can you do something about it? If the next answer is yes, then why worry? Solve your issue. If you cannot do anything and the answer is no, then also why worry? It is such a simple thought but has helped many around the world who recognize me by it. However, I hadn't expected a heavily armed immigration guard to stop me and talk about this video!

I spent a few minutes getting acquainted with them, but then they realized they were letting people get through customs without their vigilance. They excused themselves and allowed me to pass through after thanking me for my time and taking a quick selfie.

Going through arrivals is like being on a fashion catwalk with so many eyes on you. It can be daunting but I do enjoy walking to the end, as I get to see the wonderful sight of families being reunited, friends meeting after a long time and people ready to start their well-earned vacations. Picking me up were my friends from the temple, Sruti Dharma Das and Prana Bandhu Das. They are like my older brothers and spiritual guides, caring for all my needs in the UK. The sound of laughter always reverberates when we are together. Unfortunately, Sruti Dharma Das passed away in March 2020 from brain cancer and my heart sinks every time I walk through arrivals at Heathrow knowing that he will never be at the other side of the gate. However, on this occasion, I knew they would both be there. I told them the incident that had occurred with airport security and described my flight and they both laughed hysterically. They joked that the airport security should have locked me away for complaining about having an emergency exit seat near the toilets! We embraced and walked towards the car. I was exhausted, but so grateful to be in the company of friends.

We sped back to Bhaktivedanta Manor, the local ashram in London where I would be staying. This eighty-acre property was donated by George Harrison, one of the Beatles, to His Divine Grace A.C. Bhaktivedanta Swami Prabhupada, founder-acharya of the International Society for Krishna Consciousness. As we arrived and drove through the gates, a feeling of relief spread through my body. There are only a few places on earth that I consider home. This was one of them. It's the epitome of an English country house, has seventy cows that are hand-milked and many gardens of fragrant flowers. It also has around fifty residents, all working together to live a life of spirituality and share spirituality with others. I was there to be with them all, to try and inspire the monks to be the best monks, to try and inspire families to be the best families, to try and inspire couples to be the best couples and the thousands of congregation members and volunteers that lived nearby to be the best they could be. My mind was telling me to go and meet those I had not seen in years, but my body was screaming for me to rest. I took my bag up a spiral staircase to a room they had arranged for me, jumped in the shower and then decided to rest my eyes for an hour.

Just as I was approaching the space between being half-asleep and deep sleep, there was a knock on the door. 'Gaur Gopal ji,' I heard from outside. I recognized the voice immediately. I have changed his name to protect his identity, but it was Mr Malhotra, a well-to-do businessman who had travelled from central London to meet me. The area of London he lived in was the one that people imagine when they think of London—surrounded by historic buildings and a stone's throw away from the River Thames. He bowed down to me but I immediately resisted as he was my elder and this custom always embarrasses me. In the spiritual culture I belong to, bowing to an elder or someone with wisdom is a sign of respect. It represents the flow of energy and positive blessings from those who supposedly have wisdom to those who want wisdom. In many parts of India, cheeky teenagers use this custom to get a few rupees from elders as they know that it will please them, and they'll give them some cash! Nevertheless, every cultural action has a deeper spiritual meaning and a significant history.

After a few pleasantries with Mr Malhotra, I offered him a seat and asked how I could help him. I could sense from his body language something was on his mind. He was constantly wiping sweat off his head with a handkerchief and slurring some of his words. I offered him some herbal tea to calm him down. He sipped it after slowly blowing on it.

'Is everything okay?' I asked.

'This is slightly embarrassing, but I am flying for a family holiday to the Alps by a private jet tomorrow,' he said. There were worse problems in the world I thought to myself. He drank more of his tea, which encouraged him to share more. He cleared his throat. 'I usually take medication to put me to sleep, but I no longer want to do so. I have a deep phobia of flying. Several days before the flight, I feel paralysed and cannot think straight. It affects my relationships and my business. I think, what if the plane takes off, but then does not land . . .' He shuddered, which validated his concerns. I asked him to take some deep breaths.

Flying fills many with deep anxiety. In fact, that is why they call the airport a 'terminal'—you never know whether you'll make it or not. Of course, I did not tell this joke to Mr Malhotra. The top three fears for people have been dying, public speaking and flying. In the modern age, however, they seem to have changed to your phone running out of battery, poor Wi-Fi connection and your video still buffering!

Mr Malhotra had a deep fear of flying. It was not something that could be solved overnight and needed a long-term solution. In the short term, I just listened to his anxieties and took him through some meditation and breathing exercises he could do to calm his mind. One of them is as follows:

Exercise: Guided affirmation

Close your eyes.

Take a deep breath in for a count of four seconds.

Hold for a count of two seconds.

Then breathe out for a count of six seconds.

Each time you breathe in, say to yourself: 'I am not alone, the universe is with me, I can deal with whatever it is that I am going through . . .' You can be more specific about the situation that you are dealing with.

Each time you breathe out, say to yourself: 'I let go of my negative feelings. I let go of my anxiety. I feel peaceful. I feel empowered.'

Repeat this exercise ten times.

Now slowly open your eyes.

It is normal to feel anxious at different points in our life. This can be a perfectly natural emotion to life events such as sitting for an exam, getting married or going for a job interview. However, many people find it hard to control their anxiety. For them, these feelings of worry are more constant, making everyday activities difficult as they are marred by the underlying anxiety they feel all the time. Imagine walking around with a ringing in your ears. You would not tolerate it and would want to get rid of it. That is how people suffering with anxiety disorders feel; they have a 'ringing' of anxiety with every action and some people experience it worse than others.

Anxiety disorders are the most common mental illnesses in the world, and they affect approximately a third of adults at some point in their lives.[1] Anxiety itself is a specific symptom of these conditions, but the most common is generalized anxiety disorder. I am not a medical doctor, but I have counselled numerous people who suffer from this disorder and many who may have not been diagnosed formally but cannot rid themselves of constant anxiety. Symptoms of generalized anxiety disorder include feeling restless or worried, having trouble focusing or sleeping and even dizziness or heart palpitations.

Scientific literature shows that many factors can cause anxiety. Genetics seem to play a part, with people being five times more likely to suffer from generalized anxiety disorder if a family member suffers from it too. Chemical imbalances in the brain with, for example, serotonin or noradrenaline, which regulate your mood, or overactivity of some areas of the brain also seem to spike anxiety in many people. Chronic illnesses, such as arthritis or fatigue, or stressful incidents, such as losing a loved one or domestic violence, are other causes. Furthermore, drinking alcohol and smoking have been linked to heightened anxiety. The cessation of both improved symptoms for many.

There are many medicines and psychological therapies that your local doctor can prescribe, but they are beyond the scope of this book. I highly recommend that you visit a medical professional if you have been suffering from an anxiety disorder for a long period of time. We will talk more about this later in the chapter. Additionally, practices like meditation are some things that you can do yourself to help you with anxiety.

Dealing with anxiety

Rational reasoning

In this book so far, I know that I have spoken about planes, airports and flying, above and beyond the quota for any book. However, I have to tell you a story about an adventure I once had. It was one in which I got on to a plane that took off with me in it but landed with me outside of it. Let me tell you about the time I went skydiving.

The night before I was due to make the plunge, I was lying in bed visualizing myself jumping out of the plane. At first I thought, 'I cannot wait, it's going to be an incredible experience.' But then, as the night went by, I started to toss and turn. 'What if the parachute does not open? What if it opens but malfunctions when we are in the air? What if a group of birds collides with me? What if I simply free fall to the ground?' There were hundreds of these statements swirling around in my mind, chattering away and keeping me awake.

Do you know what all of these statements have in common? They may be fears and cause us anxiety, but they start with the same two words: what if. These two words govern most of our lives causing us anxiety and crippling us with inaction. What if I fail? What if we lose? What if people mock me? What if they say no? This *what if* stops us from reaching our full potential.

It is not always possible to confront your *what if* with rational reasoning. Many times, when we're anxious and approach a friend, they tell us to 'calm down'. However, telling someone to 'calm down' rarely works and in some cases, can make them even more agitated. I decided to give rational reasoning a go for myself, to myself. You can try this too for your own anxiety. The first thing I did was figure out if I wanted to experience skydiving. I deliberated and worked out that I was scared, but a resounding *yes* also came from within. Then I told my mind, 'I understand that there are many *what if*s to this scenario but whatever happens, I will be ready.' Once I gained some courage, I decided to employ my intelligence to try and calm my mind further. I made sure that I was not taking an uncalculated risk by checking the risk factors involved.

Skydiving is a popular sport in the US, and in 2020, participants made approximately 2.8 million jumps at more than 200 United States Parachute Association (USPA) affiliated skydiving centres across the country. In 2020, USPA recorded eleven fatal skydiving accidents, a rate of 0.39 fatalities per 1,00,000 jumps. This is comparable to 2019, where participants made more jumps—3.3 million—and USPA recorded 15 fatalities, a rate of 0.45 per 100,000.[2] To put this into context, there were less deaths in jumping out of a plane than car accidents on the road.

I tried to convince my mind in this way, but it protested, 'What if I happen to be one among the eleven?'

The next stage was working out *why* I wanted to have this experience.

'Then stay in the hotel room like a couch potato, missing the most exhilarating experience of your life,' I retorted to my mind. I then consoled it by saying, 'Look, your skydiving experience is not going to be all by yourself. You will be strapped to an expert who has done thousands of dives before and has not had a single casualty, obviously! Take it easy.'

My mind began to understand the rationale but needed me to repeat this multiple times so it was reinforced. The thoughts that we repeat not only are likely to become our action but also our emotions. If we can repeat our reasoning rationales, we are more likely to calm the chattering mind. Before I drifted off to sleep, I asked my mind, 'Why are you anxious?'

My mind replied, 'I am not actually anxious or nervous, I am excited.'

Anxiety reappraisal

The reason why telling people to 'calm down' does not work when they are nervous or anxious about a situation is because it is going against the grain of what our emotions want to do. Instead of trying to suppress the feeling or calm down, we should try and express this feeling as excitement. Of course, this is not a solution for generalized anxiety disorder, but it can help us in specific situations where we feel anxious, such as before an exam, a social occasion, or even skydiving!

This conversation of emotions was coined 'anxiety reappraisal' by Harvard Business School psychologist Alison

Wood Brooks. She conducted an experiment in which she made a group of people do the exact same terrifying tasks: some were doing public speaking, others were doing math problems and the rest singing their hearts out on karaoke. The results were astounding. In every task, the group that was taught to reframe their emotions of apprehension to enthusiasm had a better performance.[3]

The interesting thing is that the switch from nervousness to excitement is not a physiological one. It's not our body changing; it's our mindset changing. All the participants of Alison Brooks's study, regardless of whether they were in the control group or the group told to shift their mindset, had increased heartbeats and released the chemical cortisol, a chemical that surges when you are preparing for action. Both groups were experiencing a 'high arousal state', which is one of the reasons it is better to change our mindset from nervous to excited, than to try and 'calm down', which is a 'low arousal state'.

Although being anxious and being excited have the same physiological symptoms, the mindset differs. They both imply an uncertain future, but anxiety suggests the future should be feared, while excitement suggests it should be looked forward to. It's a state of mind that needs to be practised by reasoning with your mind the next time you have a situation that fills you with dread: 'I am not anxious, I am excited; this is an opportunity, not a threat.'

If rational reasoning does not work and the *what if*s get the better of us, there are other simple physiological things we can do that could help, namely, exercise and stopping smoking and drinking alcohol.

Exercise

Every time I tell people that exercise can help them with their anxiety, they reply that they cannot afford a personal trainer or do not have time to go to the gym. Exercise is now synonymous with lifting weights or going for long arduous runs. However, for me, exercise is getting the body moving.

Getting the body moving every day releases feel-good endorphins that enhance our sense of well-being. It can simultaneously take our mind off our worries, breaking the cycle of negative thoughts that cause us to feel anxious. It is not just anxiety disorders that exercise helps with; other mental health conditions such as depression are positively affected by staying fit.

As mentioned above, exercise could be any form of movement. The ancient science of well-being suggests that going for a walk in nature daily helps us process our emotions. With every step on the ground, our anxiety reduces. Exercise is also known to help us gain confidence by making us feel and look fit, gives us an opportunity to socialize with others by playing sports and developing relationships, and also reinforces a positive coping mechanism for us.

Stopping smoking and drinking alcohol

Many people who smoke or chew tobacco do so because they believe that it reduces stress, but scientific studies have found that this does the opposite. Cigarettes contain an extremely addictive substance called nicotine, which, at first, can improve our mood and give us a sensation of relaxation. However, over time, regular doses of nicotine can lead to changes in the brain that cause withdrawal symptoms when the supply of nicotine decreases.

Although at first, smoking can give the sensation of reducing stress, over time it increases anxiety. Science has disproved the claim that smoking gets rid of our tension. This feeling is temporary and soon caves into symptoms based on our craving. These include anxiety, stress and in some cases, paranoia.

The story is similar with alcohol but even easier to understand. Alcohol is a depressant; it lowers the level of a hormone called serotonin, which is largely responsible for the feeling of happiness. The less serotonin we produce, the more anxiety we are likely to feel. Just like smoking cigarettes, our brain builds up tolerance to the 'relaxing' sensations it produces, making it less effective and more likely to destabilize our emotions. Studies show that 20 per cent of those with social anxiety have an alcohol abuse problem and that alcohol can disrupt our sleep pattern, which in turn can trigger our anxiety.

As a monk, I do not smoke or drink alcohol. However, I do not *ever* judge those who do. It is extremely addictive and somewhat commonplace in our society. Nevertheless, science does show that if we can take the first steps to stopping smoking and reducing our alcohol intake, we can lead lives of reduced stress.

Beyond rational reasoning and simple physiological acts to help us reduce our anxiety is seeking help. We can only reason to a point—something I found with Mr Malhotra in regard to his fear of flying. If anxiety takes over, finding someone we trust to speak to about it is always a safe option.

Seeking help

Big boys do not cry is the philosophy that still permeates our society, despite the considerable movement to become aware of and eradicate mental health problems. When I was growing up, asking for help or being vulnerable was seen as a sign of weakness. It was seen as a sign that you could not cope or solve your own problems. I am now a huge advocate of changing this culture completely: big boys *should* cry and in order for big boys to cry, they have to be taught that it's fine to cry as small boys. It should be commonplace to seek help when we are struggling with our mental health.

I want to share a personal story with you. When I joined the ashram, all I had was three sets of robes and a small wooden locker. Each monk had one and they were all next to each other lining the corridor of the ashram on the first floor. Although each locker was exactly the same, the insides would be different as each monk decorated it accordingly to his personality. Some had their own personal altars of prayers, others stuck pictures of the Divine and some had personal libraries of as many ancient books as they could fit on one shelf. It's a minimalistic lifestyle, but we're happy, as we know less is often more.

The ashram is separate from the rest of the temple, but the lockers are situated on a veranda, meaning that in the monsoon, water flows off the roof of the veranda and to the ground below. Although it gets humid, sitting on top of a locker and talking to other monks can be peaceful while the rain falls. Adjacent to our corridor of lockers is a private meeting room for the monks, which in turn is adjacent to the large communal temple hall where hundreds meet weekly to pray, meditate and sing together in front of Sri Sri Radha Gopinath, *murtis* or deities in the temple and the focus of our devotion.

Many Mumbai monsoons ago, only a few years after I joined the ashram, Paresh, a young boy of nineteen years, came to stay with us. He wanted to experience the lifestyle of a monk during his summer holidays, before he went away to study abroad. We have many such requests by those who want to see how we live and gain a spiritual foundation before they move on in life. Paresh was around five-foot-six, slightly chubby around the waist, sweet, funny and eager to serve. It can be intimidating talking to monks at times, but Paresh was confident and always made us laugh. We could sense that he was having the time of his life living and serving at the temple.

One evening I sat on the floor by my locker, meditating deeply while hearing the pitter-patter of the rain against the tiled ground floor. It was the second evening of the monsoon. As I tried to focus, all of a sudden, I heard a thumping sound behind me. Paresh had fallen to the ground and was having a seizure. He was shaking uncontrollably. I jumped to my feet, shouted for help and approached Paresh whose limbs were vigorously shaking and his eyes rolling back. I had never seen anything like this and did not know what to do. Should I hold him down? Should I call an ambulance? Should I run to call another monk? No other monk was in sight. The monsoon clouds created a dark shadow across the ashram and the sound of rain was now an ominous soundtrack. I fell to my knees next to Paresh in a state of panic as I felt paralysed by my inaction. 'Paresh, Paresh!' I screamed. 'What's going on?'

At that moment, another monk who was a medical doctor came and, in a flash, performed a procedure to calm Paresh down. After a few moments, this young boy came back to consciousness slightly dazed and tired, but aware of his surroundings. 'Are you okay?' I asked. 'What was that?' He confirmed that he gets momentary blackouts and seizures. Doctors have performed tests on him but do not know why he gets them or when they are likely to happen. I was shocked while he was telling me this. I had no idea what to do and how to behave. As more monks approached the scene, I backed away and returned to the temple hall, thankful that Paresh was alive and well.

That night, as I lay in my sleeping bag covered by the mosquito net, I was having trouble sleeping. Every time I closed my eyes, the episode of Paresh having a seizure kept flashing in my mind. I tried to reason with myself that he was fine now and under the care of doctors for his condition. But the *what if* syndrome had got me. What if he was not fine and it was because I had frozen and did not know what to do to help him? If this could happen to him, what if it happened to me? The next day, I tried to brush off this feeling by keeping myself busy with my daily responsibilities, but it was to no avail. Busying ourselves with work, even if it is charity or spiritual work, will not cover up our deep, underlying emotional needs. In fact, the busier I got and the more I saw Paresh, the more I started developing a fear of this unknown disease. Just as the dark monsoon clouds covered the scene of Paresh having a seizure while I looked on, a shadow of anxiety covered my mind. It started affecting my daily activities and my quality of sleep. Reasoning did not help in this situation as the intensity of my fears was much larger than the strength of my reasoning. In this situation, the mind takes over and leaves intelligence and logic to mull in the background.

Leo Aikman said, 'Blessed is the man who is too busy to worry in the daytime and too sleepy to worry at night.' But in my case, being busy did not solve the problem. Distracting ourselves can give us relief for some time, but it usually does not heal us.

As a young monk, I also believed that intensifying my spiritual practice, meditating harder, praying harder, chanting harder would help. To my disbelief, none of it helped. Even in the name of spirituality, we can distract ourselves from our emotional needs. The purpose of our spiritual practices is not to specifically restore our emotional well-being and solve our anxieties, although they have that side effect in general. Yes, meditation can help with our stress, but if the cause of our stress is another identifiable problem, we must deal with the problem and not mask it in the name of protecting our spiritual credibility. We must not bury our heads in the sand; we must not ignore the signs that indicate we are struggling with our mental health by covering them up with our spiritual practices. Spiritual practices are meant to awaken our deeper self. They are not there to deal with our physical or mental ailments, although they may have that after-effect and can complement our healing.

An easier way to understand this is to consider the precautions we take when we are physically ill. If we fell over and broke our leg, would we pray to god for it to be fixed or would we visit a doctor? We would use our god-given intelligence to visit a doctor to place us in a cast and give us crutches. Although we do not abandon our spiritual inclinations when we have a physical ailment, we must be practical and seek the appropriate help. The same is true of mental health.

The mind is a subtle aspect of the body. This concept will be clarified in section 4. We should deal with our mental health just as we would deal with a fever: either take prescribed medication that will help our symptoms or seek help from a therapist.

My lack of sleep was significantly affecting my daily work. I could not help but think of Paresh's situation. As I write this, I think, 'Why couldn't I just get over it?' However, reverting to my previous analogy for someone who has broken their leg, you cannot tell them to simply 'get over it'. There is a way of dealing with such issues.

The common responses are fright, flight or fight. Many allow their mental health issues to linger through fright. They keep their problem switch on in the background, just as a medical clinic reception keeps the radio playing: you know it's there, but you are not quite listening. This can lead to paranoia and worsening of symptoms over time. Another group of people may decide to forcefully try and switch their problem off. They use flight to run away from their problem, turning to things like denial or being constantly busy to make their issues feel insignificant. The final group try to fight the problem. They do what they can to deal with their challenges but go about it in an unstructured manner. Fighting is great, it shows motivation and willingness to overcome the issue. But it needs structure and strategy. A boxer learns everything about their opponent and fights with a cool head. They employ structure when trying to win; we must do the same with our mental health.

We have all heard that the first step is always accepting we have a problem. Just as the first step for an alcoholic in the Alcoholics Anonymous programme is letting go and admitting they have a problem, the first step in dealing with our anxiety is admitting that we *have* or *might have* a problem. By admitting that we are powerless, even for a split second, we allow humility to settle in. It's the feeling of humility that allows us to seek the help we need. If we are anxious about something and we feel we might need help, we can take a moment to say out loud, 'I am anxious about *my problem*. I have been anxious about *my problem* for a *certain number of days or months or years*. I want to face this anxiety and get rid of it; however, I think I need help to do so.'

The first person I went to was my locker mate, Govinda Das. He was one of the first monks to join the ashram in Mumbai and I knew his wisdom was vast. I saw him every morning and greeted him, but I could not quite muster up the courage to tell him how I was feeling. It was hard to share my weakness. After all, I am a monk: was I not supposed to be above all this and be the 'enlightened one' guiding others? I was also ashamed. *What if* other monks found out and would judge me? After a few days, I realized that these monks were my most trusted confidants. Monks are human too and I am sure everyone goes through their challenges. The human mind is like our software. It can malfunction regardless of what the outer shell of gender, religion, nationality or socioeconomic status is made up of. I needed help—I admitted it and decided to meet Govinda Das privately. As a side note,

I always recommend meeting those you trust privately and not advertising your problems to the whole world. That can be overwhelming and unproductive in helping you with your anxiety.

Govinda Das is a grave person. He's strict on himself, but lenient with others. What this means is that he has the determination of a lion, but the heart of a Bengali mother. As I sat with him on the veranda of our ashram drinking hot tea, I told him how I was struggling. I spoke with my head down looking to the floor. At first, he laughed. It was not a laugh at me, but a laugh that he knew what to do. A laugh *with* me. Many times, we are so engrossed in our own problems that we are unable to take a step back and see the solutions open to us.

I finished explaining my problem fully. He paused, said some empathetic words, put his arm around my shoulders and then gave me examples of people who he had helped through similar fears. He helped me see that there was nothing I could have done to help Paresh further and that what happened to him was unlikely to happen to me. What he said next shocked me, 'Go and see a psychiatrist too.' He told me that sleepless nights and paranoia may also need to be handled with the help of a professional.

'A psychiatrist?' I thought. 'I don't think my problem is that bad. I'm fine. It's just a little thing that is bothering me. I don't need to see a psychiatrist!' For the readers of this book, were you also shocked at this suggestion? How can a monk see a psychiatrist?

Seeing a psychiatrist is taboo in many countries, but we need to work to change that. This is not only the case in India, but around the world. The stigma originates from the way mental health professionals used to treat patients and conjures up images of being in an asylum. It is especially taboo for men to seek help as they, because of societal expectations to be the breadwinners and strong, bury their mental struggles away. Stereotypes about gender can leave men damaged as they fail to live up to the dominant, in control, strong personalities that our culture portrays they should have. It is no wonder that in the UK, 75 per cent of those who commit suicide are men.[4] I admit that I also had this perception that seeing a psychiatrist is for the weak, but this could not be further from the truth. We go to a doctor for our physical ailments; we should also feel comfortable going to a doctor for our mental ailments.

I trusted Govinda Das's advice, although it was hard to digest at the time. I have never gone through anything like this or dreamed I would ever need professional help for my mind. This was not a huge issue, but it was consistently nagging at me. If you hold a barbell out in front of you for a moment, it won't bother you. But if you hold the same barbell out in front of you for an hour, it will cause significant strain. Regardless of the weight, it is how long we are carrying it that can cause injury.

Govinda Das suggested that I should go and see Dr Patel. There were many Dr Patels in our community, but I knew exactly which one he was talking about. *This* Dr Patel had been a member of our spiritual community for many years and had been training with a renowned senior for the last three years since he passed medical school. Dr Patel was incredibly bright and accomplished in his own right. But there was a catch. I had been giving lectures, a weekly talk on spiritualty,

motivation and the mind, at Dr Patel's medical school for the
past six years when he was there too. He always came to listen
and greeted me affectionately at the end. I had even done
significant discourses on dealing with the mind. How would
it look for me now to approach him with my issues? Was this
not a self-defeating action?

I returned to the first lesson we learn as monks: humility.
In fact, we pray for humility daily in our prayers: *tri nad api
sunicena*. We should have a humble state of mind so that we
can perfect our meditative state. Just as a blade of grass gets
stepped on and bounces back, we should be humble enough
to bow down so that we can gain wisdom. My prayers were
definitely working as approaching Dr Patel, my former
student, would humble me. However, it was a good thing and
an irrational hang-up. Just because someone teaches medicine
in a medical school does not mean they cannot get ill. Just
because someone is a mechanic does not mean that their car
will not break down. Just because someone is a dentist does
not mean their teeth will not decay. Just because someone is
a monk does not mean that they will not succumb to issues
of the mind and stress. The sooner we address our issues, the
better it is for us as we can get back to living a normal, stable
and fulfilling life.

At that moment, with Govinda Das, I decided to call
Dr Patel. Without a hint of superiority, he understood my
problem and I asked if I could see him in his clinic the next
day. He said that he was fully booked but offered to come
to the ashram to spend time with me personally. Another
humbling situation. At his clinic, no one knew who I was,
but in the ashram, everyone knew who I was and would see

that I was speaking with a practising psychiatrist. I snapped myself out of these thoughts. If I met a dentist in the ashram, would people jump to the conclusion that I had a toothache? Although we may introduce ourselves by our professions, humans are more than their careers.

Regardless of what people thought, I knew it was important for me to see him. At times, we live our life based on what others think of us rather than how life should be lived. The next morning, after our morning meditations, Dr Patel and I sat on the same ashram veranda where I had met Govinda Das a day before. At first, I unconsciously put up a front that everything was fine, but he was used to patients doing that. Through his communication skills, he allowed me to be vulnerable and tell him Paresh's story. I had to wipe the dust off the mirror or remove the filter from my post and show him what I was struggling with in its clean, unedited format. After hearing my story, Dr Patel said that I had been under stress, but there was no serious issue. This too would pass if I were to face my problems head-on. He had said similar things to what Govinda Das had said, but coming from a trained professional, it made me peaceful. After a few days, my anxieties about the subject started to dissipate. The processing of opening up to Govinda Das and Dr Patel was needed for me to move on.

Relief

Opening up about our problems can help us feel lighter and give us a sense of relief. If our problem is a huge box that we are carrying, opening up to someone we trust would represent them helping us carry the other side of the box. Many hands make light work. The key is that they need to know a) how to carry the box safely (be competent in listening and giving advice), and b) be trusted to carry the box (be a trusted friend who is non-biased and non-judgemental so as to not embarrass us about opening up).

We often carry so much weight on our own. This can make us feel isolated and lonely over time, harming our inner peace and joy. There is an ancient story of the jackal and the hunter that depicts this mental weight well. Once a hunter decided to cross into illegal grounds to hunt a jackal. He wanted to prove to his friends that he could catch the largest jackal of the pack. In desperation, he had crossed into a forest that was governed by another kingdom. As he walked through, he noticed the jackal in the moonlight, drinking water majestically from a stream. The hunter slowly took out his rifle, aimed at the jackal and fired.

'Who goes there?' the hunter immediately heard from the other side of the trees. It was a local officer patrolling the area. 'Drop your weapon and show yourself!' the officer shouted. The hunter immediately ran to the jackal, knowing that if the officer found it with his bullet, he would be prosecuted. He stuffed the jackal into his large coat as the officer approached. 'Who are you?' the officer demanded.

'I am a local hunter. Sorry, I am lost! Ouch . . .' The jackal was still alive! However, instead of telling the officer what he had done, he kept hiding the jackal inside his coat and allowed it to bite him multiple times. This analogical story represents mental health. The jackal is our anxiety, and the coat is our external appearance. Hiding our anxiety without dealing with it only causes pain. Letting the jackal out of our coats and admitting that we have a problem brings relief from suffering. In real life, there is no angry police officer judging us about our problems, but a trusted friend or professional helping us.

Support

Not only do we feel lighter by opening up, but we also get the support we need. This happens from three types of people:

- **Guides and friends:** These are trusted confidants who we can share our hearts with. They can help us only to the capacity they understand the problem themselves and advise us accordingly. In many cases, we already know the reason for our anxiety. We simply need someone to bounce the problem off, diminishing our uncomfortable feelings of shame and guilt.
- **Experts:** If our friends cannot help us, we should talk to a professional. It helped me and depending on your problem, speaking to a medical professional can help you see things from a different perspective, and see them rationally. In some cases, the medical expert may find it apt to prescribe medication to help us.
- **Universe:** In sharing our inner issues and seeking help, we gain the help of an additional power. When we humble ourselves and admit that we need help, our focus changes to finding the solution to our anxiety. This allows universal powers to flow through us and inspire us to succeed.

Exercise: Reflection on anxiety

Reflect on what makes you anxious. Is there a pattern that triggers you to feel anxious? If so, what is it?

Think about the last few times you felt anxious. What helped you feel less anxious and why did that help? Try and identify a pattern of things that has helped you deal with anxiety.

Mr Malhotra felt happier after hearing that I had once gone to see a psychiatrist. He had already felt better with the breathing exercise we did, but now even more so after opening up to me and discussing the issue deeply. I encouraged him to seek help for his phobia while simultaneously trying what he could do himself to solve the issue. I told him that certain fears and anxieties come from imagined problems, but others come from real issues that take a deeper insight and longer time to solve. It's important for us to tell the difference.

As I said goodbye to Mr Malhotra, I decided the next port of call for me would be to shake off my jet lag and rest. It was going to be a busy tour of the UK, meeting fascinating people who all have their own individual stories and struggles.

Chapter summary:

- Anxiety disorders are the most common mental illnesses in the world.
- The thoughts that we repeat not only are likely to become our actions, but also our emotions. If we can

repeat our reasoning rationales, we are more likely to calm the chattering mind.

- Instead of trying to suppress our feelings or 'calm down', studies show that we should try and express those feelings as excitement.
- If rational reasoning does not work and the 'what ifs' get the better of us, there are other simple physiological things we can do to help ourselves, namely, exercise and stopping smoking and drinking alcohol.
- It should be commonplace to seek help when we are struggling with our mental health.
  o Making ourselves busy with work, even if it is charity or spiritual work, will not cover up our deep, underlying emotional needs.
- Spiritual practices are meant to awaken our deeper self. They are not there to deal with our physical or mental ailments, although they may have that after-effect and can complement our healing.
- The first step is always accepting that we have a problem.
- I always recommend meeting those we trust privately and not advertising our problems to the whole world. That can be overwhelming and unproductive in helping us deal with our anxiety.
- Regardless of the weight, it is how long we are carrying it that can cause injury.
- Hiding our anxiety without dealing with it only causes pain.

FIVE

The Bird's Nest: Dealing with Depression

'Mental pain is less dramatic than physical pain, but it is more common and also more hard to bear. The frequent attempt to conceal mental pain increases the burden. It is easier to say, "My tooth is aching" than to say "My heart is broken".'

—C.S. Lewis

The heat in London is different from the heat in Mumbai. When it gets hot in London, there is a dryness to it, and it does feel as if the sun is penetrating your skin. Mumbai, on the other hand, is humid. There is a dampness to the heat that makes it difficult to sleep, especially in the ashram where we have a range of monks all preferring different climates.

When I joined the ashram in Mumbai, we did not have air conditioning in the temple hall. This hall is around twenty-five by ten metres and because of the sheer number of monks we have, around thirty of them have to sleep in this hall at night. There is simply no space in the ashram! On one hand, we would prefer they have their own space and that they don't have to sleep in the temple hall, but on the other, it's great for those who find it difficult to wake up in the morning, as the murmur of chanting monks who come to the hall way before the time it opens for worship raises them from their slumber.

To suit the range of climates preferred, we had two zones in the temple. The left side was the 'fan-atic' zone, and the right was the 'non-fan-atic' zone. In the past we did not have air-conditioning, we only had overhead swirling fans that threw the air down on those below. There were monks who enjoyed sleeping under them—the fan-atics—and those that did not—the non-fan-atics. Personally, I was a hardcore fan-atic, needing the cool breeze of a fan to get me to sleep.

One night as we were all sleeping, under our pop-up mosquito nets that make the temple hall look like a mini-city, one of the monks sleeping in the fan-atic zone woke up. He unzipped his mosquito net and jumped out of it. He crept around the other tents like a burglar snooping around a house. 'What's happening?' I whispered to him, half-asleep. It was two in the morning.

'I think I see something,' he said, startled to see me awake. Like a gazelle running away from the pounce of a lioness, the monk ran to the light switches, turned them on and shouted, 'Snake! Snake in the temple hall!' All the monks jumped out of their own mosquito nets, many of them tearing their sleeping bags in the commotion. Many simply lay there shouting 'polite abuse' back at him that it was not time to wake up yet and to switch off the lights. Others were fast asleep; not even an earthquake could wake them up.

I got up immediately, alarmed at the fact that there could be a venomous serpent among our city of tents. What if it bit someone? I went to the monk who was approaching a slithering creature. It moved away from us, almost floating on the temple floor. All of a sudden, another monk slapped him on the side of his head. 'That's a child's balloon!' he exclaimed. It was a long black balloon, the likes of which are tied into various animal shapes at parties. It had been floating around the floor due to the fans. Some monks laughed, others hurled more 'polite abuse' at him, and some missed the whole thing still being fast asleep. Relieved, we turned the lights off and went back to sleep. As we woke up at 4 a.m., he was extremely embarrassed and could not avoid the mockery of his close friends about the incident for the next few weeks.

When the lights are off, our imagination turns simple things into monsters. The pile of clothes on our chair, our jacket hanging on the door, or a balloon being blown by the wind. They can all seem like creatures from the underworld. It is only when the lights are turned on that our fears are dispelled. In the same way, our imagination can make reality out of the darkness of illusion. It can create problems that are not true. It is only when we turn the lights on—face our fears, anxieties and insecurities, or seek help from those we trust—that we really see if there is a monster there or a winter coat. This is an analogy for the difference between short-term issues of the mind that can be solved relatively quickly, like my episode with Paresh, and long-term issues that plague the mind, such as depression. The first steps are to switch the lights on to see what you are dealing with.

Exercise: Reflection on the mind's ability to trick us

Recall any incidents where you initially felt as though you were in danger but later realized that there was nothing to worry about.

Reminding ourselves of these events will train the mind to remain calm in stressful situations.

The UK is known for its universities. Oxford, Cambridge and the London School of Economics, are all notable higher education institutions training some of the brightest minds in the world. I had the opportunity to speak at University College London on my trip this time round, addressing over a hundred students on controlling the mind to get rid of stress. The auditorium was circular with red cushioned seats and large glass-paned windows looking on to the outside world. I was addressing a group of medical students and healthcare professionals on a topic entitled, 'Physician heal thyself'. Nearly everyone had a notepad and pen resting on the old wooden tables in front of them. This was an older, musty lecture theatre modernized by the insertion of two projectors beaming my presentation on to the screens above.

I have always enjoyed speaking to young people. Their minds are still fresh and malleable like young bamboo. Bamboo, much like our opinions, is flexible when it is young, but as it ages, it becomes tough and rigid. This particular group was full of energy, listening to my every word, looking for inspiration, but at the same time, also looking for the logic to what I was saying. They were not awed by my saffron robes like students in India were. Many in the audience were looking to catch a man of the cloth out in what he was saying. Young people still have the confidence to challenge a proposition until it is either defeated or understood. But once they do understand it, they have the energy to transform it into action, becoming catalysts of change to form a legacy for a brighter world. I started by explaining to the audience the fact that unless we are in a good place physically, mentally and spiritually, we cannot be good healers.

As I was speaking, an uninvited guest entered the lecture hall. It flapped its grey wings and flew to the top of the room. A pigeon with a straw in its beak startled a few members of the audience; I guess it was making a nest to lay its eggs in a corner of the old room. It was the perfect place to build a nest as no predator would think about entering a room full of a hundred healthcare professionals. I was taken aback by our new friend entering the room, but after a moment, the students focused again as if nothing had happened. I guess they were used to the pigeon entering but wary of protecting their clothes, bags and notebooks from what it may drop on them.

Inspired by what I just saw, I changed the direction of my presentation slightly. I asked the hundred-odd members of the audience, 'How many of you live in a home?' Puzzled by this rhetorical question, everyone nervously raised their hands. I continued, 'On any given day, how many of you count the pigeons flying above your homes?' Pigeons are as abundant in London as they are in India. In fact, many people make a living selling bird feed at Trafalgar Square to feed the flock of pigeons who linger around Nelson's Column. No one raised their hands to my second question. I went on to tell them of an ancient Indian anecdote regarding Emperor Akbar and his minister Birbal.

One day Emperor Akbar and Birbal were taking a walk in the palace gardens. It was a nice summer morning and there were plenty of crows happily playing around the pond. While watching the crows, a question came into Akbar's head. He wondered how many crows there were in his kingdom.

Since Birbal was accompanying him, he asked Birbal this question. After a moment's thought, Birbal replied, 'There are ninety-five thousand, four hundred and sixty-three crows in the kingdom.'

Amazed by his quick response, Akbar tried to test him again, 'What if there are more crows than you answered?' Without hesitating, Birbal replied, 'If there are more crows than my answer, then some crows are visiting from other neighbouring kingdoms.' 'And what if there are less crows?' Akbar asked. 'Then some crows from our kingdom have gone on holiday to other places.'

None of us keeps a count of the birds that are flying above the roof of our homes, but when one enters and tries to make a nest, we will notice it. In our house, they may be noisy, they may lay eggs, they make a mess! Our emotions are similar. We may have positive ones and negative ones throughout the day, but we have to let them pass just as we let the birds above our house move freely. However, when a negative emotion makes a permanent residence within our minds and starts affecting our well-being, we should address it. At that moment, the pigeon started cooing in its monotonous way and the auditorium laughed. I gave them another analogy to cement the point, which they could connect to even better as healthcare professionals. 'How do we know we are ill?' I asked the audience. A young lady at the front wearing a lab coat stood up and said, 'When the body displays symptoms, sir.'

I nodded.

'But can we actually see the cause of what is causing our illness? Can we see the virus or bacteria with the naked eye?' The audience shook their heads. 'Our bodies generate symptoms to try and fight the infection and tell us that something is wrong. Without these symptoms of pain or fever, we would not be able to seek proper treatment.' I paused for a moment, making sure that I was going in the right direction with these doctors. 'There are simple viral fevers that are cured with rest and plenty of fluids. Yet, there are others—malaria, typhoid, pneumonia . . . these diseases need extensive treatment from modern medicine at times or they could be fatal,' I continued.

I went on to explain that our mental health also produces symptoms of unease, but they are harder to spot. Many behavioural patterns are simply symptoms of an underlying emotional turmoil that needs to be addressed. Symptoms like gloom, a clouded mind, heaviness, fatigue, irritability, mood swings, lack of interest, withdrawal from our work or people, the feeling of meaninglessness, among many others, could be underlying signs of anxiety and depression. But they have an underlying cause that needs to be addressed. Just as a thermometer is used to check our temperature and a blood test is used to assess the markers of infection, we need to seek help and be assessed when we are struggling with our mind.

Exercise: Addressing negative emotions

How will you address your negative emotions so that they do not turn into a 'nest'? Write an action plan.

For example: The next time I feel a negative emotion, I am going to consciously take some time out to . . . This way, I can try and address the emotion before it lingers and creates a long-term negative effect.

Remember, this needs to be done as soon as you first identify the negative feeling.

Sadness and Depression

Studies suggest that over 40 per cent of us will suffer from depression in our lives.[1] That means every other person you meet in the street will go through this disease. However, depression is poorly understood. Many people mistake depression for sadness and sadness for depression because they share many similarities. In both, people feel lost, complain of alienation from their normal lives and cry. However, the difference is that the person who is sad has a *specific reason* for their sadness, whereas the depressed person may not. It's easy for the sad person to tell you what is bothering them: the death of a loved one, the loss of a job or the breaking of a relationship. The depressed person is just depressed; they can't pinpoint what is causing their hopelessness.

Because of this lack of clarity on *why* someone is feeling depressed, it is common to prescribe medication to lift such patients out of their state of despair. The pharmaceutical industry, and rightly so in many cases, writes that depression is due to a change in brain chemistry that needs to be corrected with cost-effective medication. The lack of a clear psychological cause of depression can also frustrate the friends and family of those who suffer from depression. These people may offer solutions that are unpalatable, or may accuse them of 'not trying to get better' or even exaggerating their symptoms.

There is another solution to depression which has a growing evidence: psychotherapy or 'talk therapy'.

Psychotherapy aims to help people understand their feelings and gives them solutions to help them face their challenges. Although it sounds similar to counselling, psychotherapists believe that there are deeper traumas that are banished to our subconscious governing our moods, actions and state of well-being. Therefore, they believe that depression *does* have a deeper cause that needs to be explored by talking to a psychotherapist. It is believed that the reason depression and sadness are closely linked is that depression *is* sadness where the cause has been unconsciously forgotten to protect you from overwhelming feelings of loss and pain. Talk therapy can help with depression, low self-esteem, bereavement, addiction and other severe mental health conditions.

Why might someone then be depressed? What could they be unconsciously trying to block out? It could be trauma from their childhood—the lack of care from a parent, trauma from their relationships—problems with their marriage or trauma from their career. The list goes on and a psychotherapist wants to uncover what that trauma is. Furthermore, a person who is depressed may not understand that they are depressed. They may not feel they need to expand their self-awareness to help themselves. This plays into the theory that people become depressed without a cause, propagating the erroneous notion that only medication can uplift their state.

People who suffer from depression can have lowered self-esteem, feel shame and guilt and, at times, have suicidal thoughts. People who are sad are generally upset about something that has happened to them and can specifically point it out. They do not feel a lack of self-worth. An interesting point is that, in some cases, depression is associated with a euphoric mood known as mania; thus people who suffer from this type of depression are labelled 'manic depressives' or more recently, as people who suffer from bipolar disorder. They seem happy but deep down, are submerged in dissatisfaction for life. You only have to search on the Internet to see how bipolar disorder affects many people regardless of their fame or wealth.

Both those with bipolar disorder, who hide their depression with 'happiness' and classic depressives, who show their depression through 'sadness' have one thing in common according to psychotherapists. With both types, feelings of pain or wrath are subdued and not directed at those who caused them. Over time this leads to self-hating to avoid the issue at hand that may have been caused by another person. Someone with depression would rather mask their true emotions than deal with them.

I am not a medical professional or a psychotherapist, but I use many of these principles when I help those who approach me as a monk. People who are depressed need someone to listen to them, someone to support them. Although medication can help them arrive at the conclusion, they need to speak to someone because I feel the disease cannot be solved just by 'fixing the brain chemistry'. Only by uncovering the cause of the depression and the unresolved trauma that lingers within, can it start to be solved. People with depression need to know that someone cares, and their emotions are allowed. They are allowed to feel angry; they are allowed to feel upset; they are allowed to feel manic. They need to mourn the life that was taken away from them just as one would mourn the loss of a loved one. For example, if someone experienced little love from their parents growing up, that person should get the validation that *that action of their parents was wrong*. It is the role of a parent to give love and the depressive should have a space to mourn that loss of love they experienced.

Within my own community, we find that those who practise spirituality can suffer from depression as well. This may come as a shock to you, as all those who practise spirituality are 'supposed to be happy' but, as stated earlier, we can fall into the trap of masking our state of mental well-being with spiritual practice.

A few years ago, a young member of our community, Ajay, approached me with the symptoms of depression. He told me he was irritable with others, did not want to serve others and really wanted to become a recluse. I probed him further and he said he would binge-eat anything he would get and just wanted to sleep, avoiding his duties. The symptoms he was experiencing were concerning.

Ajay was the oldest of four brothers. He came from a middle-class background from one of the suburbs of Mumbai. For most of his life, he had shared a room with one of his youngest brothers, never really getting space to express himself. 'The oldest always sets the example' his father would chant to him as a mantra. Although most military families are not like this, his father, who had served in the military for a few years, was strict and trained his family as if they were living in the barracks. His philosophy was, 'It is my way or the highway.' He would not tolerate anyone raising their voice at him in the house, although he would scream at the 'incompetence' of his sons.

Ajay was not smart academically. Numbers were his enemy and letters were their sidekick. However, where he did excel was with a paintbrush. Ajay was gifted at art, but that was not valued in the household. He would dread parent-teacher meetings as he knew the maths, science and English teachers would give him a 'below average' status, enraging his father. He knew that that evening his father's belt would come off and his other academically gifted siblings would laugh as he took the buckle end of it. Although his mother praised his artwork, his father would laugh at it saying that this 'is not what real men do' and 'will not get you a job in Mumbai'. His father would mock him in front of relatives telling them that it was 'first the worst, second the best' with his children.

It was hard for Ajay to open up. His mind was a fortress as his father had trained him never to reveal what he was thinking. Being tough was what mattered. Raising his voice or expressing his emotions in his parental home was forbidden. Not to say there were never good times, but the experience of a regimented, harsh and unloving father can take its toll on anyone. Being berated once or twice can be manageable, but the constant sarcastic, condescending voice of your own father can be hurtful.

The psychotherapists would understand Ajay's story as one of classic depression. Wanting to avoid addressing how his father treated him and, to some extent, did still treat him, Ajay would have probably pushed those emotions to the back of his mind. For Ajay, it was easier to live being berated than accept that his father was emotionally and verbally abusive. This is not to say parents cannot discipline and be strict with their children, but love must be the guiding force and intention. For Ajay, these suppressed feelings led to an emotional crisis and therefore his reaction was that as written above. Ajay had become a wreck. This wasn't a generalized anxiety disorder, but I understood it as depression. Only a qualified doctor would be able to diagnose it.

Listening to and understanding Ajay's problem, I realized that there were three things he could do:

- Read more about his condition and see what he could do to help himself.
- Approach a qualified psychotherapist and keep coming to me for informal counselling.
- Approach a doctor to assess whether he needed prescription medication to help him.

These three can all work together, but the ratio of how well they work depends on the magnitude of the problem.

When the magnitude of our problem is less than our ability to deal with it ourselves, self-help works. When the magnitude of our problem is overwhelmingly greater than our ability to deal with it ourselves, we need to seek help either through medication, therapy or both together. When someone is trying to lose weight, they may be able to do it themselves without any external guidance. However, in other cases, they may need to see a nutritionist or trainer or even undergo medical surgery. This analogy extends further. We have reached such a pinnacle moment in the state of our mental health as a planet. Just as morbidly obese people needing medical help have increased, those needing medication intervention to help them with their depression have also significantly increased.

One should note that we might not always be the right people to help someone suffering from depression and they might need medical help. When we are helping others deal with their depression, we should:

1. **Listen**—help the person come to a state where they can accept that they have an issue.
2. **Identify**—help the person come to a state where they feel comfortable identifying that issue.
3. **Empower**—help the person gain their sense of worth and value, and help them see how they have the power to come out of it all.
4. **Address**—find a solution to their depression by one of the three solutions given above. It is important not to try and play the role of a qualified psychotherapist in this process.

Affirmations

There is a famous saying, 'Don't speak negatively about yourself, even as a joke. Your body doesn't know the difference. Words are energy and cast spells; that's why it's called a spelling. Change the way you speak to yourself, and you can change your life. What you're not changing, you are also choosing.' You may have already heard of *affirmations* or *positive affirmations*. 'You can do it', 'You are valuable', 'You are loved', are all examples of phrases that people say as affirmations. They are positive statements that can help us overcome self-defeat and negative thinking patterns. Our thoughts become our words, our words become our actions and our actions become our character. Therefore, if we can change our thoughts and words, we can substantially improve how we behave. Positive affirmations may seem superficial and cringy, but research shows they work. Many of us do repetitive exercises to improve our health such as going to the gym, but what about exercises for the mind? Positive mental repetitions can rewire our mind to help us change our outlook. This is not to say that your depression will be cured by positive affirmations. That would be a ludicrous claim, but literature does show that it can help.

Positive affirmations can help us with stress. One study found that practising affirmations for a short period of time a day can improve the 'problem-solving abilities of chronically stressed subjects to the same level as those with low stress'.[2] But the research goes further. Another study suggested that affirmations can give us a stronger sense of self-worth that has tangible benefits in our actions.[3] For example, if we are depressed about our work-ethic, affirmations can help us cement the values we aspire to have and believe in, helping us boost our own well-being.

Three ways to avoid feeling depressed

In the spiritual culture of Bhakti yoga, we have a saying, 'It could have been worse.' This is a phrase you tell yourself, not others when they are facing a calamity. There are many things we can do to save ourselves from feeling depressed or to prevent things from getting worse if we already suffer from depression, besides consulting a professional. As bad as depression can be, we can be helped by following these given ways of avoiding it. Just as by using an inhaler, an asthma patient can prevent their wheeze from turning into a full-blown asthma attack, similarly, there are many interventions you can do that can help you move away from feeling depressed.

One thing to note with the points below is that science shows that depression can be due to genetic reasons in up to 40 per cent of people. That means that some people have a greater predisposition to the disease than others. Some people will have a harder time with their mental well-being than others due to no fault of their own. However, we still have the other 60 per cent, the majority of which can be influenced to a large extent by our actions.

Sleep

It's become fashionable to work until the point of exhaustion and scroll until the point of sleep. Getting enough sleep not only helps avoid physical illness, but also helps us with our mental well-being. On average, doctors recommend that we get between seven and nine hours of sleep a day. If we are getting quality sleep, we can avoid many of the symptoms of depression.

Health checks

Seeing a professional could be important to check if there could be an imbalance with our hormones. A qualified healthcare professional will be able to tell if there is a deficiency or overactiveness in one of our hormones. It is important that we explore concrete medical tests in addition to time with a counsellor or therapist. A simple blood test will be able to tell us our levels of oestrogen, progesterone, testosterone, etc. Many people also forget that a deficiency of vitamin D may be adding to their symptoms of depression. A simple walk in nature can boost their levels and have fantastic results over time.

Diet

Eating healthy is an important factor in preventing depression. Fresh fruits, vegetables, grains and plenty of water are key to defeating the disease. Do you snack or crave junk food when you are going through a hard time with depression? You are not alone. You are what you eat, physically and mentally. Therefore, it is important to eat fresh food. A word on coffee: avoid it after midday. This is because caffeine, the active ingredient in coffee, takes twelve hours to pass through our body. That's half the day! If we have coffee after midday, chances are we will still be awake at midnight. We want to avoid that as having a good night's sleep is essential for us in preventing signs of depression.

After I finished my lecture in London, a few medical students approached me to discuss their personal issues. They confirmed that they had also had pigeons making nests in their houses for a long time. I could not give them psychotherapy or medical advice; however, even if one of them were helped on their journey to combating anxiety and depression based on what I had shared with them, it was a success.

Chapter summary:

- The first step is to have a clear view or understanding of what we are dealing with.
- When a negative emotion makes a permanent residence within our minds and starts affecting our well-being, we should address it.
- Studies suggest that over 40 per cent of us will suffer from depression in our lives.
- Talk therapy can help with symptoms of depression, low self-esteem, bereavement, addiction and other severe mental health conditions.
- When the magnitude of our problems is overwhelmingly greater than our ability to deal with them ourselves, we need to seek help either through medication, therapy or both together.
- Positive affirmations can help us overcome negative thinking patterns and have the power to rewire our mind to help us change our outlook.
- If we are getting quality sleep, regular health checks and are eating well, we can avoid many of the symptoms of depression.

—

SIX

The Last Wish in a
Pen Drive: Dealing with Guilt

'Guilt is to the spirit, what pain is to the body.'
—Elder Bednar

Returning from my lecture in central London to the serenity of the ashram at Bhaktivedanta Manor, I lay down to rest. At times I cannot help thinking, 'Did I give that person enough time?' 'Did I say the right thing?' 'Could I have done more to help?' The burden of being the person helping is sometimes greater than the one who needs help. We have to make sure that we are giving our best to those who seek our help.

Let's take a minute to think about doctors. Although they may be seeing a number of patients a day and treating a variety of illnesses, the next patient is seeing the doctor for the first time. Therefore, they need to be focused at all times although they may be tired. At times, doctors have approached me with their guilt at not having given a patient adequate time due to being fatigued and not being able to spend enough time with their family due to their strenuous profession. Responding to this is always challenging, but I do so from a place of empathy as I have experienced a fair deal of guilt over the years in my quest to help others.

I grew up in a loving family, but we did not have much in terms of material possessions. We lived in an old housing complex called a *wada* or chawl. There were twenty-five houses in one building that had common walls. It can be likened to terraced housing in the West, but the walls were paper-thin. You could hear everything that was happening in the wada, from who was arguing about not doing the laundry to who was hosting a party; everyone knew everything about everyone else. Although this sounds bad, it did bring a sense of community to the building. All of a sudden, you had many more aunties and uncles who would look out for you. At times, this did not work in my favour as my teenage activities were quickly reported to my mother and father.

One thing that I do not miss about the wada is the lack of toilets inside the building. The toilets were situated in an outhouse that was shared between twenty-five families. Just thinking about it I can remember the stench that came from it and the queues that built up to use the bathroom. In the morning, it was not just you against your sibling to use the toilet, it was you against the entire complex! I guess this was training for when I would become a monk. We have nearly a hundred monks all living together, and we share ten toilets and shower rooms. It's first come, first served at 3.30 in the morning when we wake up. The early bird gets the worm and the early monk gets the shower.

Back to my childhood—in our house, we had six people living together. It is quite customary in Indian culture to live as a large family unit. My grandparents, my mother, my father, my sister and I lived in one of the twenty-five houses. It was congested in that house, but it was definitely a happy home as we had a common purpose to look after each other.

My father worked for the meteorological department of India in the administration department. One habit I remember about him, come rain or shine, would be his smoking. He was a chain-smoker going through packs of Charms cigarettes. His voice was coarse from it and his fingers developed callouses from where the cigarette would lie. My father knew that smoking was bad for him. Out of embarrassment, he would never smoke in front of my grandparents, but would not mind firing one up when they were not around. As children, we did not understand that smoking is so dangerous. It was just part of who my father was, a distinct characteristic that was emblematic of his personality. My mother, on the other hand, would get livid whenever he would smoke, but she would not overtly express her feelings. She would do everything she could to help him stop smoking: inspire him, help him, coax him, fight with him; literally do anything she could. However, her efforts always went in vain. Like clockwork, my father would go back to his lighter and tobacco, not being able to withstand the intense withdrawal symptoms.

I remember vividly as a teenager a conversation between my mother and her friend who was visiting from out of town. Their voices echoed through the paper-thin walls into my room. They were sipping chai, gossiping and laughing as mothers do when they get together. It's not that I was eavesdropping, but it was hard to stop listening to what they were saying. My mother's friend was talking about her husband, 'All he does is smoke all day and smoke all night.

Our son is now imitating his smoking habit to please his father.' At that point, I came downstairs for a glass of water, but with my ears still red-hot.

'Not true for me . . .' I whispered to myself. I forgot about the walls.

'What was that?' my mother said in Marwari, our mother tongue.

I coughed up my water knowing that I had been heard. 'Nothing. It's just that knowing what smoking tobacco is doing to my father's health, I would never touch a cigarette in my life.'

'You're a good boy,' my mother's friend said. Although a teenager never wants to be a 'good boy', I was a fairly obedient child and blushed.

I had a rocky relationship with my father. We were like chalk and cheese. There were many things that we clashed on, but smoking was one of the biggest. It was ruining his health and affecting my mother's happiness. Over time, as I grew through my teenage years, I stopped speaking to him. It seemed we would argue on every issue, so I thought it best to stop communication altogether. Don't get me wrong, he was a great dad and provided for us. Deep down I loved him and he loved me, but expressing ourselves was difficult. For nearly two years, we did not speak to each other. He tried to speak to me, but to no avail—I usually ignored him or brushed off his words to stop the conversation.

My relationship with my mother was the other side of the spectrum to my father. We would speak all the time; I felt comfortable opening up to her. On reflection, the love of a mother is so visible: it's active, always there with the child, nourishing them. It gets noticed, appreciated and celebrated. However, a father's love is seldom valued. Fathers also sacrifice and struggle for their children, yet because it is out of sight, it is often out of mind.

Scientists agree with this analysis. Dr Lars Perner, a consumer psychologist from the University of Southern California, told the BBC, 'Most of us simply think our mothers deserve better or bigger presents. To some extent, right or wrong, mothers are often considered to be the biggest contributor to home life.' He adds, 'People tend to understand the sacrifices they make, that's what you see. Moms have a special place in people's hearts—there's a special idea of what they offer the family.' On fathers, he says, 'Perhaps dads are also less interested in tangible tokens of appreciation. I think fathers think they don't really need expensive, showy trinkets, or anything like mom's bouquet of flowers. They're not typically gift-oriented. They generally don't expect anyone to feel an obligation to buy material items for them.'[1]

Think about the difference between Mother's Day and Father's Day. Mother's Day was first celebrated in 1908, whereas Father's Day was established in 1966. That means it was only sixty years later that the world recognized that fathers do something. I sometimes hear the ladies in the temple tell their husbands that is the same period of time it takes for their husbands to complete household chores! Mother's Day is celebrated in seventy countries, whereas Father's Day is celebrated in only fifty-nine countries. In the US, the average amount someone spends on their father is $135 on the weekend of celebrations. This is compared to around $186 on the similar weekend for mothers. This is constant around the world where both secular holidays are enjoyed. We spend a third more on our mothers than our fathers: $15.5 billion on fathers and $23.6 billion on mothers. This is not to underestimate or overstate their respective roles and both are equally deserving of our love and respect. It's just that fathers can often get neglected when it comes to their share of appreciation.

One evening as I was studying, my father came into my room and sighed. I ignored it, pretending to not hear it as I gazed into my textbook with my lamp creating shadows on my face. All of a sudden he fell at my feet, with tears in his eyes, and pleaded, 'Please stop ignoring me. I am your father and I will try and change my habits. I cannot take you not speaking with me. Please speak to me . . .'

I turned away from his sombre face as my mother entered the room.

'What is wrong?' she asked me as I tried to get back to reading my textbook. She took my dad's side, 'I think you should not be treating your father like this. You should talk to him. It's been long enough now, and you know how much he loves you!'

I could never say no to my mother, so the next day I decided to take baby steps to making conversation with him. After a couple of weeks, I was speaking to him again, but then a bombshell hit them: I left my career, my home and my family to become a monk. That was devastating for them as it was as if I had given up on society, given up on them, given up on providing them grandchildren and security. I knew that my decision was causing them a lot of pain.

However, as a twenty-one-year-old, I felt that I was serving a cause bigger than myself that would bring many more people happiness.

In the first few years of my time as a monk, I would visit my parents' home every year. Every year, on the train journey from Mumbai to Pune after taking a vow of celibacy, I would think of apologizing to them for the pain I caused when I left. But I could not do it. A three-letter word called 'ego' stopped me from saying a five-letter word called 'sorry'. I also wanted to apologize to my dad directly for stopping all communication with him, but I had convinced myself that what I'd done was right. As a matter of fact, I only stopped talking to him so that he could feel the pressure and guilt of smoking, and this was my way of urging him to quit. And I'd done that for him and my mother.

Something I did realize years later was that saying sorry does not always mean we are wrong. Even legally, apologizing is not an admission of guilt, it just means we are sorry for what the person is going through and value the person more than being right ourselves. This quote sums it up perfectly, 'What do we gain by proving that we are right? Rightness. But what do we lose? The person.' That is not to say that we apologize unconditionally at all times or become a pushover. We have to learn how to place boundaries so that people learn to change and improve themselves for the wrong they do, but as Fredrik Nael says, 'It takes both sides to build a bridge.' A genuine, heartfelt apology can work wonders to free our restrained emotions. It can mend misunderstandings, weld broken hearts and make relationships blossom again after a harsh winter. It's ironic that as a monk I preach this philosophy, but back then, even though I was a practising monk, I never apologized to my father.

Despite his reservations about my life as a monk, which is a story for another book, my father had always been kind to me when I visited him. From how I see parents behave with their children at the temple, it is easy to see why parents forgive so easily. They still see you as a small child and sometimes even treat you as one.

One year, he had asked me to bring him recordings of my talks from my tour in London. He could not travel to the temple in Pune or come to any of my lectures in Mumbai as he had been bedridden with Parkinson's disease for a few years. Parkinson's disease is horrible. It's a progressive nervous system disease that affects a person's movements. Symptoms start very slowly, with a barely noticeable tremor in just one hand. Most people suffering from it have tremors, but the disorder can also cause stiffness and slowing of movement, which deteriorates a person's quality of life significantly. I tried to cheer my father up that year telling him that he would have to meet me at arrivals when I flew in from London so that I could give him the lecture recordings straight away.

However, instead of my father rushing to the airport, I had to rush to him a few weeks after I had landed in Mumbai. I was meditating in the early hours of the morning. I usually do not take my phone with me to avoid distraction, but this morning I had accidentally taken it with me in my kurta pocket. My mother called me at five o'clock. She was an early riser but always understood that I wasn't to be called during these sacred sunrise hours. I answered. She sobbed uncontrollably down the phone, unable to speak. Another relative picked up her phone trying to calm her down. My father had just passed away. Her life, her best friend had left her alone. I was stunned. How does a monk react to the death of a loved one? How do they process these emotions? There is no amount of philosophy in the world that can cure the heartache of losing one that is closest to you and there is not supposed to be. When you are sad, you are meant to *feel* sad. You are not meant to mask it over with philosophical jugglery.

I drove from Mumbai straight away in preparation for my father's final rites. I grabbed my laptop, downloaded my talks from London that year on to a pen drive and put it in my pocket. On the journey to Pune, I held the pen drive in my hand, staring at it. I'd spoken so much on forgiveness and the art of communication. Thousands of people had listened to my lectures, yet I could not walk my talk in the case of my father. At that moment, I felt as small as the flies inside the vehicle. I was feeling the loss of someone who loved me dearly, but as I clutched the USB and tears streamed down my face, my overwhelming emotion was of guilt. The guilt of not having said sorry to him, the guilt of not having patched up my relationship with him out of ego, the guilt of the pain I'd caused him because of my attitude. I would never be able to say sorry again.

As I reached the house, the energy was heavy. It was filled with people standing around holding cups of tea, not knowing what to say or how much small talk was appropriate. In the centre of the house, however, was my family. I consoled them as the crowds of people watched my every action. I saw my father lying there still. I placed my pen drive in his hand and then grabbed his feet to offer my respects. I cried a few unseen, silent tears and whispered, 'Dad, I am sorry. I shouldn't have done this to you, I shouldn't have done this to you . . .' as we took his body to the funeral home. What happened next shocked my system.

More on that later . . .

We never know when we are going to lose those closest to us. Victories and achievements in proving that we are right are temporary, but the personal loss of someone dear is permanent. Was my apology even heard by him? Did it mean anything or was it a mental gimmick to remove the burden of guilt in my heart? These thoughts swirled around my mind as I sat next to his body.

Guilt trip

We have all gone through situations in life that we regret. Mine was most certainly with my father. My ego had blocked my path to a loving relationship with my father, causing him pain. We can let others down and feel guilty. We may speak harshly to them or deal with them inhospitably, disrupting their expectations of us. However, we may also feel guilty as we let ourselves down. We may feel disheartened as we are not able to keep up with the self-imposed expectations about our values and behaviour. Not keeping a commitment to ourselves can lead to a reduction of self-esteem as we break trust with ourselves. Would you trust someone who broke their word repeatedly? It would be hard to trust them. Similarly, when we break our own commitments and our actions do not match our ideals, we lose trust in ourselves. At times it is easier to forgive someone else for breaking our trust, than to forgive

ourselves for our own inadequacies. However, we must learn
to deal positively with the emotion of guilt to help our mental
well-being.

Guilt can be constructive and destructive. It is constructive
when it helps us correct a situation, improve ourselves
and when it displays that we have values, standards and
sensitivities to others. The lack of guilt suggests a lack of
conscience that crumbles into shamelessness in our actions
and the deviation of our moral compass. However, guilt-
tripping ourselves, or destructive guilt, can have symptoms
of a lack of self-forgiveness, magnifying the guilt out of
proportion to the problem and it does not lead to our growth
and progression.

At the same time, guilt can be reasonable and unreasonable.
Reasonable guilt is the feeling of regret we have when we have
actually wronged someone or ourselves, whereas unreasonable
guilt is the negative feeling when we are not at fault and yet
we go through regret and remorse.

Dealing with reasonable guilt

Dealing with reasonable guilt is fairly straightforward: we
can either fix the situation, fix ourselves or move on. Fixing
the situation or the mistake we made sounds easy, but as I
explained in the case with my father, it can be difficult.

While reading this, you may think that you would not
make the same mistake, but the ego makes us forget to do
the right thing because it is the *hard* thing to do. The human
mind wants to take the easy way out and follow the path
of least resistance. That means fixing a situation is left on

the back burner while the ashes of guilt pile up. A senior monk once told me, 'Repentance is passive rectification. But rectification is active repentance.' If I hurt someone or failed to keep up with a personal commitment, true repentance is about correcting that issue. That is a healthy way of dealing with guilt. A saint is not one who does not make a mistake, but someone who knows how to correctly rectify their mistake. In my dealing with my father, if I had corrected my situation by reconciling immediately after he pleaded with me, there would be no room for guilt to unpack its bags. We need to reflect and then act. The quicker the better. This will help remove the burden of remorse that weighs us down. It may be hard at first, but being unconditional in our apology is the best way to say sorry even if it may have been their fault. This is the most we can do. If a person does not accept a genuine apology, at least we can rest knowing that we did the right thing and hopefully, someday, they will be able to forgive us. But what if there is no longer someone to apologize to? Does it mean that that guilt has to stay with us forever? I did not get to say sorry to my father. To this day, this affects my mind as time has taken the matter into its own hands to relieve me of an opportunity to address the issue at hand. The only way to get rid of that guilt, when no one is there to forgive us, is genuine repentance and trying to fulfil the expectations the person may have had from us.

Fixing ourselves is even harder. If we are constantly in the wrong, making the same mistake over and over again, we should introspect and examine our behaviour patterns to check if we are insensitive to others, which in turn causes damage to ourselves. If we are able to identify that there is a common thread in all our dealings, we can then work on changing those habits and conditionings in a way that we don't end up hurting others and thereby burdening ourselves with the guilt that follows.

What if we have done everything we can, to correct the situations or ourselves? What if we are still harbouring negative feelings for our wrongdoings, which in turn are damaging our growth, peace and mental health? Believe it or not, we cannot fix every problem we come across as we are not the controllers of other people's actions or emotions. Humans are imperfect beings and can be irrational, always striving for perfection. Mistakes happen, tempers are lost, unpleasant words are spoken, harsh behaviour takes place. This is all part of the human condition that we have to accept. To err is human, to forgive, divine. If someone wrongs us and offers a genuine apology wouldn't we forgive, let go and move on? We must treat ourselves with the same level of compassion. Self-forgiveness is foundational in moving on and rising above those negative feelings. We cannot forgive ourselves if we are wallowing in guilt.

Think about it. Apart from sadists who take pleasure in seeing other people suffering, would even those that we have wronged feel happy if we held that guilt close to our hearts? My mother constantly reminds me that my father loved me dearly. Would he be happy to see me wallowing in a dark pit of guilt? Would he be happy seeing me constantly punish myself even though it was I who had wronged him? I believe he would not. Rather than only regretting our action, let us learn lessons from our experiences and avoid making the same mistake again.

Dealing with unreasonable guilt

Changing our narrative with the right type of self-talk is important, though they are not quite positive affirmations. It's a state of mind to deal with ourselves with kindness.

The ashram in Mumbai is unique as it is filled with highly educated monks who chose a life of celibacy. Many of them have a lot of professional corporate experience, as engineers, doctors and lawyers! This works well, as it means monks are able to connect with highly educated and sophisticated people. We also have some monks who are from very simple, rural backgrounds. Some are school dropouts, and some can barely speak English. When I joined the ashram, within no time I was interacting with some of the most affluent in our community. I was being respected, invited over to their homes for dinner, but monks from a simple background were not, as they would not 'fit in'. I felt extremely guilty that here were monks who were senior to me, they were more advanced in their spiritual practices and had more experience and realization compared to me and I was getting the adoration.

I remember opening up to a senior monk about this issue. His advice was invaluable. He said, 'I really appreciate your empathy towards these other monks. You must also know that you are not seeking this adoration. You have been gifted with certain abilities and they have been gifted with their own as well. Your abilities are bringing you this attention. Is that your fault? Rather than feeling guilty, be kind and empathetic to them. Never deal with them in a high-handed way with a 'holier than thou' mindset. See what you can do for their growth and benefit. That's real action and not some unreasonable sentiment. And yes, just because someone doesn't have the same opportunity that you have, that does not mean you have to squander it in misery.'

Another tool we can use to deal with unreasonable guilt is to separate the constants and the variables. Many of my classmates from university have ended up working in some of the most prestigious companies. One such friend moved to the US to work in the technology industry. Like me, he lost his father and was not there when he left the world. But his story gets worse. He could not even come for the funeral due to immigration issues with his visa. This left him with tons of guilt that kept him up all night. He felt responsible for his father's passing. His thought pattern was, 'If I wouldn't have gone to the US, I would have been around my father when he needed me. I failed him as a son. I couldn't spend the time that I should have with him. I couldn't even attend his funeral.' Imagine these words looping in your mind continuously. He approached me after six months of his father's passing, feeling like a wreck.

I told him that his father's expensive medical treatment for his rare condition was only possible because of his job in the US. He would not be able to afford it here with a job in India. And it is because of that treatment that he could live a long and medically stable life. He added quality to his father's life. I went on to tell him of the times he did visit his father and how his parents flew across from India to the US at his expense. He did not come to complete his father's final rites not because he didn't want to but because he physically could not.

In mathematical equations, we have constants and variables. For example, we have π (pi), a value that cannot be changed. There are world records for people repeating the numbers in π as fast as possible. Its value never changes so it is called a constant. However, the value of x can change depending on the equation. Therefore, it is called a variable. We must identify the variables that are within our control and work on them, but also identify the constants—things that are beyond our control—and understand they will never change. The feelings of unreasonable guilt caused by them are irrational and we should use this realization to aid our healing from them.

If all else fails, we must remember to go easy on ourselves. We would not scream at others for making simple mistakes, yet our internal voice can be our harshest critic. The rise of social media has meant that we are constantly comparing ourselves, at times feeling the guilt for what we are *not* doing. In the ashram, we sometimes have a similar competitive nature between the monks. We have one monk who doesn't eat or drink for five days straight during a sacred time of the year. I remember trying that one year but could not keep up. Instead of feeling guilty, I went easy on myself. This should be the standard for all areas of life. We often impose on ourselves idealistic standards that we cannot keep up with and then feel guilty that we couldn't do it. There are definitely ideals that we all hold in high esteem. They may be related to our diet, exercise, study, relationships and even meditation, but we have to learn how to forgive ourselves when we do not rise up to those high standards. What if we were realistic in our estimation of our capacity? What if we did what we could, and slowly, step by step, moved towards the ideal? We would live life happy and confident, rather than being miserable and guilty.

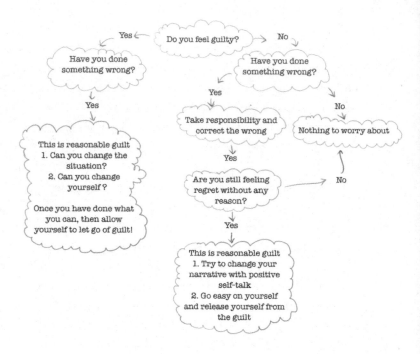

Chapter summary:

- We have all gone through situations in life that we regret.
- Guilt can be constructive and destructive.
  - It is constructive when it helps us correct a situation and improve ourselves. A lack of guilt can suggest a lack of conscience.

- o Destructive guilt can have symptoms of lack of self-forgiveness, magnifying the guilt out of proportion to the problem and it does not lead to our growth and progression.
- Guilt can be reasonable and unreasonable.
  - o We can deal with reasonable guilt by rectifying the situation, changing ourselves for the better and/or simply moving on if these two fail.
  - o For unreasonable guilt, we must identify the variables that are within our control and work on them, and also identify the constants—things that are beyond our control—and understand they will never change.
- In any case, self-forgiveness is foundational in moving on and rising above those negative feelings.

SECTION 2
OTHERS AND MY MIND

In section 1 we explored how we can learn to regulate our own mind. In this section, we will discuss how other people can affect our mind and the best tools with which to equip ourselves. We may be able to regulate our mind, but we cannot be held responsible for the actions of other people. That is why it is imperative that we learn how our mental well-being is affected by other people. We will be learning how to deal with toxic behaviour, with lingering old memories of things that have happened in the past, how to deal with criticism honourably and finally, how to deal with grief.

SEVEN

An Unexpected Humiliation: Dealing with Toxic Behaviour

'Don't let negative and toxic people rent space in your head. Raise the rent and kick them out.'

—Robert Tew

It was a beautiful evening in my hometown, Pune. It was December so there was no humidity, only a slight breeze to cool everyone off after a warm day. Pune is situated in the state of Maharashtra, and is known for its plethora of universities. There are students everywhere. It keeps the residents of the city feeling young, whatever their age. You never know what is going to happen, not just with the mischief that surrounds those coming of age, but the innovation and ideas that can only spring from those hungry to achieve.

For me, this evening was special. It had been a few years since my father had passed away and although it was hard to return, I was happy to be back. I have spoken at many gatherings around the world, but I had never spoken to members of my own community, the Marwari community. As a people, Marwaris are very charitable, but can be slightly stingy with their money for other causes. They will count every penny in the pound. I admit that this trait also flows through me as I haggle with a rickshaw or ask for a discount on a hotel room rate when I am abroad, regardless of the city I am in. I am a Marwari—we give with our hearts, but also save with all eight fingers and two thumbs.

A thousand Marwaris were sitting under one large pandal in front of a stage illuminated by bright lights to listen to one of their own, Gaur Gopal Das. I do not normally get nervous, but this time a slight sweat was gathering on my brow. As I peered through the backstage curtains, I noticed many of my friends and family in the audience. I had not seen them for many years. In fact, some I had not seen since my father's funeral. I know many had seen my work online and wanted to meet me in person and hear what a little boy that grew up to be a monk could say to impact their lives. I went back to the green room to meditate and also practise a few lines from my speech that I had prepared in Marwari. I had not spoken it in public for years; most of my lectures are in English or Hindi. I did not want to make a fool of myself or embarrass my mother by speaking sub-par Marwari. Also, my mother tongue is a very intricate language, one wrong pronunciation and the meaning can completely change. I know this from the many typos that arise from the auto-correct on my phone. I have sent countless 'Hate Krishna' messages instead of 'Hare Krishna' messages to senior monks, who have immediately called me to see if I was okay. I could not have that same problem tonight. I breathed in deeply and out deeply, praying to my spiritual teachers for strength and walked to the stage.

'Gaur Gopal Das!' the host shouted out. I walked on and was greeted by a tumultuous cheer and round of applause from my community. The appreciation was overwhelming. I felt like a soldier who had returned victorious from battle— one of their men who was trying to do something good in the world. I sat down on the stage and took a moment to look around properly. I saw some of my family members in the front row, including my mother, who was beaming as usual as any proud mother would be. Our eyes met and I paid my respects to her in my head, something I felt she understood. Other people at the front included businesspeople, political leaders and community elders.

When I was handed the microphone, I started with a special invocation prayer that I usually chant before a talk:

mūkaṁ karoti vācālaṁ
paṅguṁ laṅghayate girim
yat-kṛpā tam ahaṁ vande
paramānanda-mādhavam

This special mantra means: 'I remember with devotion the Divine who can empower you to speak with eloquence and to cross high mountains . . .' It was heart-warming to say this among an audience who followed along with the prayers. I was ready to share my heart, share everything I had learnt in my time as a monk.

I opened my eyes, but instead of seeing my mother, my eyes met those of another 'special' person. He was sitting in the front row. I had not seen him for over eight years. Isn't it interesting how your mood can change in an instant depending on who is in front of you? You can be the happiest person in the world, supported by thousands of your community who are all cheering for you, but the sight of one person can completely nullify that all.

Sensory inputs—such as the sights of people, places and things; or smells, fragrances and aromas; or sounds, music and songs—can govern how we feel. These are all things that can transport us to another part of the world as they connect with the strong memories that are associated with them. Some of those memories are very pleasing and can thrill our minds, while others are not, and can leave our minds disturbed. A severe form of this can be post-traumatic stress disorder (PTSD), which is caused by stressful, frightening or distressing events. Flashbacks and nightmares are common ways in which people with PTSD relive traumatic events. They may even be bombarded with feelings of isolation, irritability and guilt because of a serious episode in their lives. These symptoms are often severe and persistent enough to have a substantial impact on the person's day-to-day life. Although not quite as severe as the PTSD suffered by soldiers or doctors, I believe seeing that person conjured up memories that affected me.

This man was a reputed and respected leader in the Marwari community. He was also a distant family member of ours, which made matters worse as I knew he would have spread his opinions to those dearest to me. Seeing him in the audience opened a new window in the browser of my mind, accidently closing the window ready to give my lecture. For a few minutes, I stuttered. I saw him smirk and look around at his friends, as if trying to gather support to say, 'I told you Gaur Gopal Das was good for nothing.'

To explain what this man had done, I have to take you back to the day I rushed to Pune when my father passed away.

I had grabbed my father's feet that day and dropped silent tears, the way he had with me when I'd refused to speak to him. I'd then apologized and given him the pen drive of my lectures in London. I'd put it inside his hand as I paid my respects at his feet. I knew he was proud of me, and I hoped that he could listen to his son speak fondly of him wherever his soul now rested. After this episode, a few members of my family and I had lifted my father's body and taken it for cremation.

In the spiritual tradition I follow, the body is not buried, but cremated on a wood pyre. The body, made of matter, serves no purpose in this world without the spirit that drives it. Therefore, it is burnt, and the ashes are collected to be spread at the holy sites of India. As my father's body lay on the wood pyre and members of the community came to pay their respects, many people were saying kind words about him to me. Most people were wearing white and chanting sacred mantras or hymns to uplift the spirits at the funeral site. A priest led the ceremony, placing items on my father's body according to Vedic customs.

Isn't it ironic that when we are born, people love us and when we die, people love us, but in between we have to manage somehow?

As I grieved for my father, I could figure out the people who were genuine friends and spoke warmly about him, and others who only spoke well because the occasion demanded it. But I appreciated both of them. I also knew how bad some of them had been to him and how they had used his good, simple nature to take advantage of him in business, relationships and life. One of the people speaking in front of everyone was this gentleman, a de facto leader of the Marwari community in Maharashtra. He was in the front row at my father's funeral and now in the front row at my talk.

This man had nothing to do with our family; he had no involvement with us. He had not gone through the good times with us and had certainly not shown up to help us through the bad times. However, at times, we must accept the social position someone carries and allow them so as not to create a ruckus in the community. With my father's body still lying there, this man came up and spoke some pleasantries about my father as expected. However, the next thing he said made my community gasp, 'This man would have lived much longer.' He said, 'But his son, one Gaur Gopal Das, is the cause of his early death. Had he not left home to become a monk, had he not caused so much mental anguish to his father, had he not caused his poor parents so much agony, his father would still be here with us today, laughing. It is his fault that he has been taken away from us . . .'

All eyes were on me. Some were of pity, and some were angry as they believed the community leader's claims of my actions. I sank into my seat. I could not believe what I had just heard. My mind started racing, flipping between embarrassment, anger and sadness. How had this man come to that conclusion? What did he know about our family situation? How dare he criticize me in front of the whole community at my father's funeral?

The energy in the room changed from one of love to one of awkwardness. My family members looked at me in sympathy, knowing what he said was not true. However, there were others there who'd bowed their heads trying not to make eye contact. I sat there in silence. I was shocked and appalled. This was a sombre occasion, a time for reflection on the life of my father; a time for the community to look after our family. Not only was I part of the community, I was also a monk. If he did not respect me as a person, he could have at least respected the tradition that I represented. I just sat there understanding that the best thing I could do in that moment was to do nothing, to not increase the tension in the room. There was no way I would react. My mother would not want that, my spiritual teachers certainly would not want that. He was still an elder and a respected member of the community.

I remember that rain had begun to pour from the heavens right then, as if on cue. The wooden logs of the fire that were meant to take my father's body were too wet to be set alight, so we had to take his body to the electric incinerator. The doors of the furnace opened to engulf my father and then closed. As he went in, I chanted a sacred mantra to respect the fire that would take him, but my mind was still preoccupied with what that man had said. The last moments with my father's body were now tainted with the words of criticism.

My mind came back to the lecture I was giving.

I had to speak for the over nine hundred other people who were eager to listen to me and block out the memory of that gentleman who was right in front of my nose. It was not easy to do this as what he had done was exhibit toxic behaviour, which had left a deep burn in my mind. As the famous saying goes, 'What Susie says of Sally says more of Susie than Sally.' I hate labelling people as toxic. No one is fully toxic or a 'super villain' despite what we see in the movies. However, people can get caught demonstrating toxic behaviour in their actions, their energy, their words, their dealings and their insensitivity, which can hurt us.

We all know of someone who continuously demonstrates toxic behaviour. They may make us feel worse after we meet them than we did before. For me, it was a member of my community, but for you it might be someone at work, a close friend or even someone in your immediate family. 'Being toxic' is a common phrase and is thrown around in day-to-day language, but it is hard to define scientifically. Just as we discussed labelling our own emotions in the first chapter, when it comes to other people's behaviours, we should start labelling behaviours that are problematic. In many cases, it is easier to spot these behaviours in other people than it is within ourselves. Barrie Sueskind, a therapist from Los Angeles, has written about 'toxic behaviour traits':

- self-absorption or self-centredness
- manipulation and other emotional abuse
- dishonesty and deceit
- difficulty in offering compassion to others
- a tendency to create drama or conflict[1]

These might sound commonplace, but it is important to note that it is *repeatedly* demonstrating these behaviour traits that can make someone toxic. We will go into more detail further in this chapter. We can also classify toxicity by *why* it is demonstrated.

Types of toxic patterns

Everyone goes through difficulties in their life. Our emotions move up and down like the waves in the sea. It should be normalized that no one is perfect, and we all struggle in some areas of our lives. We may get into a bad mood after being stuck in traffic after work, we may be irritated by how our partner leaves their laundry all over the house, we may even go through misunderstandings with our friends over petty issues. Whatever the reason, we may also end up exhibiting toxic behaviours because of a given situation. We take note of such behavioural traits because of a situation to make sure it does not become a repetitive pattern. We have to assess whether the incident deserves our empathy or our correction.

When we know that someone's toxic behaviour is not situational, it could be a habitual toxic trait. At first, we should give them the benefit of the doubt as their habit may be unintentional. Although the responsibility of our actions is our own, we are a product of our environment. Therefore, the way we develop habits may be unconscious. If a person is toxic because of this, they also may need a dose of empathy from someone to get out of this behaviour pattern. They need help. It is important that we intervene promptly but sensitively, in a way that they do not feel embarrassed and we do not become the object of their toxicity.

The final type of toxic person is one who does so with intention. They consciously behave in a certain way that may hurt us. As stated above, they may be self-centred, manipulative or dishonest in their behaviour, purposely. With this type of person, it is important that we evaluate their value in our life and deal with them accordingly. Are they a close relative who is hard to 'cut off?' Are they a work colleague integral to our business? Are they someone that we do not need to be close to? Why this is important is that we need to make a tough decision: do we approach them about their intentional toxic behaviour, or do we move on with our life without them? This may seem harsh, but protecting our mental well-being is one of the most important things we can do. As much as we want to, we cannot be friends with a predatory wild animal. It is its nature to attack us if we get close, so we have to just respect them from a distance. I have been attacked by such 'toxic animals' in the past and have learnt the lesson that we cannot be friends with them, however much we want to.

It is imperative that, when categorizing people who carry toxic behavioural traits into these groups, we do so in a mood of not judging them, but protecting our own mental health and trying to help them.

Diving into the types of toxic behaviours exhibited by people:

- Negative:
  - They are always complaining about the smallest things.
  - They love to gossip about other people.
  - They focus on the negatives in life, which in turn makes us feel pessimistic.
- Manipulative:
  - They are political in all their dealings.
  - They seem to use everyone and everything for their own advantage.
  - They are sweet talkers, but always have an agenda.
- Irresponsible:
  - They do not take responsibility for their actions.

- They pass on many of their responsibilities to us without taking stock of how it affects us.
- They do not seem grateful despite repeated help from us.

- Self-centred and insensitive:
  - They tend to make any situation revolve around them when it does not.
  - They are blunt in their dealings.
  - They are harsh in their speech and behaviour to the extent of making others feel insulted and humiliated.
  - They are emotionally abusive.

- Emotionally over-dependent:
  - They don't want to be toxic and are generally good people.
  - They are dependent on us to help them in most situations without their own independent thought.
  - They use us as a problem-solving machine; they dump all their problems on us.

- Overly positive
  - They are over-friendly.
  - They are over-affectionate, e.g., parents who do everything for their children from laundry to tucking them in at night, sometimes even when they grow up.
  - They are over-concerned, e.g., parents who constantly check where their kids are without giving them space to explore.
  - They are over-involved, e.g., a partner who does not keep a healthy boundary between them and their loved one.

- Rigid
  - Highly opinionated without the ability to change.
  - Not flexible in their thought process to the extent of being fanatical, i.e., it is my way or the highway.
  - There is no possibility of dialogue with them—they tend to be the 'monologue guys'—we have to agree with everything they believe in otherwise they get upset, withdraw or disconnect.
- Unrealistic expectations
  - They impose their own ideals on us without caring about what we would like to do.
  - They want what they want—the way they want it, where they want it, when they want it.
- Blame game
  - They make a mistake but do not take responsibility.
  - They look for a situation, reason or person to pass the buck to.
  - They do not regret what they do or have any remorse.

When writing this list, I felt slightly odd, because when I read it, I felt that it could apply to me in certain situations as well. To an extent, we all have some toxicity within us, but it may just be situational. Recognizing that is healthy. When we point a finger at someone, three are pointing back at us. Try it: point your index finger in front of you, three are pointing back, your middle finger, ring finger and little finger. However, when we are getting to the point of seeing these characteristics repeatedly and it is affecting our mental health, it may be time to open up to someone who we trust about this issue. Otherwise, we will be left feeling angry, annoyed, frustrated, victimized, mentally drained, guilty, spiteful or wanting revenge. These emotions are not good. As we have discussed, these emotions need to be dealt with effectively. If not, we leave ourselves vulnerable to mental health problems in the future.

How to deal with toxic behaviour

I wish I knew of the healthy ways to deal with toxicity before the incident with the gentleman from my community at my father's funeral. I simply ignored him at that time, holding a stiff upper lip, but I knew it affected me as I saw him in the audience at my lecture. This is not an exhaustive list, but these are some tools to help us deal with toxic people, depending on *why* they are toxic.

Set your boundaries

India is a melting pot of different traditions with different faiths, ethnicities, cultural and religious backgrounds. However, there is one religion that everyone follows in India: cricket. It could be considered the national sport of India as it is so popular. Parents dream of their children picking up a bat or a ball and playing for the country. The players are treated like royalty or even better. I remember seeing a sign at a cricket match, 'Cricket is our religion and Sachin is our God'. This referred to one of the greatest batsmen of all time, Sachin Tendulkar.

For one who does not know the sport, cricket is difficult to explain. It is a game played between two teams, generally of eleven players each. One team is 'batting' and the other is 'bowling and fielding'. The individual batsman from the batting team faces an individual bowler who has ten other fielders on the cricket field (pitch). The bowler 'bowls' a cricket ball down a twenty-two-yard pitch in attempt to dismiss the batsman by hitting the wicket pegs on the other side, or inciting the batsman to hit the ball so that the fielders can catch it without it touching the ground. There are many other ways to discharge the batsman. The aim of the batsman, however, is to score 'runs'—the currency of the game. In football there are goals, in basketball there are points and in cricket there are runs. The batsmen must hit the ball over the boundary around the field, past the fielders on the pitch to score more runs or away from the fielders in order to run between the wickets placed on either side. After all the eleven members of the batting team have had their turn to bat or the specified number of balls, called overs, has been bowled, then the sides swap roles. Whoever gets the most runs wins.

I did mention that cricket is very hard to explain on paper. It is something that has to be seen to be understood! The reason I explained it in this context is that when we say 'boundary', most people in India will think of cricket. Just as the fielders must protect the boundary from the ball that the batsmen hit, similarly we must protect our boundaries with other people. This is the only way to win the game of mental well-being.

It is our choice to control the quality and quantity of our interactions with people. With every person in our life, we have to know where to set our boundaries. How close are we to this person? How much do we share with them? How much time do we want to spend with them? These are three important questions to answer that are dependent on our personal goals and aspirations. We do not need to be calculating and create an Excel sheet about this, but we should take stock of our relationships and boundaries with people. When we know that someone is toxic, we have to limit our interactions with them by doing the needful. Strong boundaries mean we can choose who can cross over into our lives, who has limited access and who is restricted.

Exercise:

Reflect on your interactions with people this week. Have any of them been toxic? Could you improve any of those dealings by setting boundaries?

For example: 'I spent too much time helping Josh with his problems; in one week I spoke to him for a total of six hours. Although I really want to help, I need to reduce the amount of time I am spending dealing with other people's issues as it is affecting my mental well-being. I think the maximum time I should spend on this sort of interaction is two hours per week.'

Take charge of your emotions

The hardest word to speak out, from the English dictionary, is 'no'. The human condition is such that we want to help other people and please them. Whether it is due to the need for social acceptance or out of genuine selflessness, it is difficult for us to say no. However, for hundreds of years now, the world has been transitioning from 'survive to thrive', which means that for self-actualization and spiritual growth, we need to learn how to refuse.

It is commonplace for people to agree to things to avoid the discomfort of saying no. Scientists and research also agree with this. In 2014, a series of small studies found that many people would rather commit unethical acts, such as telling a white lie even when they know it is wrong, than say no to someone.[2] Dr Emily Anhalt, a clinical psychologist, says that that is the reason why many struggle with lies in childhood. As children, they may have not learnt to speak up for themselves. She writes that people want to help others but in the process, they may forget that their ability to accommodate is not endless. Saying no in certain situations may be hurtful to our ego because it could be perceived as incompetence by the other party, especially in a work scenario. In fact, this is especially pertinent in a work-based context rather than a social context.

Even in a social context, learning to say no is important, especially if it means you are exposed to or get involved with toxic behaviour. We don't have to attend all the social drama we are invited to. In other words, just because some people are fuelled by drama, it does not mean we have to attend the performance.

To say no, we have to take charge of our emotions and reclaim our priorities. There will always be something in our lives that will make us feel compelled to say yes, but if it leaves us miserable and repeatedly strains our mental well-being, then it is not worth it. We have to step out of the passenger seat and learn to get into the driver's seat for our own lives, which means taking responsibility and accountability for our own actions.

When a person takes the back seat in a car, they can do as they please. They can take their attention away from the road. They can talk on the phone, they can look out of the window at the moving world, they can talk with the person next to them, they can eat, they can drink and even watch a video on their phone. But the driver cannot do this. If they get distracted, there will be an accident. Similarly, as we go through life, if we get distracted and do not respect our time by saying no, we can never achieve what we want. If we want to avoid getting distracted, we have to start playing the role of the driver. As long as we play the role of the passenger, we will remain distracted—in our relationships, in our work and daily duties, and in our mental and spiritual well-being. We have to start taking charge of our journey.

The way we deal with toxicity depends on why the person is being toxic. If it is situational and within our capacity to overlook the person's mishaps, we can let it go. However, if their toxicity is habitual or intentional, it must be challenged and communicated. We have to say no in order not be treated like a doormat and thereby protect our mental health. At the same time, we must also be comfortable enough to seek help from others, to learn the art of saying no, and know how to bring up a potential argumentative point with someone sensitively. I always ask for help from my close friends when I have to have a difficult conversation so that I can get a better picture of the situation. This is especially important when such toxic behaviour comes from people whom we are always surrounded by and cannot avoid being with.

A deeper aspect of dealing with toxicity is 'vibrating higher'. The best compliment we can give someone is, 'You have such great energy!' Beyond what they say, their accomplishments or how they look, this is a great compliment as it suggests that we appreciate them as a whole. The energy at which they vibrate is attractive.

According to ancient spiritual texts, we all carry a certain energy: we are both transmitting and receiving antennas. An easy way to understand this is the difference in feeling we experience when going into a hospital, a nightclub or a temple. In a hospital, we may feel morose as the majority of people are going through sickness and ill health; in a night club, people may feel passionate; and in a temple, or any other sacred site, we may feel tranquil and devotional. Although architecture definitely plays a role, as even matter in different combinations carries a certain energy, these vibes are not just created by the bricks and mortar. They are created by the people there who act as transmitting antennas.

A place of pilgrimage is wonderful in how it looks, but it seems even more tranquil because of the monks or people of high spiritual standing who reside there. Just as we can transmit energy, we can also receive energy from others. We can get affected by people's toxic energy if we are around them too long. However, if we can learn to change our frequency, to vibrate higher than them, then we can be less affected. Just as eagles that fly above the clouds are not affected by the storm, if we can learn to vibrate higher, we can definitely soar. But how do we vibrate higher? I recommend three things:

1. **Increase your association with positive people:** Every action we perform is our choice. Although we may not be able to limit our interactions with negative people in some situations, such as work or family events, and might have to do the needful, we can choose who we spend time with outside of that. For instance, do you really need to go to that work-related event if it does not serve your higher purpose?

   Making choices and saying no is tough, but as we have discussed, they are imperative to our success. We must increase our association with those who have a higher vibration. A tip to know who carries a higher vibration is to observe their habits: how they speak, how they act, what they do in their spare time. We can understand someone's demeanour by how they act in public, but we can understand their character by how they behave in private.

   Exercise:

   Identify three people in your life who you generally have positive and uplifting interactions with. Now that you have identified these people, plan ways in which you can spend more time with them. For example: Meet for lunch or dinner once a week, exercise together, speak on the phone, do an activity or course together.

2. **Focus on your priorities:** To illustrate this point, there is an interesting story. A young employee went to the head of HR at his company and said, 'I can't work here

any longer, I want to quit this job.' The HR manager asked, 'Why? Please tell me what happened.' 'The whole atmosphere is so toxic to my mind,' replied the young man. 'There are people here who are very political, then there are those who are negative all the time. Many do not work hard and spend most of their time gossiping rather than working. I don't think I can handle it any longer.' The HR manager said, 'Fine, but I have a request to make before you leave.' The man said, 'Please tell me what I can do for you, sir.' The HR manager said, 'I want you to do this one last thing sincerely. I want you to take a glass of water filled to the brim and walk around the office area three times without spilling a single drop of water on the floor. After that you may leave the job if you wish.' Though it sounded weird, the man thought he would comply. He took a glass full of water and walked three times around the office floor. Then, he came to the HR head to tell him that he was done. The HR head asked, 'When you were walking around the office floor, did you see any employee speaking badly about another employee? Any gossip? Any disturbances?' The man replied, 'No.' The HR head further asked, 'Did you see any employee looking at another employee in a wrong way?' 'No,' replied the young man. 'And do you know why?' asked the HR head. 'Because you were focused on the glass to make sure you didn't tip it over and spill any water! It's the same with our life. When we focus on our priorities, we don't have the time to see all the drama around us. The fact is, anywhere we go, we're going to find toxic people. The grass is not always greener on the other side, but where we water it. We should do what we can to positively change things around us and improve the culture. I take your point completely. But when we know we've done our best, we should shift our focus to the glass of water—our priorities, our growth, our excellence, and then we won't be as affected by the negativity around us. If it is absolutely beyond our capacity to handle, we may actually need a change, knowing well that the new job or the new situation will bring fresh complexities along with it as well.'

Exercise:

Every Monday, write down your top three priorities for that week. Throughout the next seven days, try to keep track of how much time you are giving to fulfilling these priorities. At the end of the week, tally the number of hours you spent on each priority.

We may find we are spending a minimal amount of time on those things that we have decided are most important to us. Identify stumbling blocks and/or distractions which consumed your time, and plan how you could avoid or overcome them in the future. This reflection can allow us to factually see how we spend our time and can thereby give us the impetus to implement the required changes in our lifestyle in a way that we can focus on our priorities.

3. **Increase your inner strength:** To vibrate at a higher frequency, you need to connect with a higher energy

internally. I practice mantra meditation daily to help me connect to the Divine. You may have another spiritual practice such as praying at a certain time of the day, reading spiritual texts, singing hymns and songs or other forms of meditation. The important thing is finding what works for you and being consistent in your practice. Just as going consistently to the gym is beneficial to our health, consistent spiritual practices can help us improve our inner strength, thus helping us deal with toxic energy.

Exercise:

It is important to set aside some time every day for self-reflection and spirituality. Identify an activity that draws you into that sacred space within the heart and makes you feel deeply connected. Once you have identified it, practise it consistently at the same time daily and note the effect it has on you. For example: 'I am going to practise positive affirmations for fifteen minutes every morning at 9 a.m.'

Try to help

There are two ways in which our ego can deceive us. One is by telling us, 'I am the worst human being in the world' and the other is by telling us, 'I am the saviour of every human being in the world.' Both are damaging phrases to our lives. Although we need to learn how to say no and understand that we are not the saviour of other people's lives, we can still do what we can to help those with toxic behaviour. We need to assess our own capacity to help others. Not only does this help them but it helps us as we do not have to be exposed to their toxic tendencies.

Sometimes, people are unable to see what they are doing. They are looking through the microscope of their lives, unable to zoom out and see things from a different perspective. If spoken to sensitively and with love, they may see what we see and be driven to change. However, if we do this, we need to be prepared to do it multiple times as old habits die hard. We have to dig deep to forgive and remind people of their behaviour. This can be emotionally draining so we have to be ready to vibrate higher ourselves. Please note, for those that are intentionally toxic, we must walk away and let them be. We cannot change such people and should not waste time trying to change them as they will drag us down with them. If we do not know how to swim, let us not be a lifeguard.

I finished my lecture in Pune to a huge round of applause. A crowd of people gathered around me to take pictures and ask questions. One by one, I tried my best to greet people with kindness and respect. They were my community, many of whom had raised me and seen me grow as a child. But then came the time to meet the gentleman who had berated me at my father's funeral. He approached and thanked me for my lecture while gritting his teeth. I dealt with him with courtesy and compassion but did not get overly friendly. We all need to move on and clear our heart of vestiges of unwanted negativity so we can move on, if not for anyone but our own sake. But with the heart, must come the intelligence of the brain. I made sure I kept a safe emotional distance; as mentioned earlier, sometimes we have to say 'no' and walk away.

EIGHT

A Memory Hard to Delete: Dealing with Old Memories

'My past has not defined me, destroyed me, deterred me, or defeated me; it has only strengthened me.'

—Steve Garbold

I felt rejuvenated after the event with my community. Not only did I feel appreciated by them, but I have also internally moved on from how that gentleman behaved with me at my father's funeral. It was with a great sense of relief that I walked back to the wonderful bungalow my hosts had provided for me. They had also cooked a traditional Marwari dinner for me, which reminded me of my mother's cooking when I was a child. They had made daal bati, gatta, sangri, churma, among many other Marwari delicacies. If you have seen the Disney classic, *Ratatouille*, every bite was transporting me back to sitting on the floor of our home on a straw mat and eating dinner directly from my mother's hand, just like in the film. It was good to be home.

At times, I get invited to some incredibly fancy meals at people's homes that are cooked by their expert chefs. At other times, I eat simple, traditional meals that are cooked by a loving mother. Both have their merits, but for me I really look forward to tasting the love with which someone cooks. You can taste the loving *energy* they have put into the food. When I approach these mothers who have cooked for me and show them gratitude, they usually say, 'It was no trouble at all.' But I know how much trouble it must have been! Buying the groceries the day before and then waking up at the crack of dawn to start preparing. It is their humility that says it was no trouble, but knowing the scale of the kitchen in our ashram, I know how hard it is.

Similarly, at times, I am given a luxurious hotel room to stay in when I travel, but then I come back to my small room in the ashram. We all need our physical space to be comfortable, especially when we need to accommodate more people, but it is also important to expand our mental space; otherwise, any physical space can end up feeling too small. I guess that is what it means to be accommodating, even in the literal sense of the word.

After the beautiful dinner, I went to my room ready to rest. I changed and got into bed, my head hitting the pillow and the duvets forming a cocoon around me. I looked up at the ceiling that was being illuminated by the moonlight being cut by the slowly whirring ceiling fan. The fan had to be on, remember I am a fan-atic. I went through the event in my head; everything had gone well. I had delivered all the points I wanted to say with a dash of humour. People loved it! To make other people happy and serve them makes ourselves happy. It is easy to rest when that is what we value in life. But it is not always that easy.

All of a sudden, my mind projected scenes on the ceiling. The fan changed into the front row of the lecture with the man who had screamed at me at my father's funeral appearing on the screen. He smirked as he watched me speak. It then shifted to my father's funeral as if by magic. 'It is your fault. It is your fault. It is your fault,' I heard as I saw my father's body and the man now pointing at me. I shifted on to my side so as to not look at the ceiling, but the image was then projected on to the wall of the room. Was I hallucinating? Had there been something in the food? I thought I was over the incident with this man, but I had not fully processed it. Seeing that man had brought back old memories. At the lecture that evening, I had blocked him off to make sure I delivered to the expectations of the audience. I had minimized the window of that memory, but as the adrenaline of the evening faded, that window had opened up again and was now vividly being displayed everywhere I looked.

The irony is that you could be resting in pristine comfort, in a beautiful home, but the mind can make you uncomfortable by bringing up the past. As John Milton said, 'The mind is its own place, and in itself can make a heaven of hell, a hell of heaven.' As I tossed and turned in bed, my mind continuously went back down memory lane to the night when I was restless in my family home after my father's funeral. Not only were the words spoken by this gentleman humiliating, but they were also absolutely baseless. That night, my mind was swinging from feelings of anger to justification, from resentment to letting go.

Although it's not hard for me to fall asleep on a normal day, I realized that day why so many people suffer from sleeping problems. According to the Sleep Foundation, adults need approximately seven to nine hours of sleep per night, but 35.2 per cent of all adults in the US report sleeping on average for less than seven hours per night. Around 10–30 per cent of all adults suffer from chronic sleep insomnia, which has a number of causes. Stress, anxiety, depression, physical pain and ingestion of negative substances, e.g., caffeine at the wrong time, are the main causes.[1]

As I lay in the room in Pune, I tried to remember some of the advice I had given to people when past memories invade their mental space: 'Do not allow anyone to remote-control your emotions.' We use remote controls to control our television, air conditioning and lights, but often we don't realize how other people hold the remote control for our lives, even if their actions that are affecting us are from the past. This works for both, positive and negative emotions. There are two sides to every coin. When someone praises us, they are able to generate positive feelings within us; but when they humiliate us, they do exactly the opposite. This means they can control our feelings. We should also be careful not to control others' feelings. As children we play with toys, but as we grow, we should be very cautious to not play with the feelings of others.

We must take the control back in our hands. Taking control back doesn't mean that we become stoic, emotionally uninvolved or that we stop interacting with others. It just means that we slowly minimize our dependence on others for how we feel. In a world where we seek so much validation from others to make us feel good, we can feel devastated when it doesn't come or we get the opposite of it. It comes back to the duality of the world: if we cannot control our emotions when we are happy, we will be overwhelmed when we are sad because our mind gets conditioned to react to emotions in an extreme way. It is important that we start taking charge of our feelings. The more we depend on others for feeling good, the more the scope for disappointment. And that's not because people are inherently bad, or they intentionally want to hurt us. They may just be having a bad day or going through a bad day situationally and therefore cannot reciprocate with our expectations. To err is human. Everyone has their limitations, but should we allow someone's bad mood or someone's limitations to affect how we feel? Or should we take control of our feelings, craft our own experience and help lift others up when they are going through a low phase? Emotional independence is a great strength that allows us to find our own happy space and help others find theirs.

This sounds great, but from the experience that night, I can say it is easier said than done, especially with previous trauma and past memories. The mind is triggered by external stimuli that form memories in our mind. According to the Queensland Brain Institute, neurons, the nerve cells within our brain, are responsible for our memories, thoughts and thinking patterns.[2] Our memories are dependent on how these neurons are activated. But why are some memories stronger than others? The institute explains that it is 'synaptic plasticity', which refers to the change in the strength of connections between the brain's cells—the space being called the synapse. The more these connections are activated, the stronger they become, which means that strong, active connections lead to strong, active memories. If the connection gets weaker over time, our memories can get weaker and can be lost entirely.

The strength between existing neurons—the synapse— is essential for memory formation, but the literature on it shows that brand new neurons being generated can also aid memory formation.[3] The brain is labelled into different parts by scientists. One such part is the hippocampus, which is an important memory structure. Studies have shown that the bigger the hippocampus, the better the memory. Exercise has been said to increase the capacity of the hippocampus, suggesting that increased fitness can lead to better memory.

Let's try it out now. Think of your school. What did you think of? As a teenager, you may have had a vivid picture of your school as you attended it daily, but, as an adult, you may not be able to remember all the details. This is because different ensembles of neurons are now firing for that memory. The theory is that strengthening or weakening the space between neurons makes particular patterns of neuronal activity more or less likely to occur.

In my case, the powerful memory of the gentleman berating me at my father's funeral was so vivid, it left a strong connection and neuronal pattern in my brain. This theory is also written about in ancient literature and is referred to as *samskaras* or *impressions* in the mind. Impressions are more memorable if the stimuli are a) stronger in their force or b) repeated regularly. This incident at my father's funeral shocked me and was a strong stimulus, whereas the repeated practice of a tennis player helps him build 'muscle memory' on how to play well.

Over a period of time, our memories settle down and go to the back of our mind as if nothing ever happened, just as dirt settles down at the bottom of a lake. But then, a sight or sound, an experience of a situation, can act as a stimulant to stir up the lake and bring the dirt back up again. With positive memories, such as reminiscing with an old friend, this experience can be enjoyable, such as witnessing the beauty of lotus flowers in a lake, but with negative memories, we can be traumatized and need tools to deal with that trauma.

Dealing with past memories

The past is a good place to visit but not a great place to stay. There are many things we can do to deal with memories from the past that affect our day-to-day activities.

Repeat and refine

The past may haunt us, but there are many lessons that we can learn from it. We should definitely not be imprisoned by our past; it is there to teach us lessons about how we *should* live and not a life sentence on how we are *bound* to live. We can bring back memories of things we have done that have helped us in the past and repeat them. The more we can strengthen the neurons that have helped us deal with negative memories, the more we train our unconscious brain to not be affected by such situations.

When I lecture, I practice certain points and stories as I know they have worked for me in the past. I try and repeat them, but every time I do, I get better as I refine them. I improve the quality of intonation, dive deeper into the story or improvise it. In the same way, we may also have things that may have helped us with old, hurtful memories. Is it talking to a certain friend? Drinking a type of tea? Listening to a piece of music? Going for a walk in a particular place? Developing these healthy habits and refining them over time can help us deal with past memories.

Rectify and reflect

We all make mistakes in life. In the spiritual tradition I follow, a highly spiritual person is not one who does not make mistakes, but one who rectifies and learns from their mistakes. There are countless ancient anecdotes that tell the story of highly elevated spiritualists who make grave errors but learn from them and grow.

Closer to home, I remember visiting a family's home in Mumbai. I was there to give a lecture to thirty of their family members. One gentleman in the family came up to me and said, 'I'm a big fan. I love your lectures.'

I asked him, 'What do you like about my lectures?'

'All the jokes,' he replied.

'I use jokes to make my points. What about the points?' I added.

'The points are not too bad, but the jokes are really funny,' he said confidently.

'Not too bad?' I thought as I smiled to myself.

Just then, a young boy came running towards us. I asked the man if this was his son and he said that was his eight-year-old son, Aryan. Then a young lady came up to us. I said to him, 'Is this your wonderful daughter?' The expression on his face changed to annoyance, but she had a smile that extended ear to ear.

'That is my wife . . .' he said embarrassed. He then caught his wife laughing and said swiftly, 'Don't take him too seriously. He is used to cracking jokes all the time.' His wife's face dropped, and she gently hit him on the arm.

This is a light story to demonstrate an innocent mistake. But I learnt a lesson: whenever people approach me, I ask them to introduce everyone present without any assumptions or guesses.

In all areas of life, it is important that we learn how to reflect appropriately. It is through this reflection, by revisiting the past, that we can carefully examine our mistakes and rectify them.

A structured way to do this is to follow the Gibbs Model of Reflection. This was developed by Graham Gibbs in 1988 to help us learn from our experiences in a methodical way. It examines how we went through a situation in a cyclical way to help us understand that particular incident, but also allows us to learn and plan if that incident should happen again. Gibbs originally created the model to use repeated circumstances, but the stages and principles apply equally well for stand-alone experiences too. The University of Edinburgh goes through how to answer the six questions posed by Gibbs in detail by adding the sub-questions written below:

- Description of the experience:
  o What happened?
  o When and where did it happen?

- o   Who was present?
- o   What did you and the other people do?
- o   What was the outcome of the situation?
- o   Why were you there?
- o   What did you want to happen?
- Feelings and thoughts about the experience:
  - o   What were you feeling during the situation?
  - o   What were you feeling before and after the situation?
  - o   What do you think other people were feeling about the situation?
  - o   What do you think other people feel about the situation now?
  - o   What were you thinking during the situation?
  - o   What do you think about the situation now?
- Evaluation of the experience, both good and bad:
  - o   What was good and bad about the experience?
  - o   What went well?
  - o   What did not go so well?
  - o   What did you and other people contribute to the situation? Positively and negatively?
- Analysis to make sense of the situation:
  - o   Why did things go well?
  - o   Why did it not go well?
  - o   What sense can I make of the situation?
  - o   What knowledge—my own or others—can help me make sense of the situation? E.g., is there anything I have read that can help me understand why this was happening?
- Conclusion about what you learned and what you could have done differently:

- o   What did I learn from this situation?
- o   How could this have been a more positive situation for everyone involved?
- o   What skills do I need to develop for me to handle a situation like this better?
- o   What else could I have done?
- •   Action plan for how you would deal with similar situations in the future, or general changes you might find appropriate.
  - o   If I had to do the same thing again, what would I do differently?
  - o   How will I develop the required skills I need?
  - o   How can I make sure that I can act differently next time?

We do not need to answer all these questions, but this is a useful framework to help us reflect on the past and rectify our mistakes. This is not a definitive model on reflection, but it is one that works. If you have a past memory that you are dealing with, use it to see if it works for you. If certain questions from the list above help you more than others, focus on them.

Life is like a book. The numbers of years we have in life are the number of chapters we are meant to live. Each chapter has 365 pages. Until now, there are a certain number of chapters of our life that have already been written. The ink has dried regardless of what is written. Some are beautiful: great handwriting, clean ink and the correct grammar. However, in other parts of the chapters we have already lived, the quality of the ink is low, the handwriting is illegible, and the story is quite messy. The good news is that the pages from now on are empty. We can write the chapters to come as we wish. We can re-read the good chapters of our life and use the positivity to fuel the writing of the chapters to follow. On the flip side, we can also reflect on the poorly written chapters and see what lessons we need to learn moving forward.

Recall and relive

My grandmother, like many, was defined for me by the sweet candies she used to sneak to me without my mother noticing. I still remember it: Cadbury's Eclairs! I would keep them in my mouth for hours because they were so addictive. On the other hand, the medicine that my mother gave me had the opposite effect. It was bitter and revolting—I had to hold my nose and gulp it down as fast as I could. In life, however, we tend to do the opposite. We hold on to the bitter memories and forget the joyous ones quickly.

If we can revisit the past to remember the good things, we can use it to empower the present. On a tough day, when everything seems to be going against us, we can use a specific meditation by going down memory lane. We can recall an incident that made us feel happy, an interaction that made us feel valued, loved and appreciated, and a struggle that we could successfully overcome that boosted our confidence.

The beauty of this is that if we can master this meditation, we can relive our cherished memories a million times. The physical event is gone into the past, but the memory is etched in our heart forever. We can strengthen the neurons that fire up that memory by remembering it regularly. We can rejuvenate ourselves with the positive energy of that memory whenever we want and thereby empower our present.

Release and recover

Our mental space is the most expensive real estate that we possess. There are painful memories of traumatic situations, hurtful interactions, failures and pitfalls that can be difficult to overcome with the solutions mentioned earlier. In fact, the situation with the gentleman berating me at my father's funeral was one of those interactions.

We have to be cautious that these negative memories do not make their home in our mind, just like the bird's nest we discussed before. If we spend our time on the negative memories of the past, there is no space for the fresh positivity that we can create. We have to make space for the remarkable by releasing the rubbish.

What we tell ourselves is more important than what others tell us. To release and recover from negative memories, we should first understand and tell ourselves that we cannot change people. Their core nature is hardwired from years of repeated action. It is extremely unlikely that they will change based on a few interactions we have with them. Therefore, we have to let go of the situation. This gentleman at my father's funeral is known to be blunt; he is known to ruffle feathers in the community. By accepting that and practising positive self-talk, it is relatively easy to release this toxic memory.

Another thing we need to remind ourselves is that our reality does not change because of what others have said to us or about us. People will say something regardless; whether it's gossip behind our back or to our face. There is a wonderful fable to understand this.

For people coming to India for the first time, it can be a cultural shock. In many parts of Mumbai especially, there can be organized chaos. It looks organized to the local, but is chaos to the tourists. This is especially true in the markets where vendors set up shops all across the road. Once a vegetable vendor used a whiteboard with the words, 'Fresh vegetables sold here' to attract people to buy his produce. A man passing by came up to him and said, 'Why do you need to advertise them as fresh? We can see they are fresh. Rub off the word "fresh" from your sign.' The vendor agreed with him and rubbed off the word 'fresh', leaving behind the words, 'Vegetables sold here' on his board. A few moments later, another man came up to him and said, 'I can clearly see that you are selling vegetables not fruits, why don't you wipe out the word "vegetables"!' The vendor agreed. What was left on his board now were the two words 'sold here'. A few hours passed and sales were abysmal for the vegetable vendor. An elderly lady approached him and said, 'If you're sitting in the market, you are obviously not giving your vegetables away for free. Take off the word "sold".' The vendor wiped off the word "sold". The whiteboard had only one word left 'here'. Being late afternoon by now, it was the end of the school day. A group of schoolboys passing by teased the vegetable vendor saying, 'Everyone in the world knows you are sitting here, not there, then why the "here"?' The vegetable seller erased the last word making the whiteboard clear. At the end of the day, one last person came up to him and said, 'Only a stupid man would keep such a nice whiteboard clear. Why don't you write something on it to advertise your vegetables?'

Everyone has an opinion and a suggestion. However, even with the best of intentions, this can be overwhelming. Listening to everyone really means we are listening to no one.

We may even forget what we were inspired to do in the first place. We need to ignore the opinions of people whom we do not trust, who do not love us or who we have not approached for advice. We should be respectful to people, but that does not mean we accept their opinion as gospel.

To release and recover does not mean that we do not defend ourselves. In legal arguments that are serious and affect our standing or livelihood, we should protect ourselves. But in many situations, we do not have to. People who do not like us or people who like us do not care for an explanation. It is a waste of energy explaining ourselves; at the end of the day, our peace is more important than being right.

Exercise:

Think of three things you can do to manage and heal painful memories.

For example: 'When I think of my ex-partner, I:

1. Practise journaling to let my emotions out.
2.
3.

It was a restless night in Pune, but the next morning I decided that I had to focus on releasing this memory and recovering from this incident. I had to leave this beautiful home and return to my duties in my ashram, but I also decided to leave behind these unwanted feelings and memories. Little did I know a similar situation would happen during my future trip to London . . .

Chapter summary:

- Often, we don't realize how other people hold the remote control for our lives, even if their actions that are affecting us are from the past.
- Emotional independence is a great strength that allows us to find our own happy space and help others find theirs.
- Over a period of time, our memories settle down and go to the back of our mind as if nothing ever happened, just as dirt settles down at the bottom of a lake. But then a sight or sound, or the experience of a situation can act as a stimulant to stir up the lake and bring the dirt back up again.
- There are many things we can do to deal with memories from the past:
  o Repeat and refine
  o Rectify and reflect using the Gibbs Model of Reflection
  o Recall and relive
  o Release and recover
- We need to ignore the opinions of people whom we do not trust, who do not love us or who we have not approached for advice.

NINE

A Whisper in My Ear: Dealing with Criticism

'Accept both compliments and criticism with grace. It takes sunlight and rain to help a flower grow.'

—Unknown

There is an old Sanskrit phrase: *Mitaṁ ca sāraṁ ca vaco hi vāgmitā*, which translates to, 'True eloquence is presenting the truth concisely.' One piece of work that I feel represents this phrase is an 'Ode to the Pencil' I read a few years ago. I am unsure of the author, but whoever wrote it has extracted truths from the simplest object in the world: a pencil.

The author writes of five important lessons that we can learn from a pencil, which I have expanded on and want to share with you in this chapter. The first pencil ever made came with instructions that have been lost over time. They are simple truths that, if applied, can change the trajectory of our lives.

What is truly important lies within you.

The pencil has two aspects to it. The outside—its colourful wooden casing, and the inside—the lead which is the essence of its being. The lead is the purpose of the pencil. Similarly, we all have two sides: what lies outside of us and what lies inside of us.

The outside is our persona, our appearance and our presence. It is also about charisma, our style, our presentation, how we speak, our confidence, our mannerisms. The inside is about our character, our morals, our integrity and the principles we hold dear.

The outside is about valuables. We are often accepted more for what we have than who we are. We are accepted for what we wear rather than our character. The inside is about our values. While we maintain who we are on the outside, we should not forget that what is really important is who we are on the inside. Balancing both is crucial. We live in the world; therefore, we have to give time and energy to things on the outside, but this focus should not be at the cost of our inner world as this could affect our mental well-being. We must find balance between our personality and being a genuine person, our charisma and our character, our valuables and our values.

Unless what is within you comes out, you cannot make an impact.

It's only when the lead writes on paper that it makes an impact. Similarly, in our lives, unless what is within us comes out, we will not be able to make an impact either on our own lives or on those of others. The word *educare*, from which the English word 'education' is derived, means to bring out the virtues and qualities that are inherent within us. When these qualities are expressed, we can change the lives of others. There is an anecdote about the inventor of the light bulb, Thomas

Edison, which demonstrates this point well. Once when he was a little boy, Thomas handed his mother a note one of his teachers had given him. His mother opened the little piece of paper and read it, immediately coming to tears. 'Thomas, your teacher has written that you are such an intelligent boy, you are a genius. This school does not have enough good teachers to train you. So, it's better that you do not go to school, and I teach you.' Many years later, when Thomas Edison's mother had passed away, and he was already an established inventor, he was cleaning out his mother's room. He found that small piece of paper and broke down in tears reading its contents, 'Madam, your son Thomas is a dunce, he is mentally ill, he does not fit into our school. We are discharging him back to your care effective immediately.' At that moment, Thomas grabbed a pencil and wrote another line underneath, 'Thomas was indeed a dunce, but he was made into one of the greatest inventors of the century by his hero, his mother.' His mother was not charismatic, nor a leader in society, nor was she wealthy. However, she had great character, which influenced the life of her son.

Think of your favourite teacher. They may not have been the smartest person in the room, but their sincerity to help you left an impact on your life. When the riches of what is inside of us are expressed to the world, that is what can make a difference.

Unless you go through the pain of being sharpened, what is within you will not come out.
The pencil has to be sharpened before the lead can make an impact. Something similar must happen to us in our lives.

Sometimes we have to go through the pain of being sharpened for the best in us to come out.

There is a Sanskrit text that mentions the five qualities of a student:

kāka ceṣṭā bako dhyānam śvāna nidrā tathaiva ca
svalpāhārī gṛhatyāgī vidyārthī pañca lakṣaṇaṁ.

We should all aim to possess these five qualities in our life. The word *vidyārthī* means one who seeks knowledge:

1. *Kāka ceṣṭā*—*Kāka* is the Sanskrit word for a crow and *ceṣṭā* means 'effort'. Therefore, together this means 'the effort of a crow'. This is based on the fable of the crow who was thirsty and flying across the land for water. As he flew, he saw a small pitcher of water down below in someone's garden. He swooped down towards it only to find that the water was at the very bottom of the pitcher and there was no way that he could reach it. The crow wondered how he could access the water and then had a remarkable idea. He started picking up tiny pebbles in his beak and dropping them inside the pitcher. Pebble by pebble, the crow kept working hard until the level of the water rose way up to the rim of the pitcher and the crow quenched its thirst. Kāka ceṣṭā refers to patient hard work—the effort of the crow. We have to go through the painful sharpening of kāka ceṣṭā, hard work.

2. *Bako dhyānam* is the second quality and refers to the focus of a crane. A crane stands on one leg completely still, gazing into the water at the fishes swimming around it.

The crane will allow the tiny, small fish to swim around but will not strike. The crane will be patient and wait for the big fish to come. If the crane settles for the small fish, it will scare away the big fish. And if the crane wants the big fish, it has to let the small fish passing by go free. Similarly, when we begin to focus on what is important, we should allow the small things that disturb us to pass by. We shouldn't be distracted by the little things such as petty arguments, small health issues or mishaps in our day-to-day life. We must focus on what is important.

3. *Śvāna nidrā*—*Śvāna* means 'a dog' and *nidrā* means 'sleep'. Śvāna nidrā is the third quality, referring to the level of alertness a dog has even when it is sleeping. A guard dog may be resting easy, but is ready to pounce at any moment. A small creak in the floorboards or the sound of footsteps, and the dog is ready to go. If we want to be a great student of life and want to pursue that which is meaningful, we have to practice the quality of alertness. Although we may have our eyes closed and may have a level of focus on one thing, we should not miss out on being alert to the world around us. We can learn from every experience only if we are alert.

4. *Alpāhārī*—*āhār* in Sanskrit means 'food' and *alpa* means 'less', so literally, alpāhārī means one seeking knowledge should eat less. This is the fourth quality, but it is not the literal meaning we should pay heed to. We have varieties of āhār: for our tongue we have food, for our ears we have sound, for our eyes we have things to see. For each of our senses, there is āhār. What āhār means in this case is that one who wants to be a great student has to be very careful of the sense perceptions they allow themselves to be exposed

to. As we have discussed in earlier chapters, whatever inputs we give to our senses create deep impressions on our mind called samskaras. Therefore, when we talk about alpāhārī, it means we should be very careful to choose those sensory inputs that are of value and those things that will leave positive impressions in our mind.

5. Gṛhatyāgī—Gṛha means 'home' and tyāgī means 'to give up' or 'leave'. This is the fifth quality of a student. In ancient India, students would leave their homes at early age and go to study under their teachers or gurus in the school that was called gurukula. Gṛhatyāgī means leaving home in the pursuit of knowledge. Although this is the literal meaning, gṛhatyāgī refers to leaving our comfort zone. If we are to live in our comfort zone, we cannot grow. Therefore, gṛhatyāgī refers to coming out of our comfort zone to live our purpose.

Therefore, these five qualities—the effort of a crow, the focus of a crane, the alertness of a dog, accepting the right inputs to our senses and leaving our comfort zone—are the ones that help sharpen our pencil. Living these qualities can be uncomfortable, but without them, the lead that is within us cannot come out.

There are some lessons we can learn from a pencil that can truly revolutionize our lives.

When you write you will make mistakes, but you can always correct them.

The great thing about most pencils is that they have an eraser at the other end. In our lives, we make so many mistakes, but we always have the chance to rewrite our story.

You can truly serve your purpose when you are in the hands of an expert.

A pencil cannot create a beautiful sketch by itself. It can only do so in the hands of an expert. There is a fable about a great artist. He was once walking along the road and a lady approached him and said, 'Sir, you are such a great artist, can you draw a pencil sketch of me, please?' The artist drew a sketch in less than thirty seconds and handed it over to the lady and said, 'One million dollars, madam.' She said, 'You did it in less than thirty seconds. Why are you charging one million dollars?' The artist said, 'The one million dollars is not for doing it in less than thirty seconds. The one million dollars is for the thirty years of hard work which makes me do it in less than thirty seconds.' In the hands of an architect, the pencil can make a blueprint; in the hands of a poet, the pencil can write a poem. Like this pencil, when we act as instruments in the hands of the Divine or for a purpose that is greater than ourselves, then our life can become a masterpiece.

The next lesson is powerful:

If we do not sharpen the pencil, it remains blunt and then what is within us cannot come out.

The first thing an artist would do is to make sure that their pencil is sharpened. This ensures that the ideas in their mind would manifest clearly on paper. In the same way, every morning, we need to sharpen our mental focus to make sure what we give to the world is of the highest quality. The day brings so many challenges. We need to process information fast, handle pressure and make important decisions. On top of this, we have to meet so many people, all of whom expect that we put our best foot forward. Imagine doing this without any preparation, with blunt focus. Not only would we not be able to do it well, but we would probably crack under pressure.

Meditation is one practice that has helped me sharpen my focus in the mornings. Every morning, all the monks are joined by those who live outside the temple to meditate together for two hours continuously. In our community, we practice mantra meditation or *japa*, which is the repeated chanting of mantras softly using a set of tulsi plant beads. It involves focusing the mind on a spiritual mantra, and bringing it back to this mantra whenever it becomes distracted. The mantra we chant is the Hare Krishna mantra:

Hare Kṛṣṇa, Hare Kṛṣṇa, Kṛṣṇa Kṛṣṇa Hare Hare
Hare Rāma, Hare Rāma, Rāma Rāma Hare Hare

This sixteen-syllable mantra originates from ancient Vedic texts and has the purpose of connecting us to our divine nature. Although it has been practised for thousands of years, only recently has its chanting in meditative and singing form been popularized across the world by His Divine Grace A.C. Bhaktivedanta Swami Prabhupada. I choose to practise this type of meditation, but there are many others that might help you.

I can tell the difference in my consciousness on days when I have meditated well or not meditated well. Jim Rohn says, 'Either you run the day, or the day runs you.' To begin the day with meditation means to ready oneself for the day. For me, meditating is essential, like brushing your teeth or taking a bath. Although you can meditate at any time of the day, the morning carries special weight. After a good night's sleep, the mind is less cluttered, and the passions of the day have not worn us out. Think about how you feel at the beginning of the day and then straight after work. There is a difference in energy and concentration. There is a great quote, 'Meditation is not a way of making your mind quiet. It is a way of entering the quiet that's already there—buried under the 50,000 thoughts the average person thinks daily.' If we meditate in the morning, before all these thoughts take shape, we can sharpen the mind to focus, which can help us throughout the day and guide our thoughts positively.

Let me take you back to London where the story I promised you at the end of the last chapter begins. The great thing about being a practising monk in the *bhakti* tradition is that nearly everywhere we travel in the world, there is a replica morning programme that can help us sharpen our mind for the day. It is a series of meditations that covers a plethora of devotional sentiments and lasts from 4.30 a.m. to 8.30 a.m. There may be some cultural variation, but that's four hours of preparation for the day in the exact same way found in ashrams all over the world.

One morning, I was sitting in the temple room in our monastery at Bhaktivedanta Manor, London. There were around fifty people in the room all practising mantra meditation softly, but individually at their own pace. The sun was just rising and peeking through the Tudor windows that lined the room. Some people were pacing up and down trying to focus their mind, others were sitting in a lotus position with their back straight and their eyes closed. Some were exhausted from the night before and were bobbing their heads up and down as they drifted in and out of sleep. I could not blame them; it was 5.30 in the morning! Every now and then you could hear the louder chanting of some of the monks, which would jolt you back into focus. I had to make sure to pull 'Joshua' away from external distractions around the room, but also from internal distractions that popped up: my thoughts, my creative ideas, my planning of the day, my desire for breakfast. These distractions had to be filed away safely so that I could focus on the sound of the mantra.

I closed my eyes and went into a deep state of focus, concentrating on one syllable of the mantra at a time. I felt great and was really making headway in my meditation. All of a sudden, I heard a whisper in my right ear. Was this another level of meditation where you hear voices and instructions from an ethereal realm? Unfortunately, it was not. My meditation is not on the level of self-realization just yet. The voice was right there. I opened my eyes. Sitting right next to me was one of the senior spiritualists at Bhaktivedanta Manor. He was tall, slender and wore flowing white robes. He whispered, breaking my meditation, 'Why do you crack these silly jokes in your class?' I thought he may have been joking himself, but his face was dead serious. It was a strange question to ask someone at this sacred time of the day. It was like asking questions of a Muslim during namaz or a Christian while singing hymns in a church. It was improper conduct.

Before I could answer, he continued, 'I know why! Your talk is not meant to help and serve others, but only to self-pamper your ego. All you are looking for is attention and applause. You are like that famous line which goes: Everyone wants the front seat of the plane, the back seat of a church and the centre of attention. So why don't you just stop being a jester and do something sensible?' I was shocked and you could tell that those meditating around me, whose concentration had been broken, were bewildered too.

I found this man's statements to be weird. Although he may have been a senior member of Bhaktivedanta Manor, I did not know him personally nor was he a mentor or guide. Even if what he was saying had some truth, was he the right man to say it? And if he was the right person, was he saying this at the right time? I was in the middle of my meditation. Couldn't there have been a better time of the day or a better situation to bring this up, if at all? Before I could even make some sense out of what he had just said and respond, he had walked away.

One of the outcomes of mantra meditation is to instil humility within you. That had definitely happened with this man's comments in the last thirty seconds. However, my mind would have none of it. For the next thirty minutes, it went into overdrive trying to justify the reasons why my telling of jokes to explain the points in my lectures was fine and the disqualification of this man to question me. I only use humour in my talks to lighten the mood; I am not a comedian. Philosophical truths can be a bitter pill to swallow. A spoonful of sugar helps the medicine go down. In another way, humour is the anaesthesia to make the surgical impact of the truth a little less painful. Another justification I thought of is that people are so beaten down by what is going on in their lives that should we be bringing joy, hope, inspiration and relief or should we be beating them down even more with our idealistic talk? 'Also, I am me!' my mind shouted. This was my style and my way of doing things! Isn't diversity beautiful? Should we not be ourselves and add value to the lives of others in our unique ways, rather than killing diversity and making an army of clones? In this way, my mind became defensive, paralysing me from returning to a state of focused meditation.

One thing I have learnt is that we have to accept who people are in totality. People can definitely change and grow, but at that moment, we have to accept who they are, what they do and what they say.

Criticism from others is one of the ways in which our mental well-being can be disturbed. Whether it is out of a genuine desire to help us or done insensitively, or done because of habit, or done out of malicious intent, criticism has the ability to leave our minds disturbed if we do not know how to deal with it. Gossip and criticism are so hard to stop doing, that it is said one who can stop doing both can grow rapidly in their spirituality. Just like the vegetable vendor in Mumbai, we will be criticized for most things that we do, especially if we are in the public eye and making an impact. Therefore, we have to have a process on how to handle it appropriately. My mind started to think of ways to handle the criticism, but I stopped it in its tracks right away. I still had forty-five minutes of meditation time left. This was not the time to deal with it. Right now, the priority was to focus on the sound of the mantra, to sharpen the pencil so the mind could process what happened later during the day, which was better.

Dealing with criticism

Here are some tools we can use to deal with the criticism we receive.

Don't react instantly

Patience is a virtue, and the golden word is 'wait'. This is not to say that we do not respond. In many cases, we have to do something actively to pacify the mind. However, we have to let the head cool down before we come back with a retort. As I have said in my first book, *Life's Amazing Secrets*, when the head is hot, the tongue works faster than the mind. Once words have left our mouths, they become permanent. We should never make permanent decisions based on temporary emotions. Our emotions will sway like the waves in the ocean, but the consequences of the decision based on those emotions will stay. Only on still water, when the waves have subsided, can there be steady reflection. When the mind is agitated, how can one reflect on what the right course of action should be?

Be open-minded

Could we be at fault in this situation? Are they seeing something that we cannot perceive within us? We should be open to feedback as we may have made a mistake. Our minds are like parachutes, they only function when they are open. The *Srimad Bhagavatam*, an ancient spiritual text, states that anyone can be our teacher regardless of their age, status, position and even species. We can learn from anyone, so it is important to listen to what people say as it may be an impetus to help us grow.

One of the greatest rivalries in the world was founded on the basis of one party criticizing another. I have never seen an advertisement for these two companies on television, but everyone knows their brands: Ferrari and Lamborghini. However, not many people know of their rivalry.

Ferruccio Lamborghini was born into a family of grape farmers but did not share this passion like the rest of his family. He loved machinery and after serving in the air force during World War II, he began to take old military machines apart and re-purpose them as tractors. Not only was he able to use them on his own farm, he started selling the tractors themselves, which made him very wealthy. At that time, a symbol of wealth in Italy was to own a Ferrari. It was the mark of a wealthy man and was a car that Lamborghini owned. Lamborghini had a passion for racing cars and, because he was a mechanic, he knew how to adapt his cars to be perfect for racing. When it came to racing his Ferrari, he noticed it was not smooth when driving it and was too noisy. He was also frustrated that that the interior clutch needed repairing often.

Enter Enzo Ferrari. At this point in the 1960s, Ferrari was the top-of-the-line luxury sports car in the world. Wanting to help improve Ferrari, Lamborghini approached him about the changes he could make to his cars. However, he was rudely dismissed. 'What does a farmer know about cars?' Ferrari thought as he received the criticism from the young tractor farmer. His dismissal spurred a rivalry in Lamborghini, and the rest is history. By the early 1960s, Lamborghini had become almost as powerful and wealthy as Ferrari; it could all have been avoided if Ferrari had taken the suggestions from Lamborghini with grace.

Of course, that is a simplified version of the story, but it does teach us a lesson: when we are criticized for our work or behaviour, we should be open-minded to see if there is anything we can learn.

Fact–check

We live in a world where misinformation spreads fast and the loudest voice wins. When we are criticized, we should look for an element of truth in the criticism. The first round of introspection should be by ourselves. Was anything the other person saying true? If we are not sure, the second round of introspection should be with friends, family and mentors to see if they think similarly. Those who are closest to us, to whom we can reveal our heart and speak in confidence with, will always tell us the truth about our behaviour in a way we can digest. This 'fact-check' can help us understand if there may lie an ounce of truth in the claims made by the other party.

Correct yourself

The hardest pill to swallow is that there is an element of truth to what the person criticizing us is saying. They may not be saying it in the most palatable way, but after we have discussed it with our friends, family and mentors and if they agree even partially, we should take responsibility and improve ourselves.

If we find ourselves in this situation, we have to take a moment to digest the criticism and understand that a change has to be made. In the past, I used to think that meant changing *overnight*, making a large gesture to signal to the person who criticized me that I had taken their advice. However, as I mature, I realize the only way to create substantial change over time is by taking small steps. Small, daily implementations can help us build positive habits. It becomes like compounding interest in a safe stocks and shares portfolio—you may lose a few days and you may gain massively other days, but over time, you grow steadily.

Exercise:

Think of a time you were criticized.

* How did it make you feel in the first instance?
* Was there any truth in it?
* What do you think you did well in dealing with it?
* What do you think went wrong and what can you do differently when dealing with criticism in the future?

With my own situation, as I was relatively new to the country, I wanted to make sure that my lectures were not disturbing the general masses. I did not respond directly to the gentleman who had criticized me; he had left in a flash after dropping this bombshell on me. Instead, I approached Sruti Dharma Das, my hero and mentor at Bhaktivedanta Manor. He told me that the entire community was inspired by the talks I was giving and that I was using humour only to make my points hit home, not to just make them laugh. He said the entire temple management also appreciated the way I was delivering my lectures. That was a breath of fresh air to me; however, I did not get excited too quickly. Sruti Dharma Das then went on to give me corrective advice, but it came easier from

him as he was gentle in his delivery, but stern in the outcome
he wanted. Without the blunt criticism of the man in the
morning, I would not have had the chance to get priceless
feedback from my mentor.

Chapter summary:

- Lessons from a pencil:
  o What is truly important lies within you.
  o Unless what is within you comes out, you cannot
    make an impact.
  o Sometimes, we have to go through the pain of
    being sharpened for the best in us to come out.
    ▪ Five qualities, the effort of a crow, the focus
      of a crane, the alertness of a dog, accepting
      the right inputs to our senses and leaving our
      comfort zone are ones which help sharpen
      our pencil. Living these qualities can be
      uncomfortable, but without them the lead
      which is within us cannot come out.
  o When we write, we will make mistakes, but we
    can always correct them.
  o We can truly serve our purpose when we are in
    the hands of an expert.
- Criticism has the ability to leave our minds disturbed
  if we do not know how to deal with it.
- Some tools we can use to deal with criticism:
  o Don't react instantly.

- o Be open-minded to see if there is anything we can learn.
- o When we are criticized, we should look for an element of truth in the criticism.
- o We should take responsibility and improve ourselves.
- The only way to create substantial change over time is by taking small steps.

TEN

Three's a Crowd: Dealing with Grief

'Grief is like the ocean; it comes on in waves, ebbing and flowing. Sometimes the water is calm, and sometimes it is overwhelming. All we can do is learn to swim.'

—Vicki Harrison

It had been a hectic day in London. The busier the city, the faster time seems to fly. That was true of this day: it was Akshaya Tritiya. In the Hindu and Jain calendars, it is regarded as one of the most auspicious days as it's the day of new beginnings. The word 'Akshaya' is a Sanskrit word that means inexhaustible, limitless or everlasting. On this day, people celebrate unending joy, peace and prosperity regardless of wealth, status in society and background.

I left the ashram in London that day at around five in the morning and got back thirty minutes after midnight the next day. You may recall from the last chapter that five in the morning is when I am normally meditating, but this was an especially busy day where all the engagements that came my way demanded my presence. If you were tracking my geolocation that day, I had practically crisscrossed the entire city as if I was a hardworking taxi driver.

The first event was a house-warming ceremony at six in the morning, then it was the wedding of a very close friend, then a prayer meeting for someone in the community who had departed a few weeks earlier, then to a hospital to see a newborn child, then a quick pitstop to breathe and eat some lunch. After that I had to cut a ribbon at a new jewellery shop, then sit and meet the leadership at a large corporation and finally, at the end of the day, counsel a couple who was on the brink of a divorce. It was quite a day with many people celebrating new beginnings and others grieving the beginning of the end. I got to witness so many contrasting emotions in one day from people at all stages of life. I believe all I saw was the unique list of emotions that I mentioned in the first chapter. From grumpy to disappointed, vulnerable to isolated and from thankful to relaxed, disillusioned to irritated, I saw it all on Akshaya Tritiya that year in London.

When most people think of monks, they don't think of them being so integrated into society. They think of them abandoning all forms of communication to live at the foothills of the Himalayas. Those types of monks exist, but I guess among others at our monastery, I was trained to be a monk of the people, to help normal people in their struggles. Half the battle to do this is simply showing up for the people you serve. I attend so many events and functions, it is hard to keep track. I do this to celebrate the joys of people's lives, and also to support them through times of grief.

One of the times I had to help someone through grief was when they had trouble in their relationship. Raj was insanely in love with Karishma. When I say insanely in love, I mean that when he was with her, he felt like a Bollywood star who would even want to sign her name on his hand with a knife. After years of dating and developing their relationship, Raj proposed during a beautiful sunset in Goa to Karishma. It was something you would see in a Bollywood film. She accepted, but from that moment on, the dynamics of the relationship started to change.

Karishma had a very close friend, Radhika, whom she had known since she was a child. They would do everything together; homework, holidays and even planned to one day do their wedding shopping together. They were inseparable. Radhika had helped Karishma through a rough period in her life with her parents. Because of that, Karishma always had a feeling of subordination to Radhika. It started off innocently, but over time, it started to become slightly strange, at least to Raj.

A few months after he proposed to Karishma, Raj was left in tears when Karishma did not show up for his birthday and instead went to dinner with Radhika. 'It was because Radhika wanted to,' Karishma told Raj when he called her, upset and questioning her absence. 'All of your friends were there, and they can get so rowdy. Let's do something separately!' Karishma continued on the phone.

'We could—' replied Raj.

Karishma interrupted, 'Yes, we could do something. Me, you and Radhika.'

At that point, Raj hung up the phone. Did Karishma not love him any more? Could she not see the turmoil of their relationship? He did not understand how Radhika could be dominating his relationship with Karishma so violently. He was sure that if Radhika said 'Jump', Karishma would only ask 'How high?'. What sort of person does not allow their friend to celebrate with their fiancé on his birthday? Red flags went off in Raj's head from that day onwards. He was hurt, but still madly in love with his fiancée.

The next few weeks, as the issue was not solved, arguments ensued about this one point. 'Why was Radhika interfering in our relationship?' Raj would shout. 'She's not interfering. She's just a friend!' Karishma would retort. And so that argument snowballed, and weeks of misery became months of misery for both parties. Suspecting that Karishma and Radhika could be more than friends, Raj decided to end their engagement, breaking his own heart in the process.

However, you cannot just switch off love. Raj then went through intense pain and grief. He was completely lost and unable to handle the fact that he had to give up his relationship with the person he loved the most. He had sleepless nights flicking through photos of them together on his phone. The blue glare of the phone illuminated his tears as he spent sleepless nights. Sometimes he would message Karishma on WhatsApp, but she would not reply although she had seen the message. Raj also tried to bury himself in work: taking on three projects when his seniors only expected him to take on one. Maybe more work would keep him busy, and he would forget his relationship with Karishma. But the moment the adrenaline subsided, his emotions of disillusion and abandonment came flooding back alongside his tears. It came to a stage that he would stand outside her office hoping to catch a glimpse of her, only to be distraught when he would see her with Radhika.

On one occasion, Raj took his scooter out for a ride aimlessly into the Mumbai night. Only a few stray dogs and the odd rickety motor-rickshaw could be heard at that moment. He swerved from lane to lane without a helmet, tears drying on his face because of the speed he was travelling at. He drove all the way to the Rajiv Gandhi Sea Link and stopped, looking at the black ocean below. 'Maybe that was all that was left? It's all over for me. I cannot go on,' were the thoughts swirling around his mind. He was contemplating jumping, and because he could not swim, he thought of sinking to the bottom of the abyss.

At that moment, at 1.30 in the morning in Mumbai, I remembered him for no apparent reason and dropped him a text message. Usually at that time I would be asleep. If you can imagine that we need to be awake and dressed by 4.30 in the morning, that time would be one of deep sleep for monks. However, I was in London, and it was nine o'clock in the night. He got back instantly and told me where he was and what he was contemplating. I immediately jumped up from my dinner, walked out of the family's home I was in and called Raj, speaking to him for a good hour about his grief. Fortunately, Raj went home that evening and the next day we spoke for hours as he told me the whole story and dove into the nature of his grief.

Heartbreak is a type of grief. For anyone who has gone through it with a romantic partner, friendship or even heartbreak from losing a family member, they will know just by reading this sentence the pain involved. It feels as if our heart has been ripped out of our body as we lose someone we care about more than we care about ourselves. These emotions we feel at this point are normal. It's our mind's natural reaction to being thrown into an unfamiliar phase of life . . . and it's okay to feel the way we do.

Once, I was walking in Hyde Park in London. I saw a young man sitting next to a statue. Both the statue and the man were ripped physically, but the statue stood emotionless whereas the man was crying and weeping. As stated in the first chapter, we are sentient beings, we are not Sophia. We are meant to feel pain. We are not only meant to go through it, but we are also meant to *grow* through it.

However, this growth takes time. Moving on from this pain can take time. One of the senior ladies in our spiritual community told me that when she lost her mother in her twenties, it took over ten years to feel 'normal' again. Each person has a unique situation. We all have different healing times based on the time spent with that individual, emotional involvement and our own healing capacity. That's fine too. We live in a world of instants. Instant coffee, instant streaming and instant Wi-Fi. However, with emotional healing, there are rarely any instants.

Heartbreak is especially difficult. With the number of people who ask for my counsel for their marriage, I often wonder if I have become a matrimonial therapist. I remember receiving this hilarious phone call. One gentleman called up our office and professed his love for a girl to us. He said that she was a die-hard fan of mine and he wanted to propose to her. The next day was her birthday and he asked if I could make a video wishing her a happy birthday and at the same time telling her how much he loves her. He said that if I proposed on his behalf she was bound to say yes because of how much she trusted me. Wishing people a happy birthday I had no problem with. However, I am a celibate monk—proposing on someone's behalf was a bit too much for me!

Another thing I get asked is to find a match for someone's son or daughter. I frequently get a knock on my door from an anxious father or mother asking if 'I know anyone' for their child. They come with a scroll of requirements: not too tall, but not too short; funny, but not a comedian; able to cook, but not better than me (a mother would say sometimes); healthy, but not obsessed with working out. The list would be endless. I would sometimes reply, 'I am not sure if god has made someone like that yet!'

From this you can imagine the heartbreaks, separations and divorces that I have to be a therapist for. It is my greatest privilege to help people in their time of need about these sensitive issues. Sometimes I have to give formal advice; at other times, I have to be a shoulder to cry on.

Dealing with grief in heartbreak and loss

Have you ever wondered how much pleasure our nails can give us? No one in the history of the human race would have thought about that question unless they have heard it before. We do not overly think about our nails. However, how much potential do the nails have to cause us pain? We have all slammed our finger in the edge of a door at some point in our lives and we know its excruciating pain.

Pain consumes our mind more than pleasure. Imagine being on a beautiful sandy beach in California. The weather is perfect and you're lying there reading your favourite book as the cool breeze from the Pacific blows. But now imagine having a toothache at the same time. What does your mind focus on: the great weather, the soft sand, the cool ocean, the beautiful view or your toothache? We can take painkillers for physical pain management, but what medications can we use to deal with emotional pain and grief after anti-depressant medicines stop working? I have seen people in agonizing physical pain but still smiling because they feel loved, appreciated and valued. On the other hand, I have seen people who are physically fit with no aches and pains but chronically depressed and grief-stricken, especially when they have no one to be by their side. It is their grief that can disrupt their physical health—affecting their sleep, eating and cognitive ability.

The emotions that people who are grieving experience can creep up on them over time. Shock, guilt, anger, disbelief and deep sadness are some of them. The greater the loss, the more intense the grief. The most intense type of grief is often the loss of a loved one, but as we have seen, heartbreak can also cause pain along with losing a job, retirement, miscarriage, losing a cherished dream.

One piece of advice I always give is to not be ashamed of what you are grieving for. Regardless of what society dictates, people grieve for what is significant to them. Many people approach me with deep sadness on the loss of a pet. On the outside it may not seem as bad as losing a family member, but the point is to that person, that pet *was* a family member.

It is only when we can accept that we are grieving and that it is okay to grieve, can we begin to cope in a healthy way. Through that we can come to terms with the loss, ease the suffering and in time, move forward.

Dealing with grief

The process of grieving takes time; we cannot rush the process. The experience is different for different people and depends on a number of factors, including how close we were to the person we lost, our experiences of loss, our personality, our support system and our coping mechanisms. That senior lady in our community who said it took her over ten years to 'fully heal' from losing her mother at a young age shared three things that helped her to move on:

Firstly, she said that we have to actively work on our healing. Simply ignoring the pain and distracting ourselves will only make things worse in the future.

Secondly, the emotions we experience when grieving are common to many going through similar situations. When we lose a relationship, we may feel lonely, frightened and miserable. We may cry as a result, which is a normal response, but we may not, which is also a normal response for people. People may process grief in different ways and that is okay to witness. Her sister did not cry that she had lost her mother, but she did. Not everyone will express emotions like we do and that also has to be accepted. We cannot expect everyone to cry like us as they may not hold the same relationship with the person we have lost.

Thirdly, she said that one thing that disrupted her healing process was feeling guilty about moving on. Accepting that something has happened is different from forgetting it happened. We can move on from a situation, but still cherish the person who was in our lives and the lessons they taught us. This memory can actually help us become stronger.

The stages of grief

Everyone will have to go through grief in one form or another. Psychiatrist Elisabeth Kubler-Ross understood this and introduced the 'five stages of grief'. They were based on her research in 1969 of patients' emotions of terminal illness but can be generalized to the grieving process for other reasons too, such as the loss of a pet or the breaking of a relationship. The five stages are:

1. Denial—the avoidance of the situation which can be displayed as confusion, masking deep sadness and an over-endeavour to be 'normal'.
2. Anger—looking for solutions in our wrath. The search for *why* this has happened and who we can direct our rage towards.
3. Bargaining—looking for solutions using our logic. Thinking things like, 'God if you reverse this situation, I will in return . . .'
4. Depression—feeling deep sadness and displaying a lack of motivation for day-to-day activities. This may be sadness or manifest as clinical depression.

5. Acceptance—finding peace in what has happened without forgetting that it happened.

Although these seem like neat checklists for our grief, these were not meant to be a system that people follow when experiencing grief. Kubler-Ross says, 'These five stages were never meant to help tuck messy emotions into neat packages. They are responses to loss that many people experience, but there is no typical response to a loss, as there is no typical loss. Our grieving is as individual as our lives are.' We may not experience any of these stages or may skip a few, but still be healing. Many people may read this list and now start comparing their grief, trying to find some order in the chaos and also where they fit into this model. However, Kubler-Ross encourages people to use this as a rough outline of the emotions one may feel when grieving, rather than a rigid framework.

From this model, grief may also seem linear: we go through every emotion until acceptance. However, many have found grief to be cyclical. We experience these five stages again and again depending on the events that are occurring in our lives. For example, we may have broken up with a partner and may experience deep feelings of denial to acceptance initially. However, we then may be triggered by a memory like walking past their favourite restaurant that may initiate the cycle again. As we grow and heal, we may go through the same five stages yet again, but our ability to deal with them has become stronger.

What are the symptoms of grief? Although grief is not a medical disease and is a human response to loss, there are common emotional symptoms people face. Feeling like they are in a nightmare, or 'going crazy' or even rejecting their own cherished religious or spiritual values are common. Other symptoms include feeling shocked and not being able to believe the reality of the situation. People who are shocked may expect the person to show up even though they know they are gone. This happened to one person I was counselling. He had lost his daughter to suicide and kept asking his family members to search his building for her, thinking she was hiding on the roof or in the closet.

Grief almost certainly has the symptoms of sadness. This usually comes out as people cry and feel emotionally unstable. In addition to sadness, people may feel anger or guilt. They may feel anger at the object of grief or to other people involved in the situation as a way of rationalizing the situation. They may feel guilty about not having prevented the situation from happening, not telling the person how they felt or even guilt about feeling relieved that the situation is over. Many people who have lost a loved one that they have been caring for, for many years, often feel a sense of guilt for the sense of relief they feel after the person leaves. Finally, a lingering symptom that seems to last with people experiencing grief is fear. They can feel anxious, insecure and even have panic attacks. Loss may leave people fearing the future without the person they lost and fearing their future responsibilities.

How to deal with grief

There are two types of people: people who will isolate and withdraw into their shell when dealing with grief and people who want to share their feelings with everyone they meet.

The key is to look for one-on-one support from people who care about us and those who are experts in helping people through the grieving process.

That support may come from family and friends. Being strong means asking for help, not trying to do everything ourselves. They could be a shoulder to cry on and give emotional support, but they could also help with practical arrangements such as helping us move home if we have had a relationship breakdown or a funeral arrangement if we have lost a loved one. It is important to know that people who have never experienced grief may not be so good at comforting us. They may say or do the wrong things at times, but we should try to overlook that. The rule is: if they are there, they care. We should not isolate ourselves.

Exercise:

Think of two people whom you could turn to in moments of need.

This exercise can help us feel at peace in difficult times; it is a reminder that we have people whom we can always count on.

Many people find comfort from their faith. Although a symptom of grief can be to blame our spiritual tradition, many might find peace through the mourning rituals, such as chanting, singing and praying. Talking to a senior member of our own spiritual community, one who understands grief and loss, can help us make sense of the devasting situation. There may even be a support group that we can join to help share our sorrow with like-minded individuals.

Finally, if this is not providing us solace or we need to seek additional help, there is absolutely no shame in visiting a mental health professional for grief counselling. This is their daily role, which they are experienced in. They can help us work through our grief in a healthy manner.

As we look outwards, it is also important to look inwards when we are grieving. Taking care of ourselves is crucial at these low times in life as our energy levels may already be lower due to the loss we are going through. One thing to know is that pain will never last forever. As mentioned, the mind cannot take emotional pain forever. An ancient story explains this point well.

A king once asked all his advisers in his cabinet, 'Is there any phrase, motto or mantra that works in all circumstances at all times? Is there something that can help me in the most joyous or perilous situations? When I am alone, can I call upon something to encourage me?' The advisers talked among themselves for days discussing what they would tell the king.

After a few days, the chief adviser to the king approached him and presented him with a sheet of paper folded tight into a tiny piece which fit into a golden locket. The adviser told the king, 'Please take this locket. Inside it is the phrase you are looking for, but we advise only opening the locket in the direst of situations when it seems that all hope is lost.' The king wore this locket everywhere.

One evening, the king went hunting with his army. All of a sudden, a tribe of bandits attacked the king's army, slaughtering them all and began to chase the king into the forest on horseback. A gruelling chase ensued with the bandits thinking that they would inherit the empire if they captured the king. Suddenly, the path the king was on came to a sudden halt with a cliff edge dropping down thousands of feet below. There was nowhere for him and his horse to go. The wild screams of the bandits grew louder. At this moment, with no hope, the king opened the locket and unfolded the paper. He read the words, 'This too shall pass.'

'This too shall pass?' the king thought. 'How will this situation pass?' He read it multiple times trying to decode it until he had an epiphany. 'This too will pass. Just a few days ago, I was the king of a huge empire, but today I am being hunted by savages and facing my death. Just as my luxuries have abandoned me, this danger will also pass.' The king took a deep breath and relaxed. He got off his horse and let it go into the wilderness. He then proceeded to climb down the cliff edge where he found a small cave that he crawled into. As the bandits approached, they saw his horse wandering aimlessly and looked over the cliff edge to the abyss. 'He must have jumped!' one of the bandits said as they all cheered. Little did they know that the king was thinking about this piece of universal freedom on the cliff edge: *This too shall pass*.

From that moment, the brave king planned his return, reorganized his army and then fought the bandits who had captured a part of his kingdom. He defeated them and returned victorious to his palace. The whole city was in a festive mood with the citizens of the city presenting gifts to him. The king felt proud as he rode his horse through the city with flowers being thrown on him. At that moment, sunlight hit his golden locket reminding of his motto, *This too shall pass*. He stepped down from his horse and a sense of humility hit him. 'My defeat is not mine. My victory is not mine,' he thought. 'Everything passes by. We are witnesses of all this. We are the perceivers. Life comes and goes. Happiness comes and goes. Sorrow comes and goes.'

In the same way, our pain from grief will also pass. The Bhagavad Gita mentions that just as summer turns to winter and winter turns to summer, our happiness and distress also change. We can try to suppress the pain we are feeling from grief, but it will be expressed sooner or later. If we want to heal, we have to acknowledge the pain, otherwise we can risk becoming clinically depressed, or dependent on harmful substances, or have other health issues.

Exercise:

Think of your best childhood memory—write it down.
Think of your worst childhood memory—write it down.
Think of a time you felt most scared—write it down.
Think of a time you felt most secure—write it down.
Think of a time you felt happiest—write it down.
Think of a time you felt most upset—write it down.
Now reflect: In every situation, both good and bad, that time and feeling has passed.

Often in times of grief, it is difficult to imagine feeling better; we cannot see the light at the end of the tunnel. However, by reflecting on all past experiences when we *have* come through that tunnel, we can see that there was always a light at the end, regardless of whether it was visible to us at every stage or not. Time does heal us, and though we may not believe it in the moment, it will get better. *This too shall pass.*

Other ways that we can handle our grief ourselves is by expressing our feelings creatively. Writing a grief journal, painting, singing or even getting involved with a cause that was close to the person we've lost can help. Taking up a hobby that encourages support, such as team sports or learning a new skill, can also be something that can aid the grieving process. Exercising regularly and planning ahead for 'grief triggers', such as weddings, anniversaries or birthdays, are other tools to help us grieve in a healthy way. One thing that many people tell me is the frustration they feel when people tell them to 'move on' or 'get over it'. It is important to not be disheartened by this bad advice. Most people have our best interests at heart and may want us to 'move on' as they think that that will make us happy. However, it is important we don't let others dictate our emotions. If we need to cry, we should. If we need to go through our sadness, we should. If we need to scream, shout or yell, that's fine too. We all heal at our own pace.

A day of new beginnings in London had come to an end. Not only had we had wonderful celebrations in the capital city, I had also been involved with calamities and helped a boy deal with grief who was halfway across the world.

Chapter summary:

- We are meant to feel pain, but we are not only meant to go through it, we are also meant to grow through it.

- Grief can disrupt our physical health—affecting sleep, eating and cognitive ability.
- We have to actively work on our healing.
- People may process grief in different ways and that is okay.
- Feeling guilty about moving on can disrupt our healing process.
- Grief can be cyclical; as we grow and heal, we may go through the same five stages of grief again, but our ability to deal with it has become stronger.
- We may find solace in family, friends, faith, professionals or expressing our grief in a creative way.
- The Bhagavad Gita mentions that just as summer turns to winter and winter turns to summer, our happiness and distress also change, nothing is permanent . . . *This too shall pass.*

SECTION 3
ME AND THE MIND OF OTHERS

In section 3, we will be discussing how our actions can affect how others feel. We have more power than we think. The way we behave can affect the people around us, which can affect their behaviour, thus sending a ripple of energy out into the world. Therefore, in this section, we will discuss not only how to treat people the way we want to be treated, but how to treat people *even better* than the way we want to be treated. We will start with how to develop empathy, move on to how to communicate sensitively and end with how to develop selflessness.

ELEVEN

When Sandals Meet Yeezys: Developing Empathy

'The greatest gift you can give someone is your time because that is a portion of your life that you will never get back.'

—Unknown

We live in a world where there's always a reason to be disturbed. The constant barrage of news and media means there is a campaign going on in every corner. Some legitimate campaign for social justice or against oppression. Others are not as important; they may be about children against making their beds, fathers against changing nappies or people against wearing socks to sleep. I believe that the slogan of every powerful cause should be able to fit on a T-shirt. In Mumbai, if you walk around the streets, you will see a whole host of T-shirt vendors. You have classic ones; people selling the India cricket team shirt or an IPL shirt. And then you have the counterfeit ones: people selling 'Gukki', 'BurBerri', or 'Ralph Laurice' T-shirts on the side of the road. Finally, you have the people selling funny shirts. Some of the best ones I have seen are, 'Who says nothing is impossible? I have been doing nothing for years.' Another is, 'I don't need Google. My wife knows everything!' And my favourite, and one that matches this theme, 'Do not disturb. Already disturbed.'

The first principle of empathy is to understand this T-shirt line. That although we may be going through a tough time with our mental well-being, nearly everybody we meet may be going through a tough time too. There are different degrees of problems. Not everyone's problem is the same or of the same magnitude. Nevertheless, *everyone* is suffering with something.

The ancient literatures categorize the different types of suffering in three ways in the disturbance trident:

- *Adhi-atmik:* These are disturbances that happen to us because of our own actions. Our wrong choices, wrong decisions, wrong behaviour. They can lead to suffering causing physical or emotional pain.
- *Adhi-bhautik:* These are disturbances caused by others. Our emotional well-being can be genuinely disturbed by other people: a non-cooperative neighbour, an abusive boss, a broken romantic relationship or even something as small as a mosquito. I often tell this joke to highlight this point: A baby mosquito came back home after its first time flying. His dad rushed over to him to make sure he was okay. People hate mosquitoes, so his father knew it must have been a rough day flying. 'How do you feel? Are you hurt?' the father mosquito asked his son. 'No, I feel great!' the baby mosquito replied. 'It was so wonderful to see all the humans clapping for me as I took my first flight!' We can have a positive outlook within, but it

should never be forgotten that there are forces from other living beings that will always be there to hurt us. That is the nature of the world. Although we can elevate our consciousness, there is no way to change that universal truth of the world.

- *Adhi-daivik*: These are disturbances caused by forces beyond us. In recent years, we have seen an increase in the number of natural disasters that have happened in the world. Cyclones, tsunamis, hurricanes, volcanic eruptions, earthquakes, excessive rains, drought. These are all disturbances caused by natural forces and can create immense harm for us. Nothing happens by chance, but because of the scale of these disasters, they seem to happen without any reason.

Any suffering we feel can fall into the three categories above. Just as we cannot take salinity away from salt, we cannot take suffering away from the world. Therefore, it is so important that we do not add to the suffering that people are already going through. It is important that we do not speak, behave or conduct ourselves in a way that brings more disturbance to the lives of others. Suffering is unavoidable, but we can reduce its impact on people by our dealings and actions. Rather than leaving someone in pieces, we should try and bring them peace. If we cannot be a part of the solution to end suffering, we should at least try to not be the problem. We should try and be agents of positive change in the lives of others by practising empathy.

What is the one thing that the world needs most to solve our problems? Some would say that we need to reduce the inequality in wealth. Others would argue that we need to eradicate world hunger. Yet, the majority would argue we need improved forms of government. These are all good things to strive for, and we must definitely work on them, but before we can start to 'change the world with lofty ideals', we must really work on changing ourselves. If there is one thing the world needs more of, it is people who are kinder.

We are called humankind. Therefore, the core, the essence, of being human, is being kind. Just as our mind chatters, goes through periods of sadness, depression and anxiety, feels guilt and brings us down, the mind of every other person is doing the same thing to them as well. The only problem is we do not know what others have been through and are going through right now. Our eyes can fail us. What we see on the outside does not always match what people are feeling on the inside. They could have smiling faces, but crying hearts.

A word of encouragement or an act of kindness can brighten someone's day. Science shows that not only can it help the person who receives the act of kindness, but also the person who performs the act of kindness. A study by professor of counselling psychology at Indiana University, Y. Joel Wong, found that people who encourage others naturally are just as likely to benefit from those words of encouragement as the person who receives it.[1] Not only can our encouraging other people help boost their self-esteem or 'refuel' their self-esteem but at the same time it can boost our own state of wellness. People who encourage others are more likely to be appreciated by others, thereby creating a cycle of encouragement and joy for themselves. Therefore, there are tangible benefits to learning the art of empathy and understanding how to encourage others.

It is said that being kind is akin to being a lamp post. It does not necessarily shorten the distance, but it lights up the path and makes the journey a little easier for others. After all, isn't it hard to hug yourself or cry on your own shoulder? It is important that when it rains, we share our umbrella and if we don't have an umbrella, we share the rain. Helping others does not mean we do not have our own struggles. But since we all know what pain feels like, and if someone has been empathetic to us in the past by offering us their shoulder to cry on, we also know what support feels like, and so we should learn how to extend ourselves to those in trouble.

Exercise: Random acts of kindness

Every day, at least for a week, choose to consciously do something kind for a minimum of one person. It can be a kind gesture, words of appreciation, an act of service, friendly support . . . Try to help a different person every day for a week. You should notice that you feel much happier by doing this.

I want to bring you back to my trip to London. Lecturing is fantastic but speaking in small groups or one-to-one, where I can really dive deep into people's stories, is even better. On one of my tours of London, a young man whom I know brought his friend to meet me. I could tell that he was a fan of the work I do on social media, but he was trying to not show his excitement that we were meeting. He was twenty-four years old. He was British–Indian, with jet-black long hair tied in a ponytail, green eyes hidden behind designer sunglasses and clothes from the coolest designer brands. I believe he had some 'Yeezy' shoes, which was a stark contrast to my orange robes and rubber sandals.

Most of my conversations with new people are formal. However, with this young man, it was naturally casual. It was so casual that he started using mild swear words and calling me 'dude' as if we had been roommates in university dorms. Do not get me wrong; he was a lovely young man, and his casual nature was endearing. He told me that he came from a well-to-do family, was the only child, and was now well-placed in the company he was working for. At the end of my meetings with people, I always offer them a gift in the form of sweetmeats and invite them to my upcoming public talks in the city. The young man nodded and said he would attend, the same way an old Indian aunty would say, out of formality, that they would go for tea at another old Indian aunty's house. Both know that this meeting is highly unlikely, but it is a sign of respect to extend the invite. Little did I know that he would actually come to every single talk I did in London from then on. I thought that he must have been tracking the calendar on my phone because he came for each of my talks! For most of them, he stayed until the end when everybody had left. He would sit on the stage with me and a few others chatting about the points I had raised and life in general. We became good friends; a natural rapport forming between both of us.

However, I had a feeling that he was hiding something. We had run out of small talk, we had run out of philosophical talk, we had also run out of telling jokes and anecdotes. There is a time in every relationship when you have to push forward and reveal the heart. I could sense that, behind his designer sunglasses and apathetic attitude, there was something he needed to share with me. Over the years I have learnt to stay silent until someone feels ready to share their life with me. Whether they want to go deeper in our friendship is a choice they need to make.

Life is a journey during which we meet some good people and some not-so-good people. Some treat us well and some do not. Some things go our way and some do not. Some people have lovely families, yet others come from broken homes. Who we are today is the sum total of all our experiences. Showing empathy means to understand this and to not jump to conclusions from first impressions without knowing more. As the famous phrase goes, 'It's taken a lifetime to write this story of mine, will you read me just in a day?' I waited for my new, super-cool friend to share more.

Often the vibe a person emanates speaks more than their words. It is important to trust our intuition, to sense the energy of a situation beyond everything that is seen and heard. Humans are not rational beings; we are irrational. What we say is not always what we mean because we think to ourselves, 'If I share this intimate secret, how will this person, my family and society perceive me?' It takes time to start tuning our intuition but I am sure we have all had the experience of knowing when the energy in a room is off. A classic scenario is when you walk into a room after two people have been fighting and they go silent. You could cut through the tension with a knife. Similarly, I could sense that this young man's needs were beyond just wanting to listen to my lectures. He wanted my attention and time.

All of a sudden, in the middle of an art-deco-themed auditorium, he broke down crying. It was only me, him and his best friend in the room. 'What's the matter?' I asked him with concern in my voice.

'My mother has been having an affair. I was the one who discovered it when I was twenty-three,' he said as he sobbed. 'It's been going on for a whole year and has totally devastated our family.' He took a tissue to dry his eyes while looking at the floor. 'I hear them fighting all the time. I even heard my father once shouting at her that, if it was not for him, she would have aborted me.' This was shattering information. Imagine finding out that your whole world is upside down. Everything you thought was true was a facade. His mother was having an extramarital affair and at first wanted to abort him. This young man had built himself up professionally but was struggling emotionally. He had lost faith in relationships, lost faith in the institution of marriage and lost faith in his parents. What do you say or how do you behave when someone drops something so devastating? It is a mammoth task, but we have to learn to add these three essential elements of empathy to our lives.

Understand

There is a famous saying: 'Understanding is deeper than knowledge. There are many people who know you, but just a few who really understand you.'

The first step to empathy is to understand the issue. To do this we need to learn how to listen to understand and not to reply. We have all heard the phrase, 'We have two ears and one mouth. We should use them in that proportion.' However, something even more interesting is that if we put two ears side by side, they form the shape of a heart. Also, we cannot spell heart without ear. So, if we really want to understand someone's heart, the only way is through the ears. Listen!

Often, it is hard to understand the roles others play or what they are going through in their life. I call a lady who looks after a home a 'domestic engineer'. They seem to be completing a hundred roles under one job description. There is a funny story that highlights why understanding is the first step of empathy.

A man once came back from work and was shocked to see that his kids were still playing outside and were bringing mud into the house. In the kitchen, he saw unwashed dishes, a counter with no dinner cooked, milk spilled on the floor and sugar, cereal, biscuits all over the place. In the living room, the situation was even worse. Toys, shoes, unwashed clothes and broken crockery littered the floor. He rushed to the bedroom to check if his wife was sick or had hurt herself during the day. But he was amazed to find her comfortably lying on the bed watching Netflix on her laptop. He asked her what had happened in the house. She replied, 'Every day you come back home and ask me what did I do the whole day. Well, today I thought I would give you the answer!'

We need to understand the effort, hard work and struggles that others are going through. The breadwinner in the house may not understand what the homemaker has to go through and vice versa, if both do not take out the time to listen to one another. But this is easier said than done.

Once, when I was in Mumbai, a lady came to visit me two weeks after her husband had left her. In our conversation, within the first few lines of what she was saying, I understood the problem and also came up with the solutions necessary. Like a surgeon who knows exactly what to do and where to cut from a few lines of the patient's history, I knew what she required, or so I thought. I listened to her for a grand total of five minutes and twenty-two seconds. After that time had passed, I stopped her and said I understood the problem and gave her the next steps she should take to deal with it.

Tears started welling up in her eyes. *What happened? What had I said that made her cry?* I could not understand why she was crying. There is an analogy that our body is composed primarily of water, but when the body is hurt, what comes out? Blood. And our heart is composed primarily of blood, but when the heart is hurt, what comes out? Water. We cry when we are upset, maybe because our expectations may not have been met. I tried to pacify her. At this point, there was a small crowd forming to see the lady that Gaur Gopal Das had made cry. The lady gathered herself and after an hour or so of speaking, left to go home, fairly content that I had offered her a keen ear to listen to her issues.

As I walked from the courtyard to the main temple room to pray, I could only think of one thing: her tears. I reflected on what had happened. This lady had been through incredible trauma with her husband leaving her. She had not come to me for a solution. Often, not all problems have solutions. She had simply come with a desire to be heard. She wanted empathy and kindness, not my solutions. Typically, men love to give solutions when women just want to be heard. I thought of my closest friends and family as I looked at the temple deities that evening. If they came to me with an issue on that scale, would I have even given them the same five minutes and twenty-two seconds? Probably not. With people we don't know so closely, like this woman, we are so patient, kind and tolerant. We put our best foot forward. But when it comes to those who are close to us, what happens? Is it because we think that they are our own people we can behave with them as we like? Or is it because we think that they will understand, so we do not need to spend the time trying to understand? Is it because we think that they should understand our schedules and so we do not need to make time for them? That is hardly the case. Familiarity breeds contempt, which may ruin our ability to be empathetic.

Listening requires both our will to extend ourselves to understand and also our skills to read the room, to pick up the vibes and hear the unspoken words. It requires patience; it needs restraint.

At times, a good empathetic conversation means to say nothing at all. There are words that are attributed to St Francis of Assisi which convey this message well, 'I preach the gospel at all times. I use words where necessary.' Living by example and learning the art of listening can have a more powerful effect than jumping at solutions.

That evening I called the lady up and apologized for my behaviour. After that conversation, I would not have been surprised if she had lost faith in me. She understood that I did not mean to hurt her and that, after all, I am a man 'hailing from Mars', always battling to find a solution like all men do. I mentioned that because I knew her, I became too familiar and cut her off while she was expressing her emotions. I told her that I was wrong. I did not have the right to assume I knew her problem and not be sensitive and empathetic.

After we have understood their story, through their words or through their body language, the next step is to make an attempt to feel what they are going through.

Feel

'Breathe, breathe, you are doing well. Only a few more pushes,' a husband told his wife as she was in labour giving birth to their first child. He was holding her hand, wearing surgical gloves and a gown like the three other doctors and two nurses in the room. 'You have got this!' he said. The wife smiled as she gave it her all and pushed, sweat exuding from every pore of her body and soaking her hospital robe. 'I can understand exactly what pain you are going through. You are doing really well!' the husband said to his wife. The wife stopped pushing. The doctors stopped working. The nurses looked up. Everyone was thinking the same thing, 'Buddy, you have no idea about the pain she is going through.' The room resumed their duties after a moment. His wife squeezed his hand tightly as she began to push again, causing her husband to yell in pain with her. Maybe that would be the closest he would get to understanding her pain. We should not jump to conclusions about others' lives if we have never walked a mile in their shoes

After having understood a person's situation, the next step of empathy is to intentionally feel the emotions they are exhibiting. In the first section of this book, we have discussed how we should learn to recognize our own emotions in order to have a healthy mental state. In a similar way, we must make the effort through active listening to understand the emotions others are feeling, if we want to be empathetic to them.

Once we have recognized the feeling that someone is displaying, we can then get a glimpse of what it means to remove our own shoes and put theirs on. It would mean taking off my monk sandals and putting on the Yeezys of my cool London friend. This allows us to adopt their emotions even if it is just for a few moments. What would it feel like if I was *actually* them?

The science is strong on this. The same part of the brain that is used for empathy is also used when we are experiencing another's emotions subconsciously. Think about when you see a video of someone falling off their chair or into a pool of water, belly first. What do you feel? You may wince and groan as you feel their pain as if it was your own. What is happening here is that specific 'mirror neurons' in your brain are firing when you see another person experience a stimulus that you could have been exposed to.

The act of empathy is about firing these 'mirror neurons' in the brain consciously. When we get immersed in another person's grief or sadness and learn how to feel that emotion, it tells the person two things. Firstly, it tells them that we have understood their situation. Secondly, and more importantly, it tells them that we have also understood the emotions they are experiencing as if we were swapping lives at that moment. This is a powerful connection to share with someone. It gives them the hope that they do not have to go through their suffering alone. This exercise becomes much easier if we have had the experience of the exact pain that they are going through. For example, we may never get cancer, but if we have had a very close family member go through it, we can easily empathize with others who have cancer and the turmoil it might cause in their lives.

There is an instance from the book of my dear friend Govinda Das, which highlights why it is important to not be critical of people before we have felt what it is like to travel a mile in their shoes. This can only happen through deep conversation.

A well-educated youth, the only son to his parents, decides to go to America for brighter earning and career prospects so that he can settle himself as well as his parents nicely. Soon he makes his mark and raises his own family there, while his parents continue to remain in India.

As time passes by, realizing old age is catching up, the parents can no longer be on their own, and start missing their son. Now the son is caught in a tug-of-war between his own family, which is well-settled abroad, and his parents wanting him to be with them. Trying to please the parents would upset his family but trying to please his family would mean abandoning his old parents to embrace a life replete with hurt and loneliness, eventually to die without anyone intimate around them. What would you do in such a situation? Would you have a straight answer?

Govinda Das summarizes the meaning of this example by telling the reader that it is very easy to criticize any situation or individual over a casual discussion, but mature discretion calls for putting ourselves in that situation so as to assess what we would have done. Dilemmas that are rooted in affection and duty are most difficult to harmonize. So, before hastily denouncing someone over a situation, it is imperative that we see the episode from their perspective, instead of ours.

Act

The final step in practising empathy is acting. There is a famous Japanese proverb, 'Vision without action is a daydream. Action without vision is a nightmare.' When we empathize with someone, we are showing them love and kindness. But love is not a noun. It's a verb. It's expressed through our service to others. At times, that service is offered by silent listening; at other times, through words of guidance and support. Yet, there are times when we need to, beyond words and emotional support, offer some practical actions to help them through their perils.

In a village, a farmer had some puppies that he wanted to sell. He painted a sign on the nearby highway, advertising that he had four rare breed pups that he wanted to give away. A few hours later, a crowd of people had gathered outside his door wanting to buy the puppies. 'What breed are they?' one person shouted. 'How much are they?' another yelled. 'Can we see them now?' someone demanded from the back. At the front of the crowd, a young boy grabbed his trousers and tugged at them. The farmer looked down into the eyes of the little boy, shabbily dressed.

'Mister,' the boy said sweetly, 'I want to buy one of your puppies.'

'Well, my boy,' the farmer said, while rubbing the sweat on the back of his neck, 'these puppies are a fine breed and cost a good deal of money.' Assuming that this boy could not afford the puppies, he felt sorry for the child, but there was nothing he could do about the price. He had a family to feed and a profit to make. The boy dropped his head for a moment and thought. He reached deep into his pockets, pulled out a handful of change and held it up to the farmer.

'I've got thirty-nine cents. Is that enough to take a look?'

'Sure,' said the farmer while pushing the rest of the crowd back. The farmer led the boy through his house, past the kitchen and into the backyard. The farmer then let out a large whistle. 'Here, Dolly!' he called. Out from the doghouse and down the ramp ran Dolly, the mother, followed by four little balls of fur. The little boy's eyes danced with delight as the dogs all bundled over each other thinking that it was time to eat again. However, something else caught the little boy's eye inside the doghouse. There was a smaller ball of fur crawling around inside. It was also excited, but not as fast as its siblings. It hopped down the ramp in a somewhat awkward manner; the little pup began hobbling toward the little boy doing its best to catch up.

'I want that one,' the little boy said, pointing to the most underdeveloped puppy of the litter.

The farmer knelt down at the boy's side and said, 'Son, you don't want that puppy. He will never be able to run and play with you like these other dogs would. Are your parents around to help you choose and pay for one of the healthy puppies?'

The little boy pulled up one leg of his trousers to reveal a steel brace running down both sides of his left leg attached to a specially made shoe. Smiling, he looked back up at the farmer, 'You see, sir, I do not run too well myself, and this little one needs someone who understands.' With tears in his eyes, the farmer reached down and picked up the hobbling little pup. Holding him carefully, he handed it to the little boy who was joyous beyond comparison.

'How much?' asked the little boy, holding his spare change in one hand and balancing his new friend in the other.

'No charge,' answered the farmer. 'There's no charge for love. The world is full of people who need someone who understands and helps.'

This heart-warming story shows us that there are physical acts of kindness or solutions that we can draw up if the situation requires it. After understanding and feeling, we should act to help. In our own way, big or small, we can make a difference to a person's life. We can help them with their pain and assist the healing of their mind.

One person who has acted on her empathy is Sunitha Krishnan, an Indian social activist and co-founder of Prajwala, an NGO that rescues, rehabilitates and reintegrates sex-trafficked victims into society. In 2017, she gave a ground-breaking lecture entitled, 'Shame the Rapist' where she shares her journey to help young ladies in India who have been raped and have not had justice even though the rapists themselves had posted videos online of their heinous deeds. 'When I was sent these videos, I was stunned. For a person like me who has saved over 17,000 girls from sexual slavery, I thought I would not be shocked by such a video, yet it was very shocking,' she said. From her anger and anguish in seeing these videos she started a campaign to appeal to the public to find these men. Krishnan *understands* the problem. She feels the pain that these women go through, as she was also raped when she was a child and has worked extensively to solve this problem. She also *feels* the pain of these women as the men who raped them flaunt their heinous acts over the Internet. Then, she took practical *action* to help. This is true empathy and for an incredibly worthy cause.

Although this is a huge cause and Krishnan has changed the lives of thousands of people in India, she is changing lives, one person at a time. It does not matter how big or small our empathy is; it is the quality of what we do that matters. Learning to be empathetic to our partners, friends and family can have a huge impact on them, and thus the network effects of this has a huge impact on society.

When I look at the bulb in the room, I think about how tiny the bulb is and how large the room is. And yet, when the bulb is turned on, it drives away the darkness in that room. When I spray perfume on my wrist, I think about how little the perfume is; yet, when I enter a room, the fragrance pervades the entire space. When I cook, I think about how I add only a little salt to a dish compared to all the other ingredients and yet it is the salt that makes such a large difference to the taste.

It's not just about the quantity but about the quality. It's not just about the magnitude but about the impact. If we ever think we are too small to make a difference, remember the bulb, the perfume, the salt. We should remind ourselves that we also have the ability to help others. The reason action is needed is because we have the perfect opportunity to identify what the other person needs. This is because we get to *feel* the emotion that the other person is going through, without being engrossed in the intensity of their pain. This means that we have a different perspective and increased capacity to help.

I walked out of the lecture theatre in London with the boy who had revealed how his life was falling apart. I gave him a hug and told him that I would be available to help him move through this difficult part of his life. As I approached the tube station, I saw a person selling T-shirts from a shop front. There were the classic football shirts on display, but one caught my eye that read, 'Empathy is in'.

How fitting! I thought. Maybe the tagline to that T-shirt could be: 'Understand, feel and act'.

Exercise: Improving your empathy

Think about a time someone came to you in their time of need. Audit how you think you helped that person.

How did you understand their problems? What did you do well? Did you place yourself in their shoes? And lastly, did you manage to do something practical to help them?

Now think about what you could change to increase your empathy towards someone.

1. Think about how you would like to improve your understanding of the problem a person is going through. For example, I would like to listen to the person's problem and not immediately try and offer a solution.

2. Now think about how you would like to improve on feeling what that person is going through. How can you best try and place yourself in that person's shoes?

For example: I will speak to an expert/do some research on what the person is going through, which can help me better understand the situation.

3. Once we really understand the situation the person is in by trying to feel the way they do, then we are in a better position to decide what we can actually do to help that person.

    That help may mean giving them the resources they need, or taking them away for a short break, or encouraging and helping them to seek professional/medical help.

Chapter summary:

- It is important to understand that everyone is going through some challenge or the other; in that light, we need to learn how to be empathetic.
- The different types of suffering are split into three categories: suffering as a result of our own actions, suffering as a result of another's actions and suffering imposed by nature.
- As a collective, we are called humankind. Therefore, the core, the essence, of being human, is being kind. Empathy is learning how to be kind without judgement.
- The first principle of empathy is to understand the issue. To do this, we need to learn how to listen to understand and not to reply.

- The second principle of empathy is to try and intentionally feel the emotions of another. It is one thing to understand an issue, but we need to develop an emotional connection to display empathy.
- The third principle of empathy is acting. Although being there for someone in their time of difficulty is acting, we must understand that love is a verb. Is there anything in our capability we can do to eliminate or minimize their pain?

TWELVE

Learning from 'Virus': Developing Sensitive Communication

'A knife, dagger and arrow were fighting to decide who could create the deepest wound. Meanwhile, words were sitting at the back smiling as they watched all the fun.'

—Unknown

The natural follow-on from understanding empathy is to know how to communicate it well. If there was one skill that I would recommend everyone to focus on, it is the art of communication. Communication is the art of presenting our thoughts to others. The phrase 'That's not what I meant' in a discussion is a sign that what we were thinking has not been communicated well to another person.

Communication is not only about what we say, but how we behave, which is portrayed through our body language. Body language is non-verbal; it's the unspoken gestures that reveal our true emotions and intentions. Mehrabian's Communication Model found that 93 per cent of our communication comes from non-verbal cues; the other 7 per cent includes our choice of words and the tone of our voice.

But where do we learn good communication from? There are classes we can take, but I have found that professional actors are the masters of communication. Actors immerse themselves in roles so that they can empathize with the mood, intentions and behaviours of the characters they portray. Not only do they need to understand their own emotions fully but they need to know how to communicate the emotions of the person they are acting as. That means that every word, movement and gesture is calculated to help the audience feel a certain emotion.

A few years ago, I had the pleasure of doing an event in Chennai with Boman Irani. Most of you will know him, but for those who do not watch Bollywood films, you may have to Google his name to understand who he is. He is famous in recent years for his portrayal of Professor Viru Sahastrabuddhe aka 'Virus' in the hit film *Three Idiots*. He plays a strict dean who keeps all his engineering students in line without fail. We were flying together from Mumbai to Chennai. Being an engineering undergraduate myself, when I saw him on the plane, I shivered for a moment thinking he actually was 'Virus' and was about to tell me off for my university shenanigans. But I snapped out of it and settled down to speak with him during this short domestic flight.

Boman is an interesting, wise and funny individual. Despite his fame, he was down-to-earth and friendly. We discussed everything from our upcoming event, childhood and views on the state of affairs of our planet. It was clear that he had built himself up as a successful actor from humble beginnings. As we flew above the clouds, he shared his life story and how he got to where he had. During the flight, I had to ask him one question as he was in the inner circle of Bollywood: what movie would he recommend watching? He paused for a moment, as if going into deep meditation and then laughed. He suggested that I watch the popular film, *Taare Zameen Par*, produced and directed by Aamir Khan. It explores the life and imagination of an eight-year-old dyslexic child, Ishaan, who is sent to boarding school by his parents. His art teacher, Mr Nikumbh, played by Aamir Khan himself, recognizes his disability and helps him overcome his reading disorder.

'Heart-warming!' Boman said while describing Aamir Khan's masterpiece. He went on to say that his mother taught him to watch movies to learn principles, not just for entertainment. *Taare Zameen Par* had struck a deep chord with him as he himself used to have speaking challenges as a child.

Curious to see if that film stood up to the five-star recommendation from Boman, I decided to watch it after our event in Chennai. I, too, found some wonderful principles in it and pragmatic lessons that we can apply. I learnt how our dealings can impact other people, especially children, whose minds are like putty that can be moulded by how we speak and behave. Our behaviour can make or break another person's self-esteem. We are all struggling with something. One kind word can reverberate in a person's mind for months, picking them up from a bad spell in their lives or pushing them forward to achieve extraordinary things.

One part of the movie was particularly striking; the scene where Mr Nikumbh tells Vipin Sharma, the father of Ishaan, the story of how trees are felled on the Solomon Islands. The scene starts with the father and the art teacher sitting in the art studio of the boarding school. Mr Sharma is on an office chair and Nikumbh grabs a yellow stool to face the father. Ishaan's father states very defensively that they had done all the 'online research' possible on dyslexia for their child and they do care for him, but the boy simply does not have the ability to 'make it' in the world. Nikumbh's response leaves the father dumbfounded and emotional. He tells him that a parent's responsibilities are not only bound to giving children the best toys to play with, having all the luxuries in the world or the best educational options. Loving a child means to comfort them, be with them when they need their parents the most, motivate them when they are dejected or give them affection to show you care. The conversation ends with Nikumbh telling the father, 'Isn't this what caring actually is? I am glad to hear that you *think* you do care.' Just as the father is about to leave, Nikumbh tells him the effect words can have on people. He tells him about the Solomon Islands where tribal people do not cut down the trees they want to remove; instead, they stand around the trees hurling abuses at them for hours on end, which eventually leads to the drying up of those trees and their dying within a few weeks. The tribal people believe that toxic words used against the trees instil negative emotions and beliefs within them and the trees find it difficult to survive.

This scene is very telling for us all. At times, we may feel like Nikumbh, where we do the right thing and pick people up but, at other times, we may behave like Mr Sharma, where our words drag people down. Just as trees can fall from the words aimed at them, so can people. There is a famous quote,

'The pen is mightier than the sword.' However, pens do not win battles and swords do not write poetry. Mighty is the hand that knows when to pick up the pen and when to pick up the sword. The bottom line is, words can make or break a person. The scene ends with the father crying as he sees his dyslexic son correctly reading from a whiteboard in the courtyard, showing the success of Nikumbh's encouragement and the failure of his own criticism.

The example of the Solomon Islands is a great anecdote, but many of us would find it difficult to believe it. How can intangible words travel through the air and affect a motionless tree? To understand how this works, we have to delve into the power of the mind. *The Biology of Belief* by Bruce H. Lipton explains the difference between the subconscious and conscious mind. Although the conscious mind thinks in the present, behind the scenes is the tremendous might of the subconscious mind, which is making millions of decisions a day. Our value system is what feeds into the subconscious mind. This is why it is difficult to break a habit. Although our conscious mind wants to stop biting our nails or eating junk food, this habit has been hard-wired into our subconscious mind, which overrides our will power, leading us back to having shorter nails and plumper waistlines.

Lipton states in his book that this philosophy of the conscious and subconscious mind is not new. The Buddha, 2500 years ago, talked about *Alay Vigyan*, which directly translates to 'stored consciousness'. When the Buddha said, 'You are what you think', he was referring to the Alay Vigyan, which is the part of the mind that stores our value system, beliefs and experiences that drive our life. Just as Mr Sharma's criticism of his dyslexic son breaks down his self-esteem, Lipton goes on to explain how constantly berating our children can instil a belief system in their minds that can harm them. Negative talk can have a huge impact on ourselves and others. If your friends keep saying harmful things to you, it is time to find new friends. If you keep saying harmful things to yourself, it is time to start valuing yourself.

Therefore, if tribal people in the Solomon Islands can break down the molecular architecture of a tree by disrupting its emotions, think about how words are affecting other humans. Humans have a greater frequency of consciousness. How we communicate with others does have a positive or negative effect on their mind.

How the mind affects the body

'Sticks and stones may break my bones, but words can never hurt me.' This may be the world's most believed phrase that is untrue. Studies show that psychological and emotional injuries can have as much damage to the outcome of our lives as physical injuries. In their paper 'Do Words Hurt?', neuroscientist Maria Richter and her colleagues tested how the brain responds to real and imaginary negative words in different subjects. They discovered that negative words increase Implicit Processing (IMP) within an area of the brain called the subgenual anterior cingulate cortex. What this means is that negative words in real life or even negative words that we think of, can release stress and anxiety-inducing chemicals within us.[1] Another study by Lodge and colleagues in the *Journal of Anxiety Disorders* found that children who had higher rates of negative self-talk had increased levels of anxiety.[2] Therefore, painful words that are imagined or spoken out loud can have physical effects on our body in the form of long-term anxiety and a reduction in our mental well-being.

What about positive words? Dr Andrew Newberg, an American neuroscientist at Thomas Jefferson University, and Mark Robert Waldam, an expert in communication, published the book *Words Can Change Your Brain* in 2014, in which they write, '*A single word* has the power to influence the expression of genes that regulate physical and emotional stress.'[3] They also confirm the statements written in our previous section on positive affirmations, explaining how practising the art of positive thinking can literally change the outlook of our lives. 'By holding a positive and optimistic word in our mind, we stimulate frontal lobe activity. This area includes specific language centres that connect directly to the motor cortex responsible for moving us into action. And, as our research has shown, the longer we concentrate on positive words, the more we begin to affect other areas of the brain.'

Newberg and Waldam explain that the long-term benefits of sustained positive thoughts is remarkable, as these thoughts change the function of the parietal lobe in our brain. Not only does positive thinking by holding these words in our mind help us, but it also starts training our brain to see the good in others. Therefore, what this means for us is that if we want to be more like Mr Nikumbh from *Taare Zameen Par*, we have to change how we communicate with ourselves. It is only when we do this that we can really change how we are able to communicate with others. It is a scientific fact: if we want to change the world, we have to change ourselves by communicating with ourselves positively.

Ancient wisdom has known this fact for many millennia. There is a *subhashit* or old Indian folk saying:

samsāra katu vṛkṣasya
dve phale amṛtopame
subhāṣita rasāsvāda
sangatiḥ sujanaiḥ jane

'The world is like a tree full of bitterness. But it has two fruits that taste sweet like nectar: sweet, kind, encouraging words and the company of empathetic, kind, good individuals.'

A further text from the Bhagavad Gita (17.5) tells us how to make sure that our speech does not become the cause of disturbance to others.

anudvega-karam vākyam
satyam priya-hitam ca yat
svādhyāyābhyasanam caiva
vāṅ-mayam tapa ucyate

'Speaking truthful words that are pleasing, beneficial, not disturbing to others comprises austerity of speech.'

In this context, austerity means to do that which is righteous, beneficial and uplifting for us and others, not necessarily what makes us feel good. This text shows the aspects of our communication that can be uplifting to others. Words that are truthful, pleasing, beneficial and not agitating are considered positive. At times, we may speak words that are truthful in the name of 'constructive criticism', but we may not have learnt the art of speaking them in a pleasing or beneficial way. This leads to the agitation of others.

Correcting others

Again, controlling the habit to speak untruths or harshly is the sign of a leader, as they know how to encourage others through positivity. This does not mean we do not have to explain harsh truths to people when absolutely necessary. One who is endangering their own life, or the lives of others, needs to be communicated with efficiently and strongly at times. But that does not imply that the underlying mood behind that communication is not one of kindness. When helping others is the motivation, although the words may have to be strong, only love will shine through as we have deeply considered the context in which we share them. Where are we speaking these strong words? When are we speaking them? What is the body language with which we are speaking them? Who else is around when we are speaking them? These are a few questions that a kind person will consider when correcting others.

Is a doctor not kind to a child when they give them medicine? Although it may taste bitter, this medication is protecting the child from the world's most deadly diseases. The doctor is conscious, however, to make the child feel at ease, use a technique to make it more palatable, give the medication in a comfortable setting and make sure the parents are informed. Love is in these details. Aggression does not always mean harshness and gentleness doesn't always mean kindness. Maturity is knowing what is the best course of action to help others. It means understanding the context of their problem and communicating with them sensitively. To know when to speak and when to be quiet is the hallmark of a mature individual. This takes judgement, wisdom and a deep introspection of our own nature.

There are times we must correct people but, as mentioned previously, it should be done sensitively. Often, it is not about what we say that causes pain but how we say it. As Maya Angelou says, 'I've learned that people will forget what you said, people will forget what you did, but people will never forget how you made them feel.'

Rockefeller and his encouragement

New York is considered a city that never sleeps. It's a city where opportunities can arrive in a flash, but also devastate someone as quickly. There is an old fable which mentions John D. Rockefeller, a businessman and philanthropist, considered one of the wealthiest people of all time.

On a cloudy evening, in the middle of Central Park, New York, a businessman sat down exhausted on a bench. His shirt was untucked, tie loose and face unshaven. He held his head in his hands and broke down crying. He could see no way out. Creditors were chasing him; suppliers were demanding payment. He was on the verge of bankruptcy and desperately racking his brain to see if anything could save him. As he was losing hope, an old man came and sat next to him. 'Is something troubling you?' he asked the man. The businessman broke down, telling this friendly stranger all his problems. After listening attentively, to the businessman's surprise, the old man said, 'I believe I can help you.' He then went on to ask the man his name, wrote out a generous cheque and handed it to the businessman. 'Take this money to kickstart your business. But promise me one thing: you will meet me here exactly one year from today and you can pay me back at that time.'

The old man folded the cheque, handed it directly to the businessman and walked away. Wiping his tears, the businessman saw that the cheque was for $500,000 and was signed by John D. Rockefeller. 'Unbelievable!' the man thought. He examined the cheque closely and saw it was real. Knowing that he had this cheque as a back-up to resolve all his financial troubles gave him the strength to continue working at his craft. With an invigorated sense of purpose, the businessman started striking new deals and negotiating with his suppliers over payment. Within a few months of this incident, he was debt-free and finally making a profit. He was still flying with the knowledge that he had the support of the richest man in the world with half a million dollars in his safe.

Four seasons passed and the businessman waited at the same park bench where he had received incredible kindness. He waited for hours, throughout the morning and afternoon, but the old man did not appear. In the late evening, he noticed the old man walking in the park and thought he may have forgotten their meeting. He approached him waving the cheque up in the air, ready to give the old man back his contribution plus an extra $50,000 cash as a token of gratitude. He spoke to John D. Rockefeller once again and told him all about his business.

After a while, a bewildered nurse came to where they were speaking, panting as if she had been jogging around Central Park. 'I'm so glad I caught him,' she cried. 'I hope he hasn't been bothering you. This man lives in the retirement home and suffers from severe dementia. Many times, he runs away and tells everybody that he is Mr Rockefeller. He is harmless though, do not worry.' She then escorted the old man who was now holding in his hands a cheque for $500,000 from the businessman, back to the retirement home. The astonished businessman stood in the middle of the park shocked. He did not know whether to laugh or cry. Throughout the year, he had been confidently buying and selling huge stocks and making large deals, convinced that he had half a million dollars as a fall-back option with him.

That evening as the businessman reflected, he concluded that it was the encouragement and the imagined support of 'John D. Rockefeller' that had changed his life. A simple conversation, and the belief that our friends, family or people we respect have in us, can be a powerful catalyst in helping us achieve our dreams. Our words and acts of kindness can have a ripple effect on others' lives. That may be exactly what they need at that time in their life.

Hanuman encouraged by Jambavan

The concept of encouraging words having the power to change a person's mindset to move forward is not new.

The Ramayana, an ancient history that happened several thousands of years ago, tells the story of Shri Ramachandra rescuing his kidnapped wife Shrimati Sita Devi from the rakshasa king Ravana. There is a passage where the king of bears, Jambavan, reminds Hanuman, the best of all monkeys, about the potential that is stored within him to do his duty and save Shrimati Sita Devi.

The Vanaraas, the monkey army that was recruited by Shri Rama, were struggling to find a candidate to jump over the ocean to Lanka to see if Sita was on Ravana's island. Many stepped forward, but none had the ability to jump over the ocean and make it back safely. It was at this moment that Jambavan spoke inspiring words to remind Hanuman of his miraculous abilities. After this speech and sincere words of encouragement that were full of truth, praise and honour, Hanuman, having been reminded of all his abilities, decided to jump to Lanka to find Shrimati Sita Devi. This ancient story, which is well-known all over India, proves that even the best among us need encouragement to fulfil their potential. If we can learn the art of communication, we have the ability to spark brilliance in others. Regardless of who we are, it is positive sound that motivates us.

Beware of casual fun in relationships

When we get closer to people, we tend to become looser with our boundaries. Although this can lead to greater intimacy, it can lead to more conflict. The reason nations have boundaries is to keep those who are not permitted to enter a country out. The reason we should have boundaries in our relationships is to keep friendship-breaking activities out. One of the things I suggest to enhance our communication is to set clear boundaries in our speech with people. What do we reveal to people? How much do we share? What type of language do we use? How often do we meet? Where do we meet? Do we meet alone or in a group? These are a few questions we can use to judge boundaries with people.

If we do not have boundaries, it can lead to arguments or even worse. Often, we do not know how to argue without destroying our relationships. Once a husband and a wife got into a fight while they were on a long drive. Their heads were hot, they were hungry and annoyed with each other. There was pin-drop silence in the car as they drove through the Indian countryside. The husband saw a drove of donkeys grazing by the roadside and snapped to his wife, 'Look your relatives are grazing there.' His wife snapped back, 'Yes, nice to see my mother-in-law, father-in-law and their children enjoying a good feast.'

Relationships are beautiful when there is an element of fun. Jokes and teasing are part of deeper bonding between people, but both parties need to have the same understanding and spirit to take that fun in the right way. Casual teasing and mockery can lead to emotional harm if done repeatedly even if done among good friends, let alone those who are not. Such teasing could even turn into emotional abuse, whether done knowingly or unknowingly. We must know the boundaries and limits of our jokes. Crossing that line can tarnish our cherished relationships.

Here are some principles to avoid hurting others in our casual conversations:

When we tease our closest friends in jest, be sure not to do it repeatedly as nobody likes to be made fun of all the time. We should not stress their insecurities such as body-shaming them (colour of skin, height, weight), mocking the community they come from, their ethnicity, nationality, socio-economic status, intellectual inability, etc. Finally, it is important to not make jokes about their family. Making jokes about a person's spouse, mother, father, etc., can harm our relationships.

The same principles are applied when someone makes a joke about us. If we are on the receiving end of a joke, we need to be sporting; but if they have stepped over a line and we are hurt, we need to sensibly communicate that across. That may mean being assertive enough to tell people if they have crossed a boundary in their relationship with us.

When I finished watching *Taare Zameen Par*, I thought about the principles of great communication and how powerful words can be. Just a small recommendation from my friend Boman Irani led to a profound exploration of communication for me, showing yet again the power of words.

Exercise:

Reflect on your recent communication with your friends and family.

Are you speaking the truth at the right time?

Is what you are saying pleasing as well as truthful?

Are you overstepping the boundaries of the relationship?

Think of three things you can do to improve your communication for the future.

For example: 'Last week, when my mum asked me for feedback about her cooking, I spoke the truth by telling her the issues I had about it. The problem was that I said it at a completely wrong time and in the wrong way and thus ended up hurting her. The next time she asks for feedback, I will first tell her all the positives before telling her things she can improve on.'

Chapter summary:

- Communication is not only about what we say but how we behave, which is portrayed through our body language.
- Words have the power to harm and do good, and thus must be used wisely. They are so powerful that abusive words can fell trees.
- Studies show that psychological and emotional wounds can have as much damage to the outcome of our lives as physical wounds.
- We should be careful when correcting others. It is said in the Bhagavad Gita, 'Speaking truthful words that are pleasing, beneficial, not disturbing to others, comprises austerity of speech.'
- Encouragement has powerful effects as seen in the stories of Rockefeller and Jambavan.
- Casual teasing can be an element of a relationship but can lead to emotional harm if done repeatedly, even if done among good friends, let alone those who are not.

THIRTEEN

Moving Beyond 'Oneself': Developing Selflessness

'Everything that irritates us about others can lead us to an understanding of ourselves.'

—Carl Gustav Jung

The businessman who nearly lost everything, the elderly man with severe dementia who thought he was Rockefeller, and me. What do we all have in common?

We have all experienced the intensity of living in New York City.

When I visit the Big Apple, I stay in an oasis in Manhattan, the Bhakti Centre. It's a spiritual cultural centre and ashram on New York City's Lower East Side dedicated to helping people transform through the practices of Bhakti Yoga. It looks like a simple shopfront, but inside lie valuable jewels of wisdom to help people develop themselves physically, emotionally and spiritually. From this base, I usually travel extensively, lecturing on topics of self-development, speaking to different crowds sometimes up to four times a day. I do not lie when I say that it is my greatest honour to speak so extensively, because it gives me great joy to share the life-transforming principles that I have received in my training as a monk. It's deeply fulfilling to work hard and serve people by helping them boost their mental and spiritual well-being. However, there are days when I need to unwind and focus on self-care too.

On those days, I take some time out to meditate, read and explore the city. Especially on my early visits to New York City, I was fascinated with the monuments I had only seen in textbooks or Hollywood films as a child. On one such 'self-care' day, I went to visit the Statue of Liberty and the Empire State Building, saw a Broadway show and the One World Observatory. Some of my friends had taken me to see these sights and monuments, as a treat. In fact, one of them even asked me if I wanted a green foam crown, the type the Lady of Liberty wears. But I felt that may have been an overindulgence on my 'self-care' day and also, it would not match my orange robes!

One of my favourite places was the top of the One World Trade Centre Observatory. It spans ninety-nine storeys above the ground and boasts 360-degree views of the concrete jungle surrounded by the Hudson River, East River and Upper Bay. It's the tallest building in the US with its architectural height being 1776 metres, the same number as the year in which the Declaration of Independence was signed. It was an incredible view that reminded me of how we feel when we rise above, spiritually and mentally.

When we rise above:

- The problems that seem too huge to deal with now seem tiny, like the buildings beneath us. We gain a broader perspective and are able to better cope with the things that may have fazed us in the past.

- We become immune to all the social drama that is happening down there. When I was at the top of the One World Observatory, I could see the cars and people walking on the street below, but I could not hear them. Similarly, when we rise above in our lives, we may be able to see the drama, but we are immune to it as we focus on higher principles.

- We can see the broader scheme of events in life. We were excited to see if we could find the Bhakti Centre from the top of the Observatory. After peering and searching, we did, but it seemed to be just a tiny dot as a tiny part of the entire island. When we rise above, the smaller things that we go through in our life now make sense as a part of the larger picture. I imagined what the first people that went to space thought when looking back at Earth. We are a tiny part of the large universe, but that does not mean we cannot do our tiny bit to add value to the world we live in.

Being that high above the clouds was an exhilarating and reflective experience. However, something that also impressed me was the elevator. On the way up, it showed the landscape of Manhattan in virtual reality from the ground up to the top floor while moving through the ages from the year 1500 to the present day. It was incredible to see how New York had developed industrially but devastating to see one of the Twin Towers vanishing as the timeline hit 2001. What was stunning was that this was all virtual but felt so real. On the way down, we descended from the sky to the ground in forty-seven seconds. I think it takes me longer to climb one flight of stairs to my room in the ashram in Mumbai.

These elevators had an incredible virtual view to keep us occupied and no one was looking at each other, maintaining an awkward silence. Most elevators in skyrise buildings tend to have mirrors, but this is not always the case. In another part of New York, occupants of a large residential tower started complaining about the poor elevator service in the building. They told the landlord that at peak times the wait for an elevator was excessively long. It got so bad that several tenants threatened to break their contracts and leave the building. That prompted the building management to come up with the solution to increase the speed of the elevator. The problem was that this building was built over fifty years ago; there was no engineering solution to increase the speed of the elevators. It was back to the drawing board. The management then hired a psychologist to see what could be done about the waiting time. They wondered why people would complain about waiting only two minutes and concluded that it was because people got bored waiting. For the majority of the day, they were queueing up at the supermarket or for the metro or for lunch. They did not want to have to queue up to enter their own homes, but there was no engineering feat that could change this. Therefore, the psychologist decided to tackle the problem of boredom by giving people something to do while waiting for the elevator: look at themselves in the mirror. Large mirrors were installed next to the elevators and the number of complaints dropped dramatically. Today, there are mirrors around most elevator lobbies and within lifts for this same reason.

I have seen so many people checking themselves out in their reflection in elevator mirrors. Some are doing their hair, others are quickly applying make-up and others are trying to make themselves look less tired. This happens in all mirrors. Give someone a mirror and they will be occupied for hours, whether it's rear-view mirrors in cars, bathroom mirrors or even a mirror kept in a purse. This is normal; no one wants to look bad. I often joke that no one looks as beautiful as their social media display picture or as ugly as their driving licence picture! However, mirrors don't lie. There is no Photoshop, no filters, no editing. It's just the way we are . . . on the outside at least. Mirrors do not show one thing though, our intentions on the inside.

The people around us can often act as mirrors to give us a glimpse of how we may be on the inside. Their reactions to our speech, body language, dealings and behaviour can give us a hint if we are doing the right thing. That is not to say that we live for the approval of others. That is probably the worst thing to do. But there may be some truth as to how people respond to us that highlights our inner attitude.

If we can reflect on our intentions, purpose and expectations daily, we are more likely to get to a stage where we can positively influence those around us. This is because who we are internally affects our behaviour externally and thereby the people around us. There are three main things we have to watch out for: self-conceit, self-absorption and selfishness.

Self-conceit

Self-conceit refers to taking undue pride in ourselves. It means to have an excessively favourable opinion about ourselves and our abilities. There is a fine line between being confident and being conceited. They both come from the root of our belief in our own abilities, but confidence comes across as attractive, whereas self-conceit, or arrogance, leaves an unpleasant taste in people's mouths. The difference between the two is based on our intention. Confident people have the intention to serve others. Arrogant people may serve others, but the intention of their service is to benefit themselves through the fruits of such service.

Admittedly there are cultural differences in the way people behave. I remember visiting the UK for the first time and walking past someone and not paying attention to them. That was a huge English faux pas. There is no custom in India to say 'hello' to everyone you see as you pass them in the hallway. However, by the time I had reached the end of the corridor, I had received a text message from a senior monk who was in India, about how my rude behaviour was affecting others. I may have come across as self-conceited, but it was just a cultural misunderstanding.

A few years ago, I was invited for an awards evening in Mumbai. The guest of honour was a prominent leader of the Anti-Terrorist Squad (ATS) who had been responsible for foiling several terrorist operations around the country. Through his work he may have saved thousands of lives. He was being honoured tonight as the chief guest; I was there simply as an additional guest speaker. We both sat on the stage and looked upon hundreds of young people. As he spoke, I noticed people on their phone, talking among themselves and not paying attention. They did not seem to care what he was speaking about. However, when I spoke, people were on the edge of their seats; they cheered and whistled. At the end of the event, while the organizers escorted me to the car, he was just walking by himself. The crowd gathered around me to take a selfie and he humbly stood there waiting for his car. The organizers had inconsiderately arranged for a Mercedes to take me back, but it was a Honda Civic for him. Though I smiled out of gratitude, there was only embarrassment flowing through my veins. All I could do was be kind and courteous and try to defuse the commotion around me.

On the way back, I thought that the man had been so humble despite being renowned, accomplished and successful. A person who is powerful today may become irrelevant tomorrow. Just the power of time! You only have to go to a crowd of Gen Z friends and they will ask you who is Michael Jackson or Elvis Presley. In a couple of generations, former huge stars become irrelevant. Therefore, how can we think of being conceited ourselves?

I was inspired by this man and offered a silent prayer in my heart. The same thing will surely happen to me in a few years or decades. I will be the chief guest at an award ceremony, but no one will care that I am there. There will be another hotshot on stage who wins the crowd over. Self-conceit stems from not realizing that. There will always be people who are better than us. I looked at my award with gratitude but also humility, that one day I will be irrelevant too.

In the great epic the Ramayana, one of its heroes is Hanuman. He was given the ability to jump across the ocean to save Shrimati Sita Devi and was the leader among the monkey armies then. He was ferocious, intelligent and in the limelight in the Ramayana. However, if we jump forward to the Mahabharata, another history of India, he becomes a cheerleader on the flag of Arjuna in the Battle of Kurukshetra. A once sought-after personality is now a decoration on a flag, not taking centre stage any more. However, Hanuman had deep confidence in his ability to transcend these external superficialities and so was able to focus on serving others regardless of the position. That is the difference between confidence and self-conceit.

Staying with the Mahabharata, its key villain, Duryodhana, displays endless self-conceit while one of its heroes, Yudhisthira, demonstrates quiet confidence. In that period, India was ruled by kings descending from the Bharat dynasty; hence, one of the names of India is Bharat. Yudhisthira and his five brothers, the Pandavas, were the rulers of Indraprastha whereas Duryodhana, one of the hundred Kaurava brothers, was the prince of Hastinapur. The name Yudhisthira literally translates to one who is stable even in the middle of a battle. The Pandavas were pious, righteous and spiritually inclined whereas the Kauravas were consumed by greed, arrogance and envy.

The story starts with Duryodhana asking Shri Krishna a question, 'Krishna, why am I considered a bad person while my cousin Yudhishthira is perceived as good?'

Shri Krishna replied, 'Come to me tomorrow and I will answer this question for you. However, you must return to your kingdom and bring one good man with you to see me tomorrow.' After this, Shri Krishna requested Yudhishthira to see him and requested, 'Yudhishthira, please find me one bad person in your kingdom and come with him to meet me and Duryodhana tomorrow.'

The next day the two cousins came to see Shri Krishna, both without anyone with them. 'Why have you come alone?' Shri Krishna asked them both.

Duryodhana jumped at the opportunity to reply and said proudly, 'I searched my whole kingdom, but I could not find a single good man in the whole of Hastinapur. Everyone seemed to be a cheater!'

Yudhishthira then spoke and said, 'My dear Krishna, I searched everywhere too, but I could not find one bad man. Everyone had the spark of goodness within them.'

Lord Krishna turned to Duryodhana and said, 'Here, you have your answer! You are perceived as a bad man because you only see the bad in others, because you think so highly of yourself. Yudhishthira is loved by all because he cannot see the evil in others!'

Self-conceit is thinking that I am the best and no one else is worthy of being on the same level as me. Confidence is to respect yourself, but equally give respect to others without expecting any back for yourself. This is something Yudhishthira was able to see, but Duryodhana could not.

A beautiful wisdom verse describes the four types of people who are unable to see:

> *na paśyati janmāndhaḥ*
> *kamāndho naiva paśyati*
> *madonmattā na paśyanti*
> *arthī doṣam na paśyati*

The first is a person who is born without the physical ability to see. The second is someone who is infatuated with lust and is unable to see the truth. The third is someone who is intoxicated with pride and cannot see the value of others. They do not value others' opinions or points of view. And the fourth is someone who is greedy and cannot see the risks involved in striving without proper character. They may lack the ethics or the proper process of making money.

When one is intoxicated with pride, people around can dislike us, hate us, disconnect from us and, if in a position of power, try to dislodge us. On the other hand, if we are humble, people will love us, connect with us and help us. Being humble does not mean we are pushovers. As C.S. Lewis said, 'Being humble means we do not think less of ourselves but think of ourselves less.'

There is an anecdote that beautifully explains what it means to be humble. When walking in downtown Mumbai, Mr Rashid, a wealthy businessman, spotted a young man begging on the streets. He was dressed in rags, wore shoes with multiple holes in them and smelt like he had not showered in weeks. However, his eyes were full of devotion and what he said to Mr Rashid was very sincere. 'Please sir, I am not begging for money. I am begging for an opportunity to work with you. I know I look appalling, but I have fallen on hard times. I really want an opportunity to work hard and get myself out of this situation.' Finding him to be genuine, Mr Rashid decided to employ him as a clerk in his company. Mr Rashid found this man to be straightforward and hard-working. Everything he had told him on the street had been true; he worked harder than anyone else. After a few days, when Mr Rashid was speaking with the man over a cup of chai, he found out that he was a chartered accountant and also had an MBA but things started to deteriorate for him when he lost interest in doing anything, having lost his family in a car accident a few years back. There was no other way to maintain himself apart from begging. Understanding the man's expertise and that his gesture of goodwill was actually a huge benefit for his team, Mr Rashid decided to promote this 'homeless man' to senior manager in his accounting team. A mere one year later, this homeless man was now the CEO of the company. This was a true rags-to-riches story, but trouble was on the horizon.

Seeing him rise up the ranks so quickly and becoming a trusted associate of the owner of the company, other staff members who had worked in the company for much longer began to feel jealous and insecure. *Who was this new person who had stolen the position they had been waiting for, for years?* They started to dig into this 'homeless' man's past. They noticed something particularly interesting. Although the man was well-dressed, groomed and wore smart black shoes everywhere, he carried a locked duffel bag everywhere he went. Every day, when no one was looking, he would unlock it, look inside and quickly lock it up again.

Alarmed at this suspicious behaviour, and relieved to find some dirt on the man, some of the employees approached Mr Rashid and accused the man of stealing important documents and items from the company. The owner laughed and did not believe it, but still decided to cross-check the claims. He went to the man's cabin with a mob of smug employees following him and knocked at the door. He asked all the other employees to wait outside as he walked in and closed the door behind him. The other employees looked at the interaction through the glass side-panels.

'I know this is not true, but other members of the team have suspicions that you may be taking home sensitive documents,' Mr Rashid said. The man's face dropped, and he began sweating. Mr Rashid became slightly more suspicious and asked, 'Could you please open this bag?'

'This bag,' the man said, snatching it off the table. 'There is nothing special inside. I don't see the need.'

'Yes, that locked bag. Please open it,' Mr Rashid said firmly now. The man slowly unlocked the bag after a lot of insistence from Mr Rashid. What was inside shocked Mr Rashid and brought him to tears. It was the set of torn clothes and shoes that the man used to wear when he was homeless, the same set Mr Rashid had found him in a year ago. 'Why do you keep this bag locked up? Why do you keep these clothes?' Mr Rashid asked.

'These items are my most valuable treasure,' the man started timidly. 'Every day I see them to remind myself where I was in life, where I am today and who was responsible for helping me,' he said. Catching on to what had happened, all the employees stopped gawking through the window and returned to work embarrassed. Mr Rashid gave him a huge hug while they both wept.

This anecdote is powerful as it shows the nature of someone who is not self-conceited. Such people remain humble, grateful and they dedicate double the energy for the ones who made them who they are today.

This man had gone through hard times, but picked himself up to be self-confident, not self-conceited. He did not use his position or accolades to boast, thus he preserved his character. Self-confidence means to be the best version of yourself; it means to strive for the best but keep your humility.

The apps on our phone are constantly updating. Whether we use iOS or Android, updating our apps means to use the best versions of what exists for our phones. Why would we not want to use the best? Similarly, we have to try and be the highest version of ourselves. If we stick to the older version of ourselves, we reach a ceiling in our development and start to stagnate. Stagnation does not mean we stay where we are. In reality, it means that we are actually going down than staying where we are. When we update to the highest version of ourselves, we become our competition. Nobody else is our competition. We have to compete with ourselves at every single moment to become the best version of ourselves.

The line between self-confidence and self-conceit is thin. Self-confidence makes us feel that we are the best we can be, but arrogance makes us think we are the best in the world. Self-confidence includes humility but self-conceit does not. Humility means keeping our minds, our hearts and our consciousness open to learning from the people around us. Everybody has so much to offer; arrogance stops us from learning from them. It is arrogance that makes us think that we have cracked it all, there is no more room for improvement, there is no scope for enhancing our skills.

Exercise: Humility in action

One aspect of humility is the openness to learn from the right people around us.

Think of one new thing you learnt from a different person every day for a week. The person could even be someone you would usually not expect to learn from or interact with.

For example, I learnt how to respectfully deal with someone treating me unfairly by observing how my bus driver handled a customer who was shouting abuse at him for no reason.

Self-absorbed

Another negative trait to look out for when trying to move beyond oneself is being self-absorbed. This means to be preoccupied with one's feelings, interests and situation without considering the same for others around us. There is a huge, positive movement in the world for self-care, to focus on one's own needs, growth and endeavours. This is important as it is only when we are well situated in our own lives that we can give to others. As mentioned, I have experienced this first-hand when I tour different countries. I need those self-care days to recharge so I can give my best to others. However, I fear that sometimes in the name of self-care we can be pushed over the boundary into self-absorption.

We may be self-absorbed ourselves or know someone who is. They show little interest for the care of others and find it difficult to empathize with another's perspective. The motivation for them in nearly all situations is getting *their* needs and wants met. Clinical psychologist Peretua Neo who graduated from University College, London, states that, 'We may see self-absorption in children between the ages of two and six, which is very egocentric. That is expected of children, but for adults who are self-absorbed, it's almost like they never outgrew that stage—even if they have great scripts and can mask their self-absorption.'

I want to take you back to our ashram in Mumbai. From a few simple rooms in the early days to a plethora of rooms to accommodate nearly 100 monks, the ashram has developed immensely. And it is not just in the architecture. We have many academically and professionally qualified people joining to become monks who add their own flavour and create robust systems for everything to keep things organized, whether it's how our library operates to how our *sevasthan* or medical room functions. As we age, the systems for caring for monks have evolved too. As many seniors grow elderly, their changing needs need to be accommodated. Even for me, everything from food to laundry, accommodation to travel and healthcare to insurance is taken care of. For me as a monk, I have never had to really feel the pain of paying bills, to shop for groceries or book tickets for a flight. I agree that this seems luxurious, but there are other struggles monks face that people outside the ashram do not. Staying with nearly 100 other people is a different kind of challenge.

Nevertheless, I deeply empathize the battles families in our community have to fight. It is hard to survive in Mumbai as salaries can seem stagnant and prices become inflated. If you are a middle-class person, buying a house can seem a far-off dream. There are mortgages to be paid, education expenses for kids, healthcare payments, taxes and travel expenses. We have not even mentioned the simple luxuries in life like eating at a restaurant or going on holiday.

At one point in time, I realized that, in our ashram, we seemed to have too many privileges. Many of us were becoming out of touch with the real world and the struggles that people go through. The facilities we had freed up our time for spiritual endeavours. That same time was not available for people of our community who were non-ashramites. Our lectures used to come from the view of those in the ashram and started to go stale as we said things that did not make sense to the growing family communities. The symptoms we were experiencing were signs of 'ashram self-absorption'. It is not as if we are horrible people, but in our bubble, we did not understand how others were living or the hardships they faced.

I decided to speak up and share this with our temple leadership. Monks need to interact with families to understand and empathize with the challenges they face. This can help us be down-to-earth and also serve them better. When we find ourselves becoming too self-absorbed and unable to relate to people, we should think, 'Is there something I am missing? Is there something I am doing which means that I cannot relate to or empathize with this person's needs?' We can also book time out to solely focus on other people. People have their 'me time' or 'self-care time'. To move beyond oneself, I recommend booking out 'them time', which means for that period of time, I am solely focused on the needs and wants of others, beyond my own tasks and projects.

Selfishness

The last of the three character traits that stop us from moving beyond ourselves is selfishness. A self-absorbed person is only interested in their own life, but a selfish person deeply cares only about their own personal profit and pleasure.

People who are self-absorbed are too focused on their own lives to have time, energy and care for the lives of others. However, selfishness is an advanced form of self-absorption. It represents people whose thoughts, words and actions do not exhibit any consideration for others' feelings, likes and desires.

A baby fish and its mother were once swimming near the shore. The baby asked its mother, 'Why can we not live on land and roam the earth?'

The mother replied, 'Child, the land is not a place for fish, it is the place for the selfish.'

Selfish people are mainly takers and rarely give to others. They do not care for others' interests or their well-being. They want to enjoy themselves as much as they can and suffer the least. They do not have a genuine interest in others but may fake that they do to take care of their own needs. Although they have some ethical boundaries, their consciousness is pervaded with self-interest.

The opposite of selfishness is selflessness. This is where the operating system for that person is focused on the genuine well-being of others. Such a person is willing to go out of his or her comfort zone and make serious sacrifices for another's pleasure.

Staying with stories about the ocean, a man once went sailing with his friends. The sea was choppy and the boat was rocking. All of a sudden, a one-pound coin fell into the river. In a flash, the man jumped into the waters to retrieve it, unmindful that he did not know how to swim and did not have a life jacket on. As he began to drown, one of his friends shouted at him, 'Give me your hand so that I can pull you out.'

The drowning man refused. Another friend on the boat who was watching this told the rest that he knew how to save him.

'He only understands the take-language, not the give-language,' he laughed. After the first gentleman changed give to take, asking him to 'take his hand', the man agreed, and reached out to be saved. He was pulled back on to the boat, and was able to breathe normally again.

Our breath is something we are born with, and we die with. As we breathe in, our chest expands and as we breathe out, our chest collapses. There is no such thing as *just* breathing in or *just* breathing out. There is a natural rhythm of giving and taking within our body and in life as well. No one wants to be around a person who is only taking; whether it is resources, help, time or attention.

A wisdom verse says:

> *pibanti nadyaḥ svayameva nāmbhaḥ*
> *svayaṃ na khādanti phalāni vṛkṣāḥ |*
> *nādanti sasyaṃ khalu vārivāhāḥ*
> *paropakārāya satāṃ vibhūtayaḥ ||*

'Rivers do not drink their own water and trees do not eat their own fruits. Likewise, rain-bearing clouds do not eat the grains they help grow. Surely, the aim of great noble and righteous persons in their lifetime is to do selfless service to humanity.'

The story of Kamalamma demonstrates what it means to move beyond ourselves. The picture that surfaced of her on social media displays the depth of her selflessness. In the second wave of the Covid-19 pandemic, India went through a hard time. Families were ravaged by the disease, which took their loved ones away. At that time, we had seen incredible initiatives of humanity to help others, but one such contribution impressed me. It was the contribution made by seventy-year-old Kamalamma. Kamalamma, a resident of Chennagiri Koppal in Mysuru, had donated Rs 500 out of her Rs 600 monthly pension to the Chief Minister's Covid-19 fund. This amounts to nearly 90 per cent of the sum she received as a pension even though she herself is a destitute. What is important is not how much we give, but how much we hold back.

Self-awareness

I am not propagating selflessness to an extent where we burn out. That is not sustainable. However, when self-care remains only for oneself without extending into the service of others, it morphs into selfishness.

The way to accept self-care without being selfish is through self-awareness. This is when we try to consider our wants and needs with the same force as we consider other people's wants and needs. Imagine if all the needs we must attend to in a day were written on a whiteboard and we had to prioritize them. Some of those needs would be our own and some would be the needs of others. It is not the case that our needs are always at the top of the list as a priority, but sometimes they are and that's okay.

Life is busy for everyone, regardless of who we are, but it's not busy for all at the same time. There may be times when life is hurting us and we need to prioritize our own needs, but there may be times when we have a greater capacity to shift our attention to the needs of others. For most people, it is hard to think about their own needs because we do not want to be labelled selfish by society. The way to be more compassionate to ourselves is to think: if someone else puts their own needs first, would we brand them selfish? Therefore, why would we do it to ourselves? It is okay to refuel and recharge. It is okay to take a walk instead of doing chores. It is okay to say that we are out of office instead of replying to that work email.

Being self-aware is the secret to moving beyond ourselves and giving to others sustainably. When we are self-aware, we can understand if we are being self-conceited, self-absorbed or selfish and then correct that appropriately. It sounds like a paradox, but when we are self-aware, when we take time out to refill our tanks of compassion, that is when we can have a huge impact on aiding the well-being of others. It is in this state of balance, we will feel great about ourselves; we will feel higher than the clouds as if we have taken a virtual elevator up to the top floor of the One World Observatory.

Chapter summary:

- Just as a mirror can reflect our externals well, we have to continuously place a mirror on ourselves internally through deep introspection to see if we are moving beyond ourselves to really help the mental well-being of others.

- To develop self-awareness, we must look out for three things: self-conceit, self-absorption and selfishness.
- Self-conceit refers to taking undue pride in ourselves. It means to have an excessively favourable opinion about ourselves and our abilities.
- Self-absorbed means to be preoccupied with one's feelings, interests and situation without considering the same for others around us.
- A selfish person deeply cares only about their own personal profit and pleasure.
- The way to accept self-care without being selfish is through self-awareness. When self-care remains only for oneself without extending into the service of others, it morphs into selfishness.

SECTION 4
THE UNIVERSE AND MY MIND

The final section of this book focuses on how the mind is affected by the universe around us. We have already learnt how our own mind can affect us, how other people can affect our mind and how we can affect other people's minds. However, in this chapter, we discuss forces in the world that can have an influence on how we think, feel and behave and can affect our emotional well-being. Let's dive deep into ancient concepts of identity that can create outcomes for our modern way of living.

FOURTEEN

We Are a Universe within a Universe

'When I discover who I am, I'll be free.'
—Ralph Ellison, *Invisible Man*

My travels take me through many different cultures. One of the most interesting places I have visited on the planet is Moscow, Russia. It is considered the world's northernmost megacity and regained the title as the capital of Russia from St Petersburg under Soviet rule in 1918. Moscow has a population of approximately 12 million.[1] The people I met in Moscow were straightforward, to-the-point and extremely hospitable. The intensity with which the monks in Russia practice mantra meditation and listen to wisdom lectures is unparalleled anywhere in the world!

During one of my trips to Moscow, one of the Russian monks presented me with a gift. He handed it to me at the airport as I was just about to leave for India. I was wearing my saffron robes, a thick puffy jacket and a woolly hat. Just as the devotion of the monks in Russia is unparalleled, so are their winters! When I opened the box, I was surprised to find a small wooden doll. I looked at the monk with confusion, meaning to convey, 'I am a grown-up and I do not play with dolls.'

He sensed my confusion and began smiling. 'This doll is a very special one,' he said. 'It is hand-carved, oak wood and is called a *matryoshka* or *babushka* doll. Everyone who visits Moscow takes it back as a souvenir for their loved ones as it represents the feminine, softer side of Russian culture and strong family values.' Matryoshkas are a set of wooden dolls of decreasing size placed inside each other. The one he presented me had nine nested layers, one inside each other and getting smaller. The largest doll that held the others was four inches long; the world record for the largest set of matryoshka dolls is a 51-piece set painted in 2003 with the largest doll measuring twenty-one inches. My dolls were hand-painted with reds, greens and yellows and had images of a motherly lady as is traditional. Some of you might have seen these dolls as they are quite popular.

I opened the dolls up at the airport lounge and placed them next to each other. The craftmanship was quite remarkable. The nested dolls reminded me of a beautiful concept about identity from the ancient literatures that was taught to me at the beginning of my monastic training.

Am I the senses?

Just as the Russian doll has layers, each getting smaller and more intricate, our identity also has layers. The Bhagavad Gita explains that we have five external layers—earth, water, fire, air and space—which together make up the physical body. There are also five knowledge-acquiring senses—smell, sight, taste, sound and touch—which are subtle and help us interact with the world. As I sat at Sheremetyevo International Airport in Moscow, I looked around to see how all my five knowledge-acquiring senses were engaged.

My sense of smell was picking up the fragrance of duty-free perfumes, coffee and the odd person who had not used deodorant! My sight was engaged in seeing people from all around the world walking around with their carry-on luggage. Some were looking at designer shops, some were engrossed in their phone and others were eating. What were they eating? That is how their sense of taste was engaged. Burger King, McDonald's, Pizza Hut were all there as choices. Other lesser known names were Kroshka Kartoshka, Teremok and Buy&Fly. My ears were engaged in the sounds: general hubbub, announcements for flights and the undertone of classical music that reverberated through the airport. The final sense was touch. My own arms were against the cushioned airport chair, but I saw signs for an airport spa and a fish pedicure.

Just being in an airport lounge, we can engage all our senses. It's a whole experience of the senses for us to enjoy before we jet across the world. But the real question is *who* is enjoying that experience? Who is that *us*?

The things we see in the world are made out of matter, which is inert, that is, it contains no life. Wisdom states that our senses are also made out of the very same matter. Therefore, the questions can be raised: Are our eyes the ones experiencing the beauty of the world? Are our tongues experiencing the taste of coffee? Are our noses smelling the roses in the garden? Are our hands touching the freshly mown grass? No, they are not. It is *us* who is experiencing that.

We see through our eyes, we smell through our nose, we taste using our tongue. As matter cannot experience other matter, this implies that we are something beyond the senses. We are simply utilizing the body and the senses as a tool to interact with things and people in this world.

Am I the mind?

While I was watching the inner workings of the airport and how all of my senses were being utilized, I was about to put my headphones on to zone out of the external world, when I saw something interesting. I saw airline staff at the check-in counter behaving really rudely with a passenger. 'Your bag is 0.5 kilograms overweight, sir. Please remove some items immediately or we won't allow you to board,' the staff said abruptly. The passenger began to raise his voice, talking about how he was feeling slightly cheated having seen the person before him being allowed 5 extra kilograms in their luggage without being charged.

Different people may have reacted in different ways to this situation. One person may have felt hurt and given them the silent treatment; someone else may have ignored the situation, paid the bill and gone on with their travel. Each one of us feels a different emotion and may respond very differently to a stimulus that acts as a trigger.

Who is feeling those emotions? Who is going through those experiences? The mind is such a powerful voice within us that it is natural to feel that we are the mind. As the philosopher René Descartes said, '*Cogito, ergo sum*', which translates as, 'I think, therefore I am'. The mind is a tool that accepts or rejects what comes to us in our lives on a moment-by-moment basis. When it faces a sense stimulus, the mind is the one that considers the possibility of engaging with it. When we walk by a cake shop, it tells us to go in or walk past. The mind also projects the emotions we are experiencing front and centre into our thoughts, just as an LED projector shows a movie on a screen.

However, ancient wisdom states that we are not the mind. How can we explain this? It is easy with the senses. For example, the eye does not experience beauty; we know that it is something within. However, the mind *is* within. So how can we explain that the core of our identity does not start with the mind?

At times, I walk to the beach from our ashram in Chowpatty, Mumbai, and sit to see the beautiful sunset. In those moments I am just present—no phone or priorities—just savouring the experience. I have no thoughts at this time; it feels like my mind is switched off. It is a deep experience, albeit a very brief one, where you are just there. But all of a sudden, you come back and your mind reboots again, projecting multiple thoughts and making sense of all the sense perceptions around.

This can also happen when top athletes or performers are 'in the zone' or 'in a flow state'. In psychology, this is a mental state when a person is fully immersed in a feeling of full concentration, hyper focus and enjoyment in the process of a certain activity. It is the complete absorption in a process, a feeling where we move beyond the day-to-day interactions our senses experience. Examples of being in the zone and moving beyond the mind are when top athletes compete.

They are focused on their sport—thoughtless for a moment as their mind does not speak to them as it would casually. After the race or event, when they leave that flow state, their emotions and thoughts come rushing back.

A similar experience may happen to someone who loses a person very dear to them. That state of shock stuns them where nothing registers, the mind stops functioning and it takes them a while to come back to their senses. This is an experience beyond the mind.

Also when the mind gets disconnected from the particular sense, even though the sense is in contact with the sense object, we don't perceive that sense object. That is why there is the concept of being absent-minded, that is, the mind is elsewhere. Since the creation of video games, mothers have been shouting at their children to stop playing and come down for dinner. Even though the sound of the mother shouting is entering their ear, sometimes the mind of the child is so disconnected with their hearing that they do not even perceive that their mother is calling them.

Therefore, it is the mind, which is used by the Self, that explores the objects around in the pursuit of pleasure. It is also a vehicle in which we experience feelings and emotions.

Am I the intelligence?

Let's dive deeper into the matryoshka dolls of our personality. According to ancient wisdom, the next layer is the intelligence. Back at the airport in Moscow, I saw many people had their headphones on and were watching movies on their phones. In fact, many couples had one earphone each and were watching things together.

When we watch films, we disconnect from that aspect of our intelligence which analyses if things are true or false, so that we can just enjoy the movie. We all know someone who always ruins a film for you by whispering, 'That would not happen in real life because . . .' They have not disconnected that aspect of their intelligence which is calculating reality and thus, they lose the entertainment value of the film. When we watch *Mission: Impossible*, we know for certain that this is fiction. Tom Cruise, although he does all his own stunts, is not actually saving the world. However, for the two hours we are watching the film, our whole being is engrossed in the action. We feel as if it is real as we allow our intelligence to stop analysing it.

People in love can also stop analysing things. When a couple is deeply in love, we say that they are 'loved up'. Others viewing their relationship may see things are not right with them. They may not be compatible for multiple reasons, but they cannot see that. Their intelligence stops working because of the powerful emotions they are experiencing. As Jules Renard says, 'Love is like an hourglass, with the heart filling up as the brain empties.' If they are compatible, that is fine, and all is well. But as the intelligence reboots again, they may realize that this relationship has flaws that they overlooked. I sometimes joke that love is blind, but marriage is the eye-opener.

Therefore, even the intelligence is an instrument that is used and can get shut off. Whether we are watching a film or are madly in love, the intelligence can also stop working and is therefore not the essence of our identity.

Am I the ego?

The next layer is the ego. The ego represents the multiple roles and identity labels that we all have. To understand the ego, where we forget ourselves as we get preoccupied with the role we are playing, let's discuss the award-winning Daniel Day-Lewis. He is widely considered to be one of the most accomplished actors of all time, having won three Academy Awards for Best Actor, four BAFTAs and two Golden Globes, among others. His technique of acting is called method acting, where he lives as if he is in the role he is playing. He literally loses his own identity when he is immersed in this method-acting process. For example, in 2012, he starred in Steven Spielberg's acclaimed biopic of President Abraham Lincoln as the President himself. Not only had he done extensive research about the man he was playing, he understood his mannerisms in depth. He changed his entire ego for a while to behave like Lincoln himself, asking his co-stars to call him 'Mr President' and even texted them back as 'Abe'. For this performance, he received an Oscar for Best Actor.

Wisdom states that we are all method actors. 'All the world's a stage, and all the men and women merely players: they have their exits and their entrances; and one man in his time plays many parts, his acts being seven ages.' This quote by William Shakespeare explains the ego perfectly. We all have multiple roles to play in life: our personal, social, professional and community roles, among others. We need to play our roles well. Daniel Day-Lewis immerses himself in the roles he acts, but never forgets that he is Daniel Day-Lewis. Similarly, we need to play our roles in society well, but we should not forget that they are *just* roles and we are not our roles. We are the ones who are playing those roles.

The words 'I am' represent the ego. 'I am a human, I am a man or woman, I am Indian, Russian or American, I am Hindu, Christian or Muslim.' 'I am' encompasses a whole range of identities, but one has to question if 'I am' is the ego, who is that 'I'?

I am the Self!

The final layer within the Russian doll of our identities is the Self. It is the 'I' who uses the body and the senses, the mind and the intelligence. It is the 'I' who has the ego—our sense of identity—but who is that 'I'?

Ancient wisdom tells us that permeating throughout our whole body is consciousness. This consciousness is the only thing in the universe that is not matter or as physicists may say, it is 'anti-matter'. It is generated from the area around the heart from the spark of life that gives energy to the other layers of our identity, the senses, mind, intelligence and the ego. In many traditions, this spark is called the 'soul' or the 'spirit'. In ancient wisdom, it is called the 'atma'. They are all synonyms, but are just called different things based on time, place and circumstance. It is when the spark leaves the body that life comes to a standstill. It is the driving force of life.

An ancient text, the Linga Purana, defines the atma very precisely: 'to obtain or, to eat or, to absorb or, to enjoy or, to pervade all'. Even in popular culture, it is easy to understand the atma. I remember on my 'self-care' day in New York, the Broadway show we went to watch was *The Lion King*. In this classic film and show, there is a concept of the main character Simba being extremely powerful but forgetting who he is. Rafiki, the mystic healer, takes him to the top of the mountain where the spirit of Simba's father Mufasa reminds him of who he is and gives him the power to achieve what he sets his mind to. 'Just remember who you are,' he tells the lost Simba. If we decide to, and truly connect with the atma, moving beyond our external identity labels, not only do we have the ability to reach our aspirations, but also handle everything that comes our way by connecting to a spiritual energy that is not known by many.

This knowledge is incredible as it is the basis of the universe. This may sound very lofty, but ancient wisdom dictates that we have the macro-universe and the micro-universe. The macro-universe is composed of matter exactly like the micro-universe, our own body. However, what is driving the macro-universe is this energy of consciousness or the atma of the world. This divine force drives the macro-universe; the micro-universe is driven by the spark of consciousness within each of us. The more our micro-universe within and our macro-universe without are in sync, the more we can experience physical, mental, emotional and spiritual well-being. The ability to do this is called holistic wellness, which will be covered in the next chapter.

The giving of gifts is a tradition that can give joy, spark creativity and fuel wisdom. For me, receiving a matryoshka doll from my friend in Russia sent me on a trail of thoughts that helped me understand our identity even better. Let's take it further in the next chapter.

Exercise: Identity reflection

Think of how you looked when you were ten years old. What has changed? How has your hair, face, height, weight, etc., changed?

When you were ten years old, what was your view on life and what were your aspirations? How have these changed over the years?

Think of your personality traits when you were ten and compare them with the ones you have now. How have they changed?

Despite all these changes that have happened over the years, are you still the same person?

Your body, your thinking, your personality, your sense of purpose and worth change with time, but you still remain the same person.

That 'YOU' remains unchanged.

Chapter summary:

- Just as the Russian doll has layers, each getting smaller and more intricate, our identity also has layers.
- The physical body has senses—sight, touch, smell, taste, sound—which interact with sense objects. We may interact with sense objects using our senses, but we are *not* our senses.
- The mind interacts with the senses and is responsible for thinking, feeling and willing, but we are *not* the mind either.
- The intelligence is another subtle part of our being which is used to discriminate how to act; it analyses a situation. Nevertheless, the essence of our being is *not* the intelligence.
- The ego represents the multiple roles and identity labels that we have. It is even more subtle than the mind and intelligence, and something that we deeply identify with. However, we're *not* the ego either.
- The real self is called the atma or spiritual consciousness. It is the final layer within the Russian doll, which is the essence of our being.

FIFTEEN

A Holistic Approach to Wellness

'Knowing yourself is the beginning of all wisdom.'
—Aristotle

On my flight from Moscow back to Mumbai, as I looked down at the clouds and the land below, I thought about the world we live in. I peered outside my window and I thought how everything was moving with a certain rhythm. The universe seems to have a certain tempo by which everything moves. At school we are taught the fundamentals—maths, science and a range of languages. I believe that alongside these topics, it would be great if we were to also include topics such as how to manage our time or how to deal with our emotions, and even more crucial aspects like holistic well-being and the rhythm of our world. Learning these concepts can dramatically improve our lives.

We can see evidence of the rhythm with which our universe operates in a variety of activities around us: in the changing of the seasons. In many parts of the world, flowers bloom in spring, thrive in summer, dwindle in autumn and die in winter, only to come back again the following spring.

Even in the things we create as humans there is an aspect of the circle of life, e.g., watches, a Ferris wheel, etc.

One of the most interesting inventions is the compass. It uses the magnetic field naturally present in the earth to direct our travels. It works on the energy of the universe. Like the compass, if we master the science of tuning into the energies of the universe, we will learn the art of living and prosper.

Isn't it a fascinating concept that we all live our lives as the main characters in our own stories? It is true that we all have our own narratives within the larger narrative of the universe. We are a tiny universe within a larger universe. Each of us is receiving energy from the larger universe. An easy way to understand this is through our circadian rhythms. They respond primarily to the rising and setting of the sun and affect all living beings. This light-related circadian rhythm means that we sleep at night and are awake during the day. It gives us an idea why, in general, we are more alert during the morning, and we have a slump after lunch. Each cell in our body responds to the circadian rhythm as they all have their own natural timing devices, or biological clocks. If we can tune in to live according to this natural rhythm of life, we can live happier, fulfilling lives as we are in sync with the world around us.

If our morning is in sync with the universe, the rest of our day usually is in sync. And if our day is in sync, our night and sleep will also be in sync. Think why is it that the birds go to sleep when the sun sets and they wake up when the sun rises, without fail? They are following their natural circadian rhythm. We switch off our lights at night to follow that universal rhythm, but the glow of artificial lights or the glare of our smartphone screens can disturb our sleep and thus ruin that rhythm. Our universes within cannot cope when they are swimming against the current of the universe without. Many issues with our mental well-being occur because we do not live by the concept of being in sync with the outer universe; when to do certain things and when not to do certain things. Even the birds get confused whether it's day or night when they see the artificial lights around at night.

One of the easiest ways of syncing with the universe is to start our mornings right. Just as we charge our phones so that they last us the whole day, charging ourselves up in the morning is what we need to fuel us for the rest of the day.

Our morning charge

Start with gratitude

Kick-start your morning with a boost of positive energy. This happens when we consciously and realistically empower ourselves with a positive emotion such as gratitude. This is not about artificially trying to think of huge things that are going right in our lives because, at times, many things may feel like they are going the wrong way. But even if we can spend five minutes in the morning focusing on our blessings instead of our problems, we can start to train our minds to stay in a state of gratitude. I recommend not making any lists of gratitude on your phone or technology. They are more likely to distract your mind than focus it. Use good old-fashioned pen and paper!

Exercise:

Do this exercise first thing in the morning.

List three things you are grateful for that morning.

Remember it doesn't have to be 'good' experiences; sometimes the things that appear 'bad' teach us the most meaningful lessons too.

Make a commitment to see the positive

Allow yourself to see the positive in your day ahead. Things will go wrong during the day, there is no denying that. I am not saying that we should not correct things that are within our control. However, if we are of the mindset to see the positives, we will start to accept that things that are beyond our control are going to happen. We will accept that they are meant to happen to us, but to teach us lessons in life. They are part of a bigger picture and when we zoom out of the incident, we will see they are there for our good. Most of us have been practising seeing the negative for the majority of our lives, which means we are experts at it. We need to start practising seeing the positive, especially in the mornings. It is only then can we start taking steps to good mental well-being.

Exercise:

When you wake up in the morning, think of three things that you are looking forward to during the day ahead and why you are looking forward to them.

Do small things right

Try and accomplish small things in the morning that will boost your esteem. Folding your clothes or making your bed perfectly every morning is a small action but can lead to a disciplined attitude. As US Navy Admiral William McRaven says, 'Making your bed in the morning will reinforce the fact that little things in life matter. If you can't do the little things right, you will never be able to do the big things right. And, by chance, if you have a miserable day, you will come back home to a bed which you made and the made bed gives you encouragement that tomorrow will be better.'

Decide to help one person

Make a list of people who may need your help and choose at least one person to help. By investing our energy in empathy, love and kindness the first thing in the morning, we will feel that same energy for ourselves throughout the day. Everyone is going through a battle we know nothing about. Make a resolution that you will try to be kind to yourself and every person you meet. Not only will this boost your endorphins in the morning, but it will also attract people into your life who will wish the best for you.

These four things help condition our mindset for positivity. Try them every day for one week and you will experience a tangible benefit in the joy you feel during the day. Be compassionate with yourself, however. We will have our late nights and events we must attend. It is not easy to become an early bird right away, but we can take baby steps to implement these positive habits in our lives.

Let us take these principles a step further to see how they fit into the ancient holistic model of well-being, the pyramid of needs. This model is over 5000 years old but can have a significant impact on our modern lives.

The pyramid of needs

This model is found in the Taittiriya Upanishad but has been adapted by many modern philosophers, psychologists and even economists over thousands of years. This model of needs and identity discusses how our true self is covered by five *koshas*. Kosha translated into English means sheath, covering or layer. They wrap around our true nature with each sheath getting closer to our true self, thus making them subtler and harder to differentiate from the Self. Ancient wisdom suggests that if we can understand these sheaths, we can find peace; if we can apply them, we can find fulfilment; and if we can transcend them, we can achieve self-realization.

The first sheath: *Annamaya Kosha*—the sheath of pleasure

The first kosha is annamaya kosha, which means the sheath of pleasure. From the native Sanskrit it is literally translated as the sheath of food. It is the most physical and visible layer over us, our own body that is made up of the food we eat. We have discussed this previously, but this layer is made up of our senses, which have their foundation in the five elements: earth, water, fire, air and space. These senses are nourished by the food we eat, the water we drink and the air we breathe.

There is a famous phrase, 'You are what you eat.' It means that what we ingest becomes what we are. If we eat healthy, we become healthy. Indeed, a thinker once said, 'You are nothing, but food rearranged.' The phrase 'You are what you eat' came from the 1826 work *Physiologie du Gout, ou Meditations de Gastronomie Transcendante*, by French author Anthelme Brillat-Savarin who wrote: 'Tell me what you eat and I will tell you what you are.'

Though many spiritualists tend to ignore this outer layer of our identity, it should be cared for as much as the other layers that are within. For example, when driving a car, not only does the driver need to be cared for through a proper meal and rest so that he or she can be alert, but we also need to take care of our car.

Both the driver and the car have different needs. It is very important that we address both. The car needs the right servicing—the oil needs to be correct, the windscreen wipers need to work and it needs the right amount of fuel—to help us reach our destination. Yet, at the same time, we recognize that we are not the car itself. We are the driver within.

Our bodies need the proper nourishment and care. We need nutritious food, sound sleep and regular exercise to keep the annamaya kosha healthy. The ancient literatures say that each of the five aspects of this kosha need to be nourished in specific ways.

The element of **earth** is present in the form of the foods we eat and the things we see; everything that is manifest in creation has the element of earth. This concept is easiest to understand through what we eat, however. Eating the right foods is vital to keeping us healthy. The ancient literatures suggest that we have a compassion-based diet, full of fruits, vegetables, beans, lentils, etc. Not only does this keep us energized, but it also has a subtle effect on our mind, keeping it focused too. The easiest way to understand this is through beer. Drinking too much alcohol might physically give us a pot belly, but it also can cloud our mental judgement by inebriating us. Similarly, other foods can have different effects on both our physical and mental states too. Every morning when I wake up, I say a prayer of gratitude to the Earth that has provided everything we need to eat and drink for our health.

samudra vasane devi
parvata stana maṇḍale
viṣṇu-patni namas tubhyaṁ
pāda sparśaṁ kṣamasva me

This translates to seeking forgiveness from the Earth for touching our feet on her even though she gives us so much. Science has also found that walking barefoot on any natural surface such as soil, sand or grass has a lot of benefits for our well-being. As we have discussed, the Earth has its own natural energy. When we are in direct contact with it, our health improves. A study published in the *Journal of Environmental and Public Health* found that by walking barefoot, we are drawing electrons from the Earth that can help us with chronic pain, skin conductivity, improved glucose regulation and reduced stress, and support our immune systems.[1]

Another study in the *Journal of Alternative and Complementary Medicine* states that walking barefoot on the natural ground increases the surface charge of our red blood cells.[2] This means that our red blood cells are less likely to clump together, reducing the risk of heart disease as our blood 'flows better'. Many people take an aspirin tablet every day for the exact same reason: to help their blood become thinner and thus reduce the risk of heart disease. Therefore, we need to be in touch with the Earth to nourish our annamaya kosha.

Water is the second element. The importance of water in our lives is pretty self-explanatory.

We should drink around 2.5 to 3.5 litres of water a day to replace net water loss, but studies find that most people do not drink nearly that amount. Water physically hydrates us; not drinking enough means that we go through our day dehydrated, which can lead to physical and mental health issues. On the outside, even the sight, touch or sound of water can calm the mind. Having a shower can make us feel rejuvenated. Listening to the sound of a babbling brook can give us peace. Or watching the waves in the ocean can instil a sense of calm within us. Water is an important element to nourish our sheath of pleasure.

Fire is the third element that we must nourish. It provides heat to give us warmth when we are cold, aids our digestion and boosts our mental well-being. There are risks of getting exposed to too much sunlight, but there are notable benefits too. An increase in vitamin D, improved mood and higher quality sleep are some of the benefits of being in the sun. There is evidence that as little as five to fifteen minutes of sunlight a few times a week can supply us with the vitamin D our bodies need. Science also shows that those who do not get enough sunlight, especially in winter months and in countries that have shorter days, can suffer from Seasonal Affective Disorder (SAD), anxiety and depression as they miss out on the serotonin the sun provides.

The fourth element is **air**. We will elaborate on this aspect of our being in the next layer in the form of breath work meditation, but the simple act of breathing in fresh air can work wonders to help us feel balanced and better about ourselves. Fresher air contains more oxygen and the more oxygen we breathe in, the happier we feel, as our body releases more serotonin. There is also evidence to show that fresh air helps with our digestion, lowering our blood pressure and strengthening our immune system.

The final element is that of **space**. This is related to how different sounds can heal us. Sound is one of the most powerful forces in the world. Scientists have found that sound healing therapy can use music to improve our emotional and even physical well-being. This can be something as simple as listening or singing along to music, to guided meditations or neurological music therapy, a method designed to help people become less anxious and reduce post-operative pain.

Although these five elements of the annamaya kosha need attention, its deeper aspect is related to any other form of nourishment that our body needs. It is interesting to note that within each sheath there are subtle layers. For example, look at the door nearest to you. That door is made up of wood, that wood is made up of fibres, those fibres are made up of billions of atoms; each layer becomes progressively more subtle. In the same way, when annamaya kosha becomes subtler, beyond just the needs of the five elements, it also includes all those things that give comfort to our body to help it find pleasure, relax and recover.

When we neglect the needs of our annamaya kosha, our minds can become disturbed. When we are hungry or thirsty, when we do not get proper food, when we are in extreme or austere conditions, we tend to become agitated and irritable. Therefore, it is important that although we are not the body, we care for it, knowing that it's the vehicle that can help us with our purpose in life.

Exercise:

Annamaya kosha log

Day	Sleep (write down the hours)	Have you eaten your fruits, veg, lentils?	How many litres of water have you had?	Have you had some connection with Mother Nature today?	Have you had any exposure to sunlight?	Have you spent time on guided sound meditation?
Monday						
Tuesday						
Wednesday						
Thursday						
Friday						
Saturday						
Sunday						

The second sheath: *Pranamaya Kosha*—the sheath of energy

Underneath the annamaya kosha is the second layer called the pranamaya kosha. Ancient wisdom explains that this is the energy sheath or the sheath of life forces. It is responsible for blood flowing through our veins, oxygen being assimilated in the blood and the food we eat being converted into the energy that sustains us. This sheath keeps our body functioning and maintains it by giving it the energy that it requires. Prana is like a tide surging within the body. It makes us go through the experience of breathing, hunger, thirst, good health or the lack of it. Our health is dictated by the quality of our prana. In fact, holistic medicines act less on the body and more on the pranamaya kosha.

The ancient literatures talk about the five primary life airs circulating within the body called prana vayus. They give our entire body the strength and the energy to function both externally and internally. This energy, called prana in India, is known in the ancient Chinese system of medicine as chi and in Japanese as ki. When people are fatigued, anxious or stressed for no apparent reason, it is believed that their prana is imbalanced. When our prana is strong, it can give us energy and strength; but if it is weak, it can make us feel stagnant and also make us ill.

Prana is affected by many things. Not eating correctly, a lack of fresh drinking water and a lack of sleep can reduce the strength of our prana. Subtle things like a lack of loving relationships, social interaction and a lack of the right kind of mental activity can also affect our prana.

When we are fatigued, overworked or feeling under the weather, this could be a sign of a disturbed pranamaya kosha. This can also affect our mental well-being. Doesn't our mind feel disturbed when we are weak, tired, chronically fatigued and exhausted? There are many ways to help balance this sheath of energy that is vital to our health.

The ancient Chinese understanding of prana, called chi, includes a series of exercises and breathing techniques that can improve our posture, circulation, balance and muscle tone. This is called tai chi. It teaches self-discipline and opens up blockages in our life airs. Yoga can also help do the same. Although tai chi and yoga both help balance our prana, they are different in their approach. Tai chi is about fluid movements whereas yoga is about holding postures for a prolonged time and thus becoming aware of the blockages within us. In yoga, holding a pose helps prana accumulate, creating an artificial 'blockage'. Releasing from that pose clears the blockage and allows our life airs to flow freely. Different poses have different effects on our prana and prevent blockages over time.

Another popular way of improving the circulation of our life airs is through pranayama or conscious breathing. This balances our energies to give us instant relief. The exercise below can help you feel the immediate effects of pranayama. By being conscious of our breath, we are able to tune into our prana. As we breathe in, we are not just breathing in air but also prana, which are both circulated around the body. That is why deep breaths help us when we are under stress as they attempt to restore the pranamaya kosha. Focusing on our breath through pranayama is a form of meditation that can help our prana keep flowing to avoid blockages. A final thought about how we can physically restore our pranamaya kosha is through the amount of sleep we get. Good quality sleep directly restores our pranamaya kosha. Getting a minimum of six to eight hours of sleep a night is crucial to keep our prana circulating without concern.

Our pranamaya kosha is also affected by the more subtle aspects of life. As we move from being teenagers to adults, we must remember that life is not a race to win, but a journey to evolve and experience. Our energy sheath can be disturbed by emotions such as fear, insecurity and the competition to win the rat race. The more we feel secure in our income, in adequate facilities where we live and in our opportunities for growth, the stronger our pranamaya kosha will be. The people we surround ourselves with also makes a huge difference. The more we surround ourselves with people who want us to grow and prosper, who support us and who are rooting for us, rather than those who are envious, insecure, trying to pull us down and always competing against us, the more our energy sheath will feel nourished and therefore our mind will feel peaceful.

The pranamaya kosha and the annamaya kosha are closely related. It is the energy that we have from the pranamaya kosha that helps us enjoy the pursuit of our pleasure from our annamaya kosha. For example, imagine you are at a romantic beachside restaurant with your partner and the chef is preparing the freshest, most authentic Italian pizza for you. If you are feeling ill or are under a lot of stress, will you enjoy that experience? It is doubtful.

Annamaya is the tool to get pleasure—the body—and pranamaya is the energy to empower the body to get that pleasure.

Exercise: Alternate nostril breathing

Alternate nostril breathing, also known as anulom-vilom pranayama, can help us physically by enhancing the quality of our breathing and blood circulation and psychologically by calming our mind.

Although this breathing technique is safe, it's recommended that one learns it from and practises it under the guidance of an authorized yoga teacher.

Practise it on an empty stomach, three to four hours after you have taken any meal.

- Choose a quiet, comfortable space and sit with your spine and neck erect and eyes closed. You may sit on the floor cross-legged or on a chair if you have trouble sitting on the floor.
- Rest your left wrist on your left knee.
- Fold the middle and index fingers of your right hand towards its thumb as if to touch it. Now gently place the thumb on your right nostril and the ring finger above your left nostril.
- Close the right nostril with your thumb and inhale gently and deeply through your left nostril, until your lungs are full.
- Now, release your thumb, close your left nostril with your ring finger and exhale slowly through the right nostril.
- After this, do the exact same thing in a reverse manner, now inhaling through the right nostril and exhaling through the left.
- With every repetition, make sure that you stay focused and are conscious and aware of your breathing.

Initially, start this practice based on your comfort level for as long as you can and slowly increase the duration and repetitions.

The third sheath: *Manomaya Kosha*—the sheath of emotions

The third sheath is called manomaya kosha or the sheath of emotions. It literally translates to the 'sheath of the mind'. It is within this sheath of the mind that we have thoughts, emotions and feelings, and where our memories are stored.

Our deep nature is to love and be loved. Getting the opportunity to do both keeps us emotionally healthy and we certainly *need* both to be healthy. A positive and loving childhood is where we experience a lot of love from our parents and siblings. This affection, through deep and stable relationships in our family, is the foundation of a balanced manomaya kosha. On the contrary, those who have had a negative childhood, through abuse, a broken home or unstable relationships, could be more vulnerable to a disturbed sheath of emotions that will have long-term consequences on their mental well-being.

This does not mean we cannot heal if we experienced trauma in our childhood. We can still begin to heal our sheath of emotions. Previously, we discussed the validity of counselling and therapy. It is okay to seek help when necessary. Other methods of healing are through finding love through fruitful relationships. This is powerful, as a stable, loving relationship can put our mind at ease. That is why so many people have pets—the unconditional love from a pet is an attempt to experience the love that heals our manomaya kosha.

Another aspect of this book that comes back into play now is self-love. This is different from self-obsession and goes beyond our bodies, looks, minds, abilities and talents. Self-love is about appreciating ourselves and accepting ourselves the way we are. It means to pardon ourselves for the mistakes we may have made and to even pamper ourselves with a healthy indulgence. It is to act for our own welfare. Imagine the person we love the most. Would we not want these things for them? We would want them to not feel the burden of their mistakes, accept their physical features and even treat themselves to the things that they love. We need to get into the habit of doing the same for ourselves. That is self-love. People who try to love others without loving themselves have an imbalanced manomaya kosha and are frequently disturbed as they lack self-worth and self-esteem. They are experiencing a phenomenon called *compassion fatigue* and need to swing the pendulum back to restore their sheath of emotions through self-love.

The manomaya sheath is used to experience emotions in the pursuit of pleasure. The damage of this sheath is the most prominent reason for a disturbed mind. It is the true self that experiences a situation, but it is through the platform of the manomaya kosha.

Exercise: An assessment on self-love

Write down three things that you love about yourself and why you love these about yourself.

What makes you feel the most loved?

How much time are you spending on the things that make you feel the most loved?

How can you increase the time you spend on these things?

How are you giving love to others?

The fourth sheath: *Vijnanamaya Kosha*—the sheath of wisdom

As we move deeper into the different layers of our being, things get more subtle. The vijnanamaya kosha is literally translated as the 'sheath of intelligence'. The intelligence has three functions: to decipher or understand, to discriminate between right and wrong, and to decide the next steps to take. As soon as we are born, our intelligence starts acting to acquire the knowledge required to survive in this world.

We begin with basic knowledge, such as where we can find food, who likes us and who does not like us. We then start to pick up language from our parents and family members as we learn how to crawl, walk and run. We even learn how to ride a bike! As we grow, we start to undergo formal academic training at school or university. We continue our learning when we start working. There is a huge industry for seminars, conferences and continued professional development.

However, there is knowledge that is more 'fun' and 'casual'. I remember visiting a university in the UK where a lady was handing out leaflets for students to join the 'Harry Potter Discussion Club'. This was a place to learn all about Harry Potter and his wizarding friends. They would dress up in capes and carry broomsticks and discuss the theories of the magical world. Then there is knowledge about the world around us. We may want to know the truth behind what is happening in the world. Political knowledge, business knowledge and current affairs grip us as there are multiple sources to discover the intricacies about the state of our planet.

Another way our intelligence is gathering knowledge is by trying to gain more information about another person before committing ourselves to a relationship. We have to discriminate if that person is compatible with us: whether they will be a good life partner, will remain a friend or be a negative influence in our lives. It is intelligence that discerns between the three options.

Finally, there is existential knowledge. Where do we come from? What is the purpose of life? Who am I? How was the world created? These types of questions are about life itself. As humans, we want a reason for the existence of life and the purpose of our being. This delves into the world of spirituality and faith.

We live in a world full of information. My spiritual teacher, HH Radhanath Swami, repeatedly says that we live in a world of 'mass distraction'. We seem to have *too much* information now at our fingertips that is hard to sift through. This makes it difficult to make a decision as our intelligence cannot cope with this bombardment of information. This is known as 'infobesity' or 'infoxication' or 'information anxiety'.

When information is distilled, it becomes knowledge; when knowledge is applied, it becomes experience; when experience becomes the guiding force behind our choices, it becomes maturity and when maturity ripens with years of practice, it becomes wisdom. It is wisdom—our own or from other sources we trust—that should be the basis of the choices we make in our life.

Things that make our wisdom sheath weaker and, at the same time, may be symptoms of a weak wisdom sheath are confusion, the inability to make proper decisions, speculation, laziness and a lack of either motivation or a proper value system.

We can strengthen our wisdom sheath in three different ways: Firstly, by reading the wisdom literatures that create focus within us and which help direct our intelligence into action. Regularly reading from these literatures and reinforcing our intelligence with this guidance can help us deal with our real-life situations. A simplistic example takes us back to the cake. If we are reading about the dangers of heart disease and eating too much sugar, and if we are well-informed about matters of nutritious food, we are more likely to walk past the cake shop and buy an apple instead. This is where our knowledge becomes action.

Secondly, listening to wise guides, mentors and gurus who have wisdom is imperative for us to protect our intelligence. They can give the practical application of the wisdom literatures that we may not be able to grasp. Such mentors who are impartial, mature and can take a step back to look at our lives are crucial for our success. We need this guidance to solidify our wisdom sheath.

Finally, our own experiences in life can be a big teacher to leave imprints on our intelligence of what is correct and what is incorrect. A common story that explains this topic well is that of the billionaire's answer to the reason for his success. At a press conference, a journalist asked a billionaire about the secret of his success. He answered, 'Two words: right decisions.' The journalist retorted, asking how those right decisions are made. He answered, 'One word: experience.' The journalist then asked him how that experience is developed, and he replied, 'Two words: wrong decisions.' Life is a powerful teacher, but we should be careful as she can also be a cruel mistress. Regular consultation with our mentors and the wisdom literatures can make sure that the lessons we think we are learning from anything life throws at us are in alignment with universal values.

It is the vijnanamaya kosha or the intelligence that is used to discriminate between good and bad, right and wrong, to make decisions in our pursuit of pleasure.

Exercise:

How much time per day do you devote for:

- Reading books that add value to your life?
- Watching/listening to uplifting content?
- Interacting with wise and mature individuals whose experience can teach you what no books can?

How do you think you can increase the time you spend doing one/all of these?

What will you do to maximize what you gain from these?

The fifth sheath: *Anandamaya Kosha*—the sheath of bliss

The final sheath that covers our true identity or atma is the sheath of bliss. This goes beyond the pleasure that is derived from sense objects. Ancient wisdom explains that we have four states of existence:

1. *Jagrati*: This is our waking state. In this state, both our mind and senses are active and all koshas are alert. To understand this, imagine your body is a smartphone. In

the jagrati state, your phone would be working to its maximum capacity; in full battery mode, with the Wi-Fi connected and Bluetooth ready to pair.

2. *Svapna*: This is our dream state; the senses are inactive, but the mind is active. One experiences dreams in this state. We have our phone in airplane mode so no one disturbs us. This is when the annamaya kosha is inactive.

3. *Shushupti*: This is our deep sleep state where both the senses and mind are inactive. There are no dreams during this deep sleep experience. In fact, the first four koshas or sheaths of our being are inactive. This is analogous to our cell phone being turned off. This is something that people rarely experience. It is the freedom from any physical pleasures or pains, thoughts, feelings or emotions and intellectual analysis. We are totally 'turned off' with only our anandamaya kosha still active. This complete disconnection from the outside world leads to a state of deep, complete relaxation. Most of us struggle to achieve this state today. One activity to try to get you into this state is during yoga nidraa or sound baths where the mind stops. This yoga practice and experience is created consciously to promote our experiencing this state of our being by disconnecting us from the world. It is hard to explain in writing, but a powerful experience.

We will come to the fourth state of existence, but this state of anandamaya kosha is balanced and realized through meditation. Meditation can take us closest to ourselves where we feel as if we are in a state of nothingness. This is an extremely powerful experience of peace, but it should be noted that we are still not connected to ourselves. This is still a covering of our true identity, but it's so close that it feels satisfying. We are still one small matryoshka doll away from our true identity. It is likened to a surgeon's innermost glove. It is so thin that it feels as if it is their actual hand, but it is not. The glove is not the hand. Many spiritual paths choose to end there as this 'shutting off' and 'feeling nothing' is such a powerful experience that it becomes addictive. But we have to dive deeper to experience the fourth state of reality, our true self.

This state beyond wakefulness, dream and deep sleep, is called *Turiya*. It is synonymous to a samadhi, a liberated state or freedom where we realize the true identity of our own atma. This spark that drives our entire being is fully understood at this point and we disconnect from anything material, and achieve the state of moksha or liberation. This is a totally spiritual state, but it does not end there.

Exercise:

Take out a minimum of ten minutes a day in the morning to practise meditation.

Write down how you feel after your meditation practice and assess your level of absorption and connection.

Ancient wisdom says that *Turiya-atita* is one step higher. Here the Self is disconnected from matter, but also in touch with the supreme being, the *paramatma*. This connection with our own self and a connection with the Divine is the absolute state of awareness. It is the spark being connected to the fire, the light bulb being connected with the electricity generator or the drop being connected to the ocean. It is a state where all our koshas are balanced and satisfied, and is also the highest state of spiritual experience as we are connected to the Supreme. It is a state where our joy endures timelessly. Many ancient books have explained this state in detail. It is beyond the scope of this book, but something I plan to write about in future. However, before we get to this lofty platform, we must understand that we need to live holistically on this planet by balancing our koshas. This can create a sense of true mental well-being for us in the here and now.

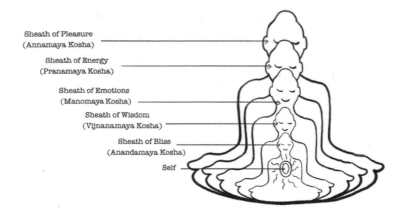

Balancing the koshas

There are five different koshas or sheaths that we discovered in this chapter. The first layer was annamaya kosha or our body that wants to experience pleasure from the senses. The second was pranamaya kosha or the energy that drives the body to experience pleasure. The third was the manomaya kosha or the sheath of the emotions that is experienced from the mind itself. It is where our thoughts, feelings and memories are stored. One step deeper is the vijnanamaya kosha or the sheath of wisdom. This is our intellect that informs the rest of the layers about right and wrong; it discriminates, understands and thinks about the next steps to take. And the final layer is the anandamaya kosha or the sheath of bliss that disconnects us from the senses, mind and even intelligence, and gives a state of bliss in nothingness. This deep state can be achieved through practices such as meditation, yoga nidraa and in sound baths.

For holistic wellness, we need to address the needs for each of these koshas in a balanced way. Balance is a dynamic principle. It is a concept difficult to understand, but necessary for a healthy life. It is like walking a tightrope with a bamboo stick to balance us. When we lose balance, one side of the bamboo tilts over so we understand that we need to tilt it to the other side so we can regain our composure. However, we cannot specifically define how much we need to tilt it over. We cannot say that at three feet from the start of the rope, the walker has to tilt the bamboo thirteen degrees to the right to make it safely across. You could calculate it mathematically, but that isn't how life works. There are so many intricacies to it that we can only apply the principles of balance. Life is such that at every point during this tightrope walk one kosha may need more attention than the other. In doing so, sometimes, something else may get neglected. For example, sometimes our annamaya kosha for physical comfort may need more priority than our vijnanamaya kosha or intellectual understanding. Sometimes our manomaya kosha or our mental well-being may need more priority than our pranamaya kosha. Although they are all related, we must accept that just as a tightrope walker tilts to the left and right, but keeps on walking, we will also have moments of imbalance that affect our well-being. But we must keep on walking forward. These five koshas are there for us to understand and utilize for our holistic well-being. We dipped our toes in the water of what is beyond those five koshas in the pursuit of peace and joy, but I strongly believe that if we can first master balancing these five koshas, the mental state of humanity would be uplifted.

As I landed in Mumbai from Russia, thinking about these states and holding these dolls, I walked off the plane feeling invigorated. I knew that I had to write about this topic as it has changed my life completely. As a monk, I have the luxury of thinking and researching these topics. However, I make it my duty to share it for the betterment of the world. Feeling the humid Mumbai air hit my face again as I walked into Arrivals, I saw a friend whom I had not seen in a long time.

She was sliding along the floor of Arrivals and attracting a huge crowd around her. She spoke with such conviction and there was an evenness in her voice. I felt that she did not have to deal with her mental well-being as I had to. She was beyond the koshas, beyond guilt and beyond envy, and beyond anxiety and depression. I was impressed with her and felt oddly jealous that she did not have to cope with all these emotions. However, I then realized that the beauty of life is in the journey of discovery. It is discovering how to deal with our emotions and how to enrich our lives by helping others deal with their own. It is discovering and accepting that we have flaws, and we all struggle with different things, but there is always hope. The hope to do better and the hope that there is always a way forward. And finally, I pitied her as she did not have the opportunity to *feel* like you and me.

She was Sophia.

Chapter summary

- Everything in the world is bound by a certain rhythm. It is important to tune into these natural circadian rhythms that the universe provides so that we can thrive. Getting our morning right to sync with these natural circadian rhythms occurs by starting with gratitude, making a commitment to see the positive, doing small things right and deciding to help others.

- The pyramid of needs is an ancient model of identity that can help us understand the Self. It explains that the Self is covered by five koshas or sheaths that wrap around our true nature.

- If we can understand these sheaths, we can find peace; if we can apply them, we can find fulfilment; and if we can transcend them, we can achieve self-realization.

- The first kosha is annamaya kosha, the sheath of pleasure. It is the visible layer over our true Self, our own body that is made up of the food we eat. This layer is made up of our senses, which have their foundation in the five elements: earth, water, fire, air and space. These senses are nourished by the food we eat, the water we drink and the air we breathe.

- The second kosha is the pranamaya kosha. It is the sheath of energy or life forces. It helps with the experience of breathing, hunger, thirst, good health or the lack of it. The pranamaya kosha empowers the body to gain energy to seek pleasure.

- The third kosha, the manomaya kosha, is the sheath of emotions and literally translates to the 'sheath of the mind'. It is within this sheath that we have thoughts, emotions and feelings.

- The fourth kosha is the vijnanamaya kosha, the sheath of intelligence. The intelligence has three functions: to decipher or understand, to discriminate between right and wrong, and to decide the next steps to take. It is within this sheath that we start acquiring knowledge and understanding which actions to take and not to take.

- The fifth kosha is the anandamaya kosha, the sheath of bliss. This is a state of pleasure that goes beyond the body, mind and intelligence, but is still a covering over the true Self.

- The state of turiya and turiya-atita are truly spiritual states beyond matter. That is where the atma or true Self is realized.

- We must balance the different sheaths that cover us while at the same time aim to discover our true Self.

Acknowledgements

I offer my heartfelt respect and gratitude to His Divine Grace A.C. Bhaktivedanta Swami Srila Prabhupada, my grand spiritual master, and Radhanath Swami, my spiritual master. Their teachings, wisdom, and life have, and will always be, the inspiration behind everything I do.

My endless gratitude to Govinda Das for his friendship, mentorship and continual support in all my endeavours. Even the most casual interactions with him have always enriched my understanding of life.

Thank you to Radha Gopinath Das, Shyamananda Das, Sanat Kumar Das, Late Sruti Dharma Das, Pranabandhu Das, Gauranga Das, Siksastakam Das, Vraj Vihari Das, Shubha Vilas Das for their continued encouragement.

My gratitude to all my friends in our ashram and the community members of the Radha Gopinath Temple, Mumbai, my spiritual shelter and my place of residence. Thanks to all my friends and the community members of Bhaktivedanta Manor, London, my second home.

Huge thanks to Dr Vinay Raniga, who, beyond being an accomplished dentist in London, is also an expert writer and editor. This book would not have been possible without his immense help and tireless efforts.

Huge thanks to Dr Bhavik Patel from London for all his help with the practical exercises and his continued support in everything I do.

A big thank you to Shyamgopal Shroff for all the logistical help required to get this book done and for his tireless hard work in my efforts to serve all of you.

Thanks to Kush Boradia for designing this book's graphics and artwork.

Gratitude to everyone at Penguin Random House India for their support in publishing this book. A special thanks to Vaishali Mathur for her expert help in seeing the book to completion and Ralph Rebello for the expert copy-editing. Thanks to Gunjan Ahlawat for the cover page design.

Thank you to my loving parents, family, friends and well-wishers for their love, prayers and blessings.

My sincerest gratitude to all our online and offline followers, whose continued encouragement and support inspire me to keep going in my work.

My heartfelt thanks to all the readers of our first book, *Life's Amazing Secrets*, for making it such a huge success. I can't thank you all enough for your love.

And finally, a massive thank you to you, who have chosen to read this book. My humble wishes and prayers are that the principles shared here may help you energize your mind and transform the way you live.

Notes

Introduction
1. https://fullfact.org/health/mental-health-spending-england/

Chapter 1: You Are Not Sophia: How to Feel, Deal and Heal Our Emotions
1. https://hbr.org/2016/11/3-ways-to-better-understand-your-emotions

Chapter 2: Stuck in Economy—Dealing with the Fear of Missing Out
1. https://www.statista.com/statistics/272014/global-social-networks-ranked-by-number-of-users/
2. https://www.addictioncenter.com/drugs/social-media-addiction/
3. https://www.ncbi.nlm.nih.gov/pmc/articles/PMC3032992/
4. https://www.oecd.org/els/health-systems/Children-and-Young-People-Mental-Health-in-the-Digital-Age.pdf
5. https://www.gla.ac.uk/news/headline_787680_en.html
6. https://selfdeterminationtheory.org/wp-content/uploads/2014/04/2013_PrzybylskiMurayamaDeHaanGladwell_CIHB.pdf
7. https://www.rsph.org.uk/static/uploaded/d125b27c-0b62-41c5-a2c0155a8887cd01.pdf
8. https://www.pnas.org/content/118/4/e2016976118

Chapter 3: Joshua Slips Away—Dealing with Mental Chatter
1. https://journals.sagepub.com/doi/abs/10.1177/1087054720961828

Chapter 4: Jumping at 18,000 Ft: Dealing with Anxiety
1. https://www.psychiatry.org/patients-families/anxiety-disorders/what-are-anxiety-disorders
2. https://uspa.org/Discover/FAQs/Safety

3.   https://www.apa.org/pubs/journals/releases/xge-a0035325.pdf
4.   https://www.mentalhealth.org.uk/a-to-z/m/men-and-mental-health

Chapter 5: The Bird's Nest—Dealing with Depression
1.   https://www.who.int/news/item/28-09-2001-the-world-health-report-2001-mental-disorders-affect-one-in-four-people
2.   https://www.mindtools.com/pages/article/affirmations.htm
3.   Ibid.

Chapter 6: The Last Wish in a Pen Drive: Dealing with Guilt
1.   https://www.bbc.co.uk/news/business-40260169

Chapter 7: An Unexpected Humiliation: Dealing with Toxic Behaviour
1.   https://www.healthline.com/health/how-to-deal-with-toxic-people
2.   https://psychcentral.com/lib/learning-to-say-no#why-its-hard

Chapter 8: A Memory Hard to Delete: Dealing with Old Memories
1.   https://www.sleepfoundation.org/how-sleep-works/sleep-facts-statistics
2.   https://qbi.uq.edu.au/brain-basics/memory/how-are-memories-formed
3.   Ibid.

Chapter 11: When Sandals Meet Yeezys: Developing Empathy
1.   https://journals.sagepub.com/doi/abs/10.1177/0011000014545091

Chapter 12: Learning From 'Virus': Developing Sensitive Communication
1.   https://www.researchgate.net/publication/38027140_Do_words_hurt_Brain_activation_during_the_processing_of_pain-related_words
2.   https://pubmed.ncbi.nlm.nih.gov/9560177/
3.   https://www.everydayhealth.com/columns/therese-borchard-sanity-break/420/

Chapter 14: We Are a Universe within a Universe
1.   https://www.macrotrends.net/cities/22299/moscow/population#:~:text=The%20current%20metro%20area%20population,a%20 0.5%25%20increase%20from%202019.

Chapter 15: A Holistic Approach to Wellness
1.   https://www.ncbi.nlm.nih.gov/pmc/articles/PMC3265077/
2.   Ibid.